Edward MacRobbie
1872 Arizona Ave
Ottawa Ont
1-613-731-4866

ANALOG SYSTEMS FOR MICROPROCESSORS AND MINICOMPUTERS

Patrick H. Garrett

RESTON PUBLISHING COMPANY, INC.
A Prentice-Hall Company
Reston, Virginia 22090

Library of Congress Cataloging in Publication Data

Garrett, Patrick H.
Analog systems for microprocessors and minicomputers.

Includes bibliographies and index.
1. Automatic data collection systems. 2. Electronic instruments. 3. Analog-to-digital converters. I. Title.
TS158.6.G37 621.3819'57'2 77-17392
ISBN 0-87909-035-9

To my father

A Prentice-Hall Company
Reston, Virginia 22090

10 9 8 7 6 5 4 3 2

Printed in the United States of America.

CONTENTS

PREFACE

Progress in analog instrumentation and signal processing has been especially rapid since the introduction of the Fairchild 709 monolithic operational amplifier in 1965. This advancement is highlighted by the fact that all five of the first-generation linear integrated circuits went to the moon aboard the LEM. Recent emphasis on microprocessor and minicomputer applications involving data acquisition and process control has resulted in a significant intrusion of the analog-digital interface and its manifold considerations into the realm of the user. For example, frequent requirements include upgrading signal quality between sensors and computer inputs to the equivalent number of binary bits of interest within a known confidence, while simultaneously conserving system complexity and cost.

This book was undertaken to present a compendium of key topics which address the preceding and related requirements for applications-oriented readers. The ten chapters are organized in a sequence to provide a gradual development of subjects which involve analog input and output systems for digital computers as they are nominally encountered in practice. The chapters can also be used on an ad hoc basis, such as for active filter design, signal conditioning operations, or process controller tuning. Many specific examples have been included to impart a sense of practicality that a more formal or generalized approach might lack, with the intention of communicating some of the excitement of the possibilities for analog systems.

The book is intended for use in a one term course on instrumentation at the 400-500 level, as an adjunct text for a sequence of computer courses, and as a reference for practitioners. It should provide gap-filling information for engineers and technologists whose competence lies in other fields, and help for the digital specialist. The author accepts responsibility for shortcomings in the writing, organization, editing, or ideas presented, and wishes to acknowledge the helpful discussions with Messrs. Lewis A. Drake and Robert L. Young. The author is also indebted to the Industrial Environmental Research Laboratory of the U.S. Environmental Protection Agency at Research Triangle Park, North Carolina, whose leave with that organization resulted in ideas for this book.

Pat Garrett

1

ELECTRICAL TRANSDUCERS

1-0 INTRODUCTION

The purpose of this chapter is to survey present electrical transducer techniques and practices for both laboratory and industrial process measurements. Key sensor characteristics are of interest, since these devices represent the starting point in sensor-based data acquisition and real-time control systems. Sensors for measuring temperature, pressure, and flow are presented plus displacement and positioning actuators. Photometric and radiometric devices are also described, and chemical analyzers introduced, including some on-line applications to process streams. The chapter concludes with a presentation on grounding and shielding practice for low-level transducer signals.

1-1 TEMPERATURE SENSORS

Temperature sensing constitutes one of the more frequently required industrial and laboratory measurements. The specific application and temperature-measurement range largely dictates the choice of sensor. However, thermocouples, resistance thermometer devices (RTD), semiconductor sensors, and pyrometers are dominant. Table 1–1 presents an orientation of temperature measurement devices.

TABLE 1–1. Temperature Sensor Orientation

Type	Range (°C)
Glass stem	−50 to +600
Bimetallic	0 to +500
Filled element	−50 to +300
Semiconductor	−100 to +100
RTD devices	−100 to +300
Pyrometers	+100 to 5000
Thermocouples	−250 to 2000

Thermocouple transducers are the most widely used temperature sensing devices because of their ruggedness and wide temperature range. Two dissimilar metals are used in this Seebeck-effect temperature-to-EMF generator with repeatable results, as illustrated in Figure 1–1. Proper operation does require the use of a reference junction, or the electrical equivalent, in series with the measurement junction in order to polarize the direction of current flow and maximize the EMF at the measurement junction. Various dissimilar metal combinations are utilized, depending upon the operating environment and range of operating temperatures required. The more frequently applied combinations are tabulated in Table 1–2. Wide-range temperature measurements usually require linearization of the transfer characteristic. This is considered in some detail in Chapter 5.

When accurate thermocouple measurements are required, it is common practice to reference both legs to copper wire at an ice-point reference junction. Since a reference-junction temperature change influences the output signal and since ice baths are inconvenient, practical

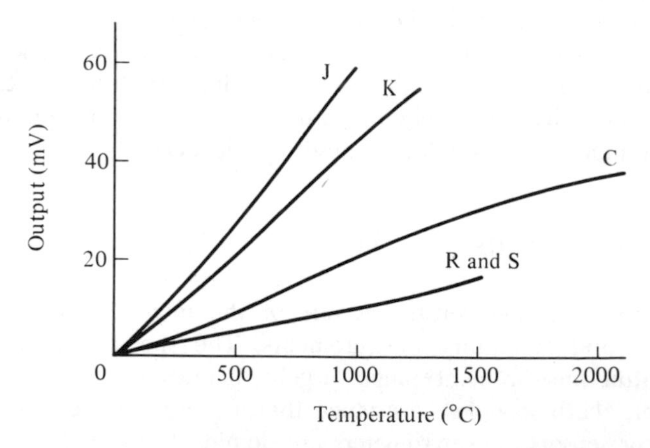

FIGURE 1–1. Thermocouple Characteristics

TABLE 1–2. Thermocouple Comparisons

Type	+ Element	−	mV/°C	Range (°C)	Feature
J	Iron	Constantan	0.04	−250 to 1000	Economical
K	Chromel	Alumel	0.03	−250 to 1400	Most linear
R and S	Pt–Rh	Platinum	0.01	0 to 1500	High temperature
T	Copper	Constantan	0.04	−250 to 400	For moisture
C	Tungsten	Rhenium	0.02	0 to 2000	High temperature

alternative methods are usually employed. The electrical bridge method utilizes a self-compensating network to cancel error as the temperature surrounding the reference junction varies (Figure 1–2). A possible disadvantage is the requirement for a mercury battery with a typical 60-day continuous life or a stable dc power source. For less stringent requirements, copper-terminated compensating junctions placed on a stable heat sink at ambient temperature provide performance adequate for many industrial applications. This arrangement is frequently available integrated into a single thermocouple housing assembly.

Resistance thermometer devices provide greater resolution and repeatability than thermocouples and operate on the principle of electrical resistance change as a function of temperature. The platinum resistance thermometer is frequently used for industrial applications and offers good

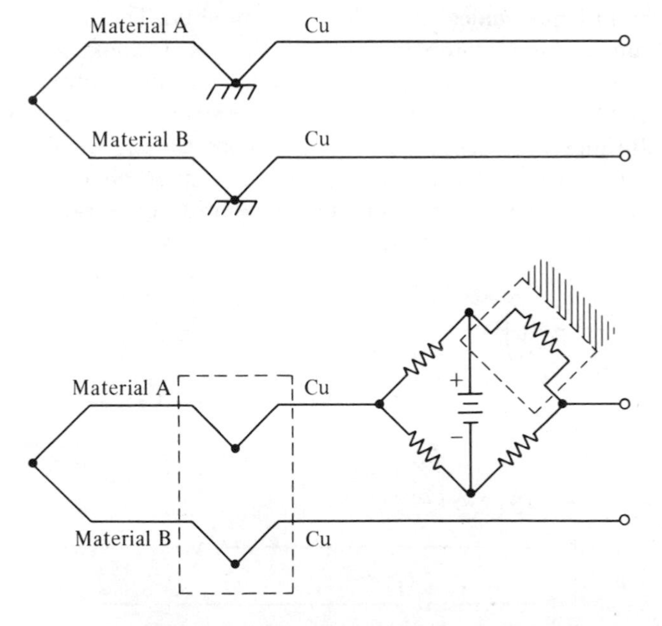

FIGURE 1–2. Thermocouple Reference Circuits

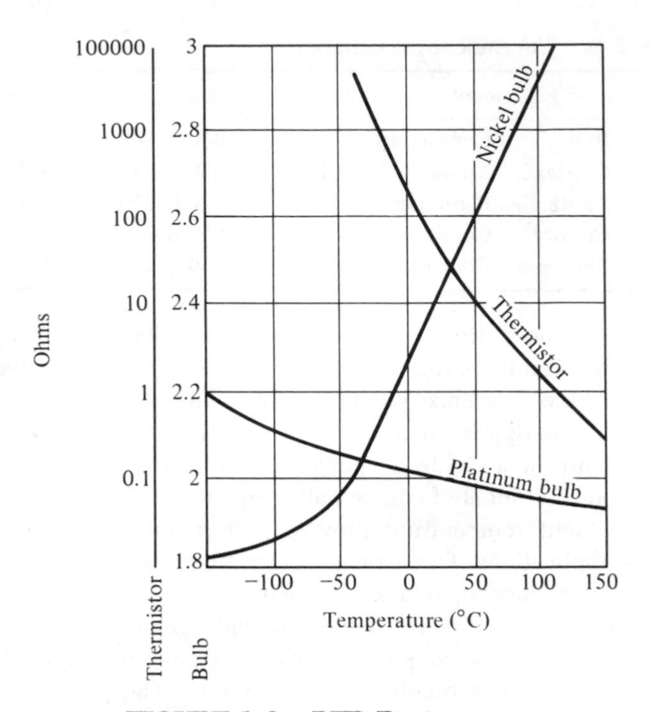

FIGURE 1–3. RTD Devices

accuracy and mechanical and electrical stability. Thermistors are fabricated from a sintered mixture of metal alloys, forming a ceramic that exhibits a large negative temperature coefficient. Metal film resistors have an extended and more linear range than thermistors, but thermistors have about 10 times the sensitivity. The signal conditioning usually required is conversion of the resistance change into a voltage change and possibly linearization. Figure 1–3 presents the temperature-to-resistance characteristic of popular RTD devices.

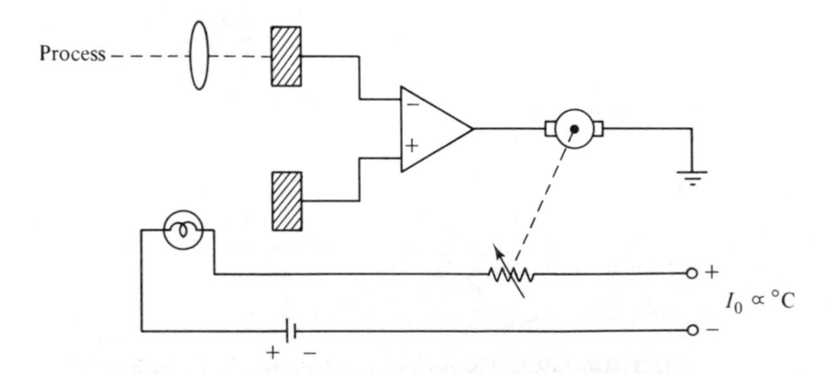

FIGURE 1–4. Automatic Pyrometer

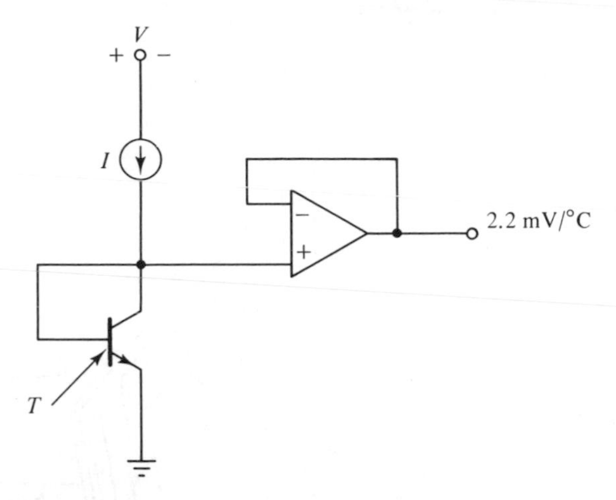

FIGURE 1–5. Semiconductor Temperature Measurement

The optical pyrometer is useful for temperature measurement when mechanical sensor contact with the process is not feasible but a direct view is available. Measurements are limited to energy within the spectral response of the sensor used, whereby a radiometric match between a calibrated reference source and the process provides a current output corresponding to a specific temperature. Automatic pyrometers employ a servo loop to provide this balance, as shown in Figure 1–4. Operation to 5000°C is common.

Temperature measurement using forward-biased semiconductor devices (Figure 1–5) is a recent technique which is capable of accuracy to 0.1°C over a useful range of about ±100°C. Although this is a limited span, it is in the range of frequently required temperature measurements. The negative temperature coefficient of the bipolar transistor base-to-emitter voltage drop varies by 2.2 mV/°C and can be made very linear by means of a constant-current supply.

1-2 PRESSURE AND FLOW TRANSDUCERS

In the beginning there was the potentiometric device. Its low cost and high output have kept it popular in simple systems, but its high sensitivity to shock and vibration and mechanical nonlinearity errors (typically in excess of 3%) limit its utility. An early technique for overcoming the limitations of potentiometric pressure sensors centered around the unbonded strain gage. This device provided substantial improvements in accuracy and stability with typical errors $\frac{1}{2}$% of full scale. However, it was delicate and difficult to fabricate and has an output in the millivolt range, usually requiring a preamplifier.

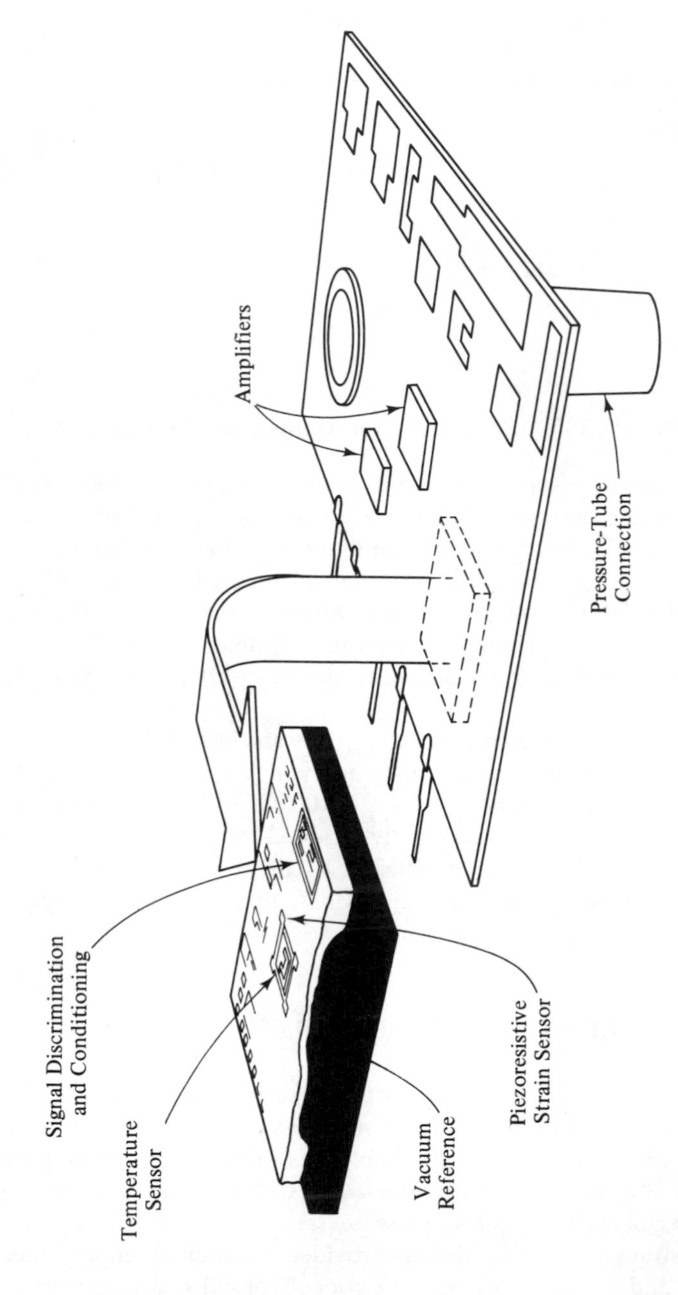

FIGURE 1–6. Integrated-Circuit Pressure Transducer (*Courtesy* National Semiconductor)

An alternative to the unbonded gage transducer is the semiconductor gage bonded directly to the pressure diaphragm, eliminating the mechanical linkages. Frequency response and sensitivity to vibration are improved with accuracy equivalent to the unbonded implementation. However, its low output also requires a preamplifier, and its low sensitivity makes it suitable only for pressures of 100 psi and above. An improvement on this is the use of a crystal diaphragm with diffused piezoresistors. The advantage of this technique is the freedom from measurement hysteresis exhibited by the other methods, since when errors are reduced to the order of $\frac{1}{2}$%, hysteresis becomes the limiting factor.

Current developments in pressure transducers include the incorporation of piezoresistors with hybrid integrated circuit techniques to compensate for the various error sources (Figure 1–6). National Semiconductor pioneered this development with their LX-1700 and LX-3700 series devices, providing an order-of-magnitude price reduction for devices of 1% accuracy. The hybrid device contains a built-in vacuum reference, internal chip heating to minimize temperature effects, and piezoresistors arranged in a Wheatstone bridge sensing circuit with preamplification and signal conditioning included in the device.

Fluid-flow measurement is generally implemented by one of two methods: differential pressure sensing and mechanical contact sensing, such as by turbines. Flow rate F is the time rate of fluid motion with typical dimensions in feet per second. Volumetric flow Q is the fluid volume per unit time, such as gallons per minute. Mass flow rate M for a gas is defined in terms of, for example, pounds per hour.

Differential-pressure flow sensing elements have been referred to as head meters or variable-head meters, because the differential pressure across two measurement points is equated to the head. This is equivalent to the height of the column of a differential manometer. Flow rate is obtained from its relationship with the 32 ft/s^2 gravitational constant g and differential pressure. Liquid flow in open channels is normally obtained by head-producing devices such as flumes and weirs. Head measurement is obtained by measuring the height of the flow over the weir. Volumetric flow can then be obtained by including the cross-sectional area of the flow as described in Figure 1–7. Figure 1–8 shows examples of differential-pressure-sensing elements.

$$F = \sqrt{2g} \cdot \sqrt{\Delta p} \qquad \text{feet/second} \tag{1-1}$$

$$Q = \sqrt{2g} \cdot L \cdot H \cdot \sqrt{H} \qquad \text{cubic feet/second} \tag{1-2}$$

The majority of flow rate, or velocity, measuring instruments are point sensors, such as the pitot tube for gas streams. Single-point measure-

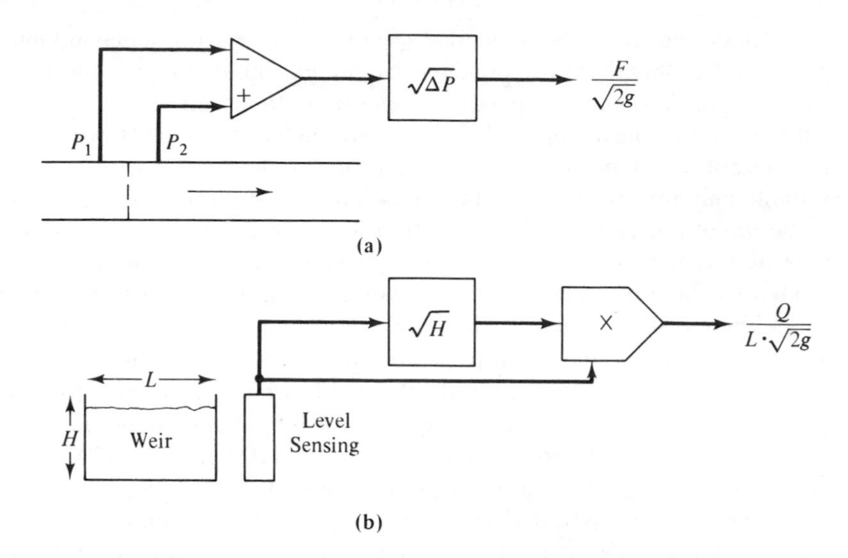

FIGURE 1–7. Flow Rate and Volumetric Flow

ments are generally inaccurate representations of a process stream, however. Multipoint sampling or line averaging sensors such as an annubar are more accurate. Differential-pressure measurements of gas flows at small pressures are another possible source of uncertainty and may require the application of sensitive LVDT-coupled pressure sensors.

Supplementary static temperature and pressure sensing are required for mass-flow-rate measurements. Temperature must be measured at each point where velocity is acquired for accuracy, whereas static pressure can be considered constant across a duct (Figure 1–9). Ideally, velocity sensors should incorporate integral temperature sensors. It is common practice to associate a calibration factor with the probe, as described in the following equations.

$$K = \sqrt{R \cdot \frac{\Delta P_0}{\Delta P_x}} \qquad {}^\circ(\text{K/second}^2)^{1/2} \tag{1-3}$$

where ΔP_0 = true differential pressure $P_0 - P_\infty$ torr
ΔP_x = measured differential pressure
R = universal gas constant

$$M = K \cdot \sqrt{\frac{P \cdot \Delta P}{T}} \qquad \text{pounds/second} \tag{1-4}$$

Mechanical contact flow sensors include turbine and gyroscopic transducers which derive flow rate from angular momentum, thermoelec-

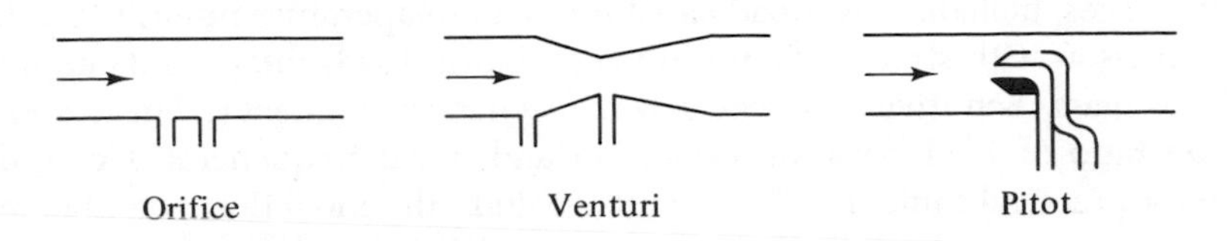

FIGURE 1–8. Differential-Pressure-Sensing Elements

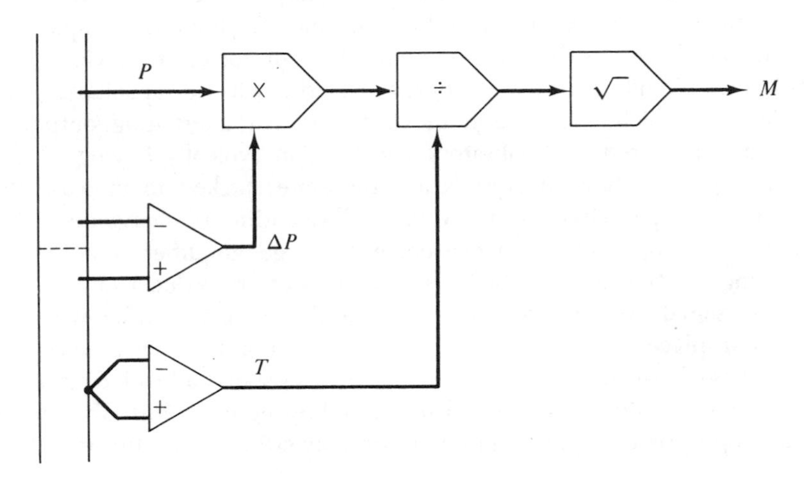

FIGURE 1–9. Mass Gas Flow Computation

tric cooling-rate transducers, electrical resistivity measurements, and beta decay methods. The turbine flowmeter is a popular device which implements the following basic equation to acquire flow rate.

$$F = \frac{\omega R}{\tan \alpha} \quad \text{feet/second} \tag{1-5}$$

where ω = angular rotor velocity
R = average rotor blade radius
α = rotor blade angle

1-3 DISPLACEMENT SENSORS AND ACTUATORS

Accurate position, shaft angle, and linear displacement sensing are possible with the linear variable displacement transformer (LVDT). With this device an ac excitation introduced through a variable reluctance coupling circuit is induced in an output circuit through a movable core which determines the amount of displacement. The LVDT offers distinct advantages, including overload capability and temperature insensitivity, in comparison with strain gage transducers, but a disadvantage is its appreciable mass. Sensitivity increases with excitation frequency, but a minimum ratio of 10:1 between excitation and signal frequencies is considered a practical limit. LVDT variants include the induction potentiometer, synchros, resolvers, and the microsyn. Null balance can be improved with a capacitor across the ac output terminals. Figure 1–10 presents the basic LVDT circuit for both ac and dc outputs.

Acceleration measurements are principally of interest in industrial applications for shock and vibration sensing. Dashpot and capacitive transducers have largely been supplanted by piezoelectric devices. The equivalent circuit is a voltage source in series with a capacitance, the product of which is a charge in coulombs. An alternating output is generated as a result of vibratory acceleration typically having a very small amplitude. Several crystals are therefore stacked to increase the transducer output. Owing to the very small quantities of charge nevertheless transferred, a low input-bias-current charge amplifier is employed following the transducer, which also converts the transducer output to a velocity signal. An additional integrator and precision rectifier will provide a displacement output which may be calibrated, for example, in millinches of displacement per volt. Figure 1–11 shows a block diagram of such a circuit, which is described by the following equations. The choice of an appropriate amplifier and ac-to-dc convertor circuit are described,

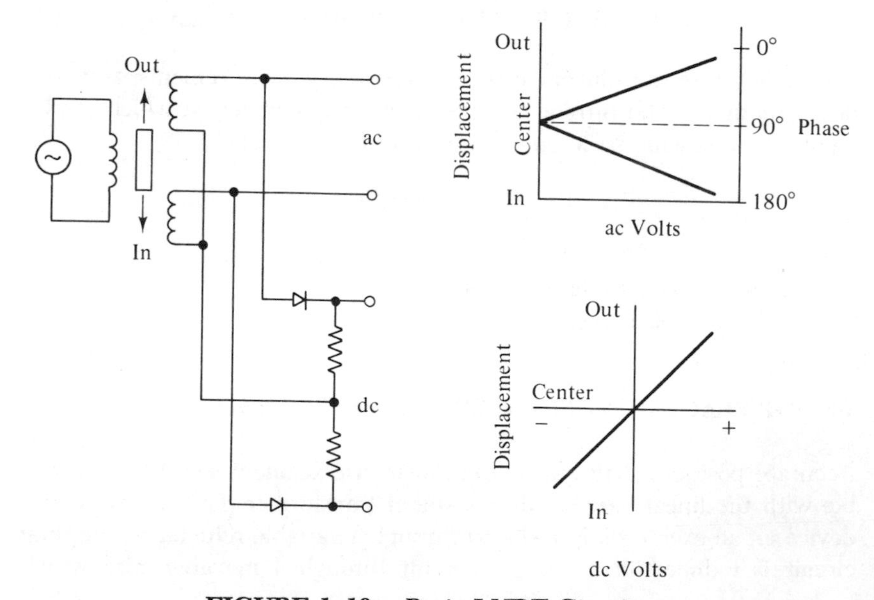

FIGURE 1–10. Basic LVDT Circuit

respectively, in Chapters 2 and 5.

$$\text{acceleration} = C \cdot \Delta E \qquad \text{coulombs} \tag{1-6}$$

$$e = \frac{C}{C_f} \Delta E \qquad \text{volts} \tag{1-7}$$

$$E_o = \int_0^t K \cdot \Delta E \qquad \text{volts} \tag{1-8}$$

Liquid and quasi-liquid (granular solids) levels are process measurements frequently required for tanks, pipes, and other vessels. From level measurements, liquid volume and mass can also be determined if the tank geometry and density, respectively, are known. Sensing methods of various complexity are used in measurements of continuous and incremental-height liquid levels. Float devices and differential-pressure, ultrasonic, and radiation transducers are widely applied.

Float devices offer simplicity and various ways of translating motion into a level reading. However, they are usually less satisfactory for viscous fluids. A differential-pressure transducer can also measure the height of a liquid when the specific weight of the liquid W is known and the ΔP transducer is connected between the tank surface and bottom. Height is given by the ratio $\Delta P/W$. Ultrasonic level sensing can be implemented by an echo-ranging system, which is especially useful for tall tanks, and discrete-height sensing by means of emitters and receivers horizontally opposite each other along the tank height. Difficult fluids, such as cement and paper mill digesters, are best served by nuclear devices that operate similarly to the discrete-height ultrasonic sensors.

Ac-servo positioning systems provide useful actuator mechanizations because they require no periodic calibration. An example system is illustrated in Figure 1–12. To achieve a new output position, the input

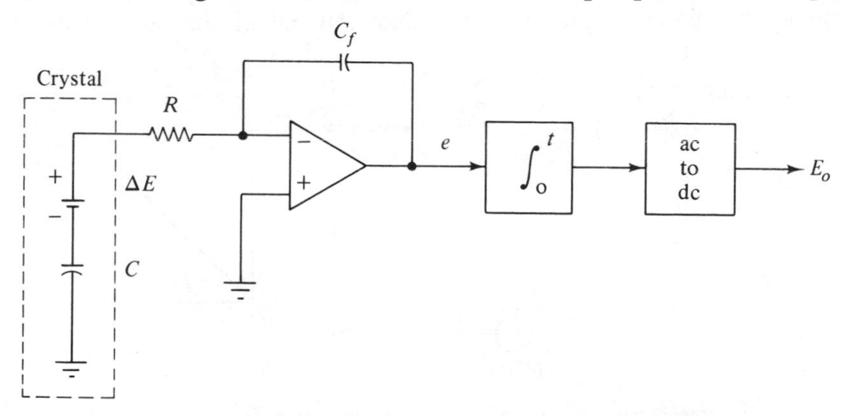

FIGURE 1–11. Vibration Measurement

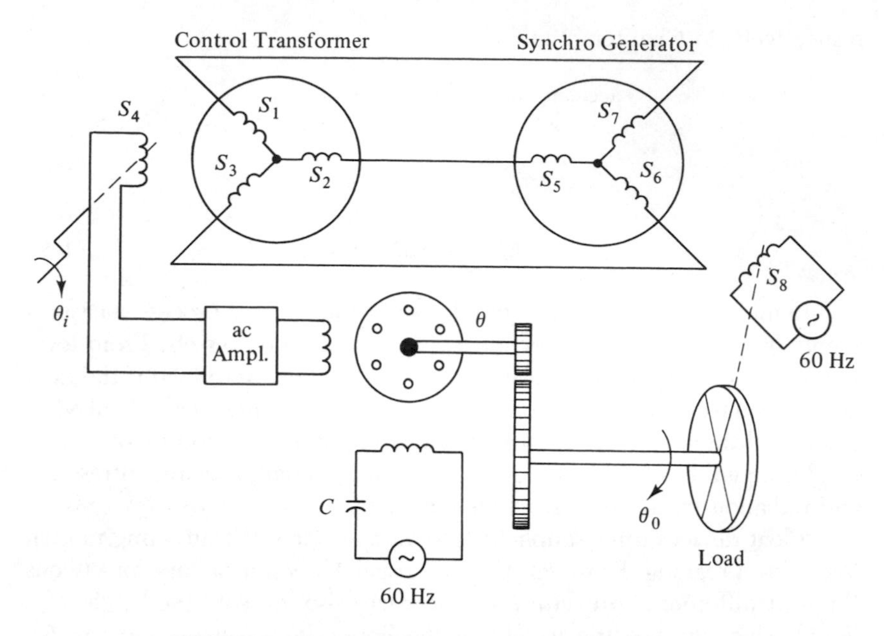

FIGURE 1–12. AC Servo Positioning System

crank displaces the LVDT control transformer winding S_4, upsetting the existing null condition and applying excitation to the servomotor. The motor drives the load in the appropriate direction as determined by the excitation polarity of winding S_4, thereby repositioning synchro winding S_8 until a new null is achieved at S_4. This action removes excitation from the servomotor, or the error voltage, with the positioning system having "answered out" to the input angle θ_i. Further insight is available from Figure 1–13. For small inertia rotors typically encountered in servo positioning systems, the shaft-angle motion for a two-phase induction motor will closely approximate the time integral of the motor control

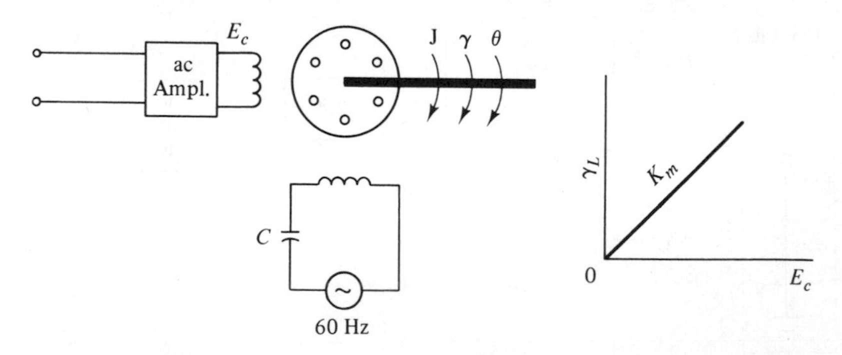

FIGURE 1–13. Induction Motor Relationships

voltage and its gain constant, as follows:

$$\theta = \int_0^t K_m \cdot E_c \cdot dt \tag{1-9}$$

where τ_L = locked rotor torque
J = rotor inertia
θ = shaft angle
K_m = motor gain constant
E_c = motor control voltage

1-4 CHEMICAL ANALYZERS

On-line measurements of industrial processes and chemical streams frequently require the use of dedicated analyzers to obtain variables important to the control of a process. Examples are oxygen for boiler control, inorganic sulfur oxide emissions from combustion processes, and organic hydrocarbons found in petroleum refining. Laboratory instruments such as gas chromatographs generally are not used for on-line measurements, primarily because they analyze all compounds present simultaneously, rather than a single one of interest.

The dispersive infrared analyzer is perhaps the most widely used analyzer, because of the range of compounds it can be configured to measure. Operation is by the differential absorption of infrared energy of the sample stream in comparison to that of a reference cell. Detection is by deflection of a diaphragm separating the sample and reference cells, which, in turn, detunes an oscillator circuit capacitively. Oxygen analyzers are usually of the amperometric type, in which oxygen is reduced at a gold cathode, resulting in a current flow from a silver anode which is a function of this reduction. In a second paramagnetic wind-type device, a wind effect is generated when a mixture containing oxygen produces a gradient in a magnetic field. Measurement is derived by the thermal cooling effect on a heated resistance element, which is a thermal anemometer mechanization.

Hydrocarbon analyzers usually employ the flame ionization method, whereby a regulated sample gas passes through a flame fed by regulated fuel and air. Ionization of hydrocarbon compounds into ions and electrons ensues, which are then collected and measured with polarized electrodes. Chemiluminescent reaction analyzers produce specific light emission when electronically excited and oxygenated molecules revert to their ground state. A summary of these methods is tabulated in Table 1–3 and an example analyzer implementation is shown by Figure 1–14.

TABLE 1–3. Chemical Analyzer Methods

Compound	Analyzer
CO, SO_x, NH_x	Infrared
O_2	Amperometric, paramagnetic
HC	Flame ionization
NO_x	Chemiluminescent
H_2S	Electrochemical cell

Electrochemical analytical sensors detect the electrical potential generated in response to the presence of dissolved ionized solids in a process stream. Included in this group are pH, conductivity, and ion-selective probes. The principle of operation is based on the Nernst equation, which typically provides a 60-mV potential change for each tenfold change in the activity of a monovalent ion. For pH sensors, the ion-selective electrode is sensitive to free hydrogen ions in the stream, thereby reflecting the acidity or alkalinity of the sample. pH and oxidation–reduction (ORP) sensors, in which the latter detects the ratio of reducing agent to oxidizing agent, are important in effluent measurement and treatment

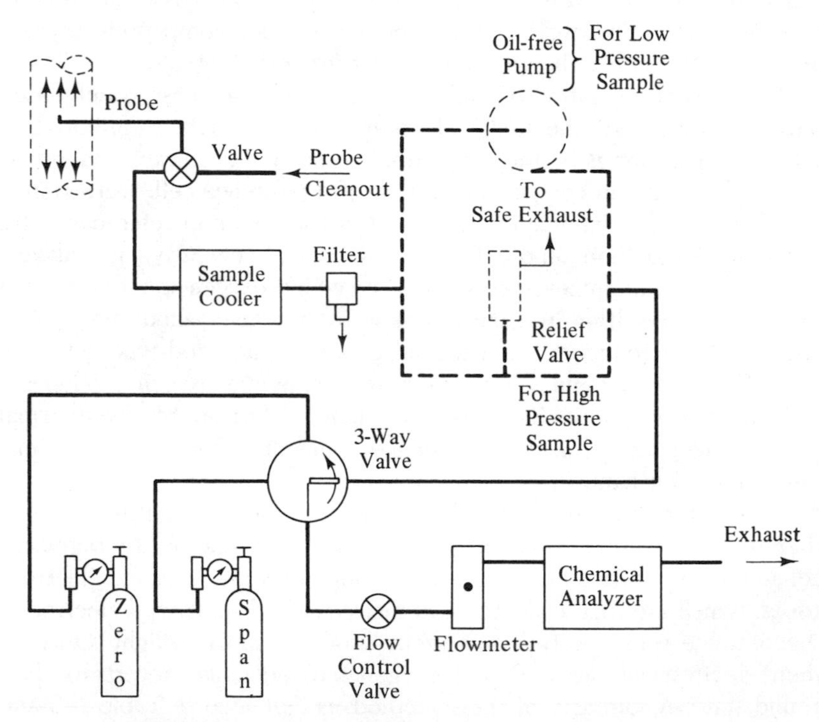

FIGURE 1–14. Typical System Flow Diagram

control. Equation (1-10) describes the Nernst relationship.

$$E = E_0 + \frac{F}{n}\log(ac + s_1 a_1 c_1 + \cdots) \qquad \text{volts} \tag{1-10}$$

where E = voltage between sensing and reference electrodes
E_0 = electrode base potential
F = Nernst factor, 60 mV at 25°C
n = ionic charge, one monovalent, two bivalent, etc.
a = ionic activity
c = concentration
s = electrode sensitivity to interfering ions

1-5 PHOTOMETRY AND RADIOMETRY

Photometry and radiometry have been described as difficult fields of precise measurement. Much confusion has resulted from the use of archaic terms, qualitative definitions, and incorrect substitutions between photometry and radiometry. Planck's basic assumption was that light was not continuous, but consisted of discrete photon quanta, whose energy is a function of frequency. For this reason energy E falling on an arbitrary photosensitive material will exhibit a spectral response peak, a function both of the specific material and equation (1-11). It is therefore necessary to spectrally match sources and sensors to optimize the transfer. This can be aided by a lens that gathers parallel rays and focuses them on the area of the sensor (Figure 1–15). The gain associated with this transformation is approximately given by equation (1-12). Table 1–4 presents common photometric and radiometric definitions, where a source of diameter $\frac{1}{10}$ the separation distance is considered an area source. A sphere has a surface area of $4\pi R^2$ and a total solid angle of 4π steradians.

$$E = hf = (6.626 \times 10^{-34}\ \text{J/s})(f\,\text{Hz}) \tag{1-11}$$

$$\text{sensor gain} = 0.9\left(\frac{\text{lens radius}}{\text{sensor radius}}\right) \tag{1-12}$$

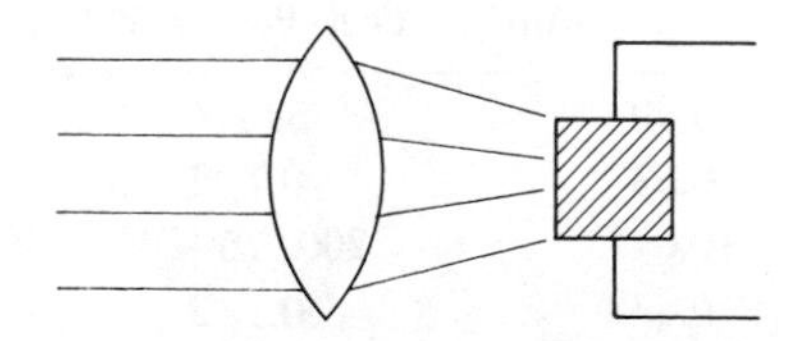

FIGURE 1–15. Sensor Gain with Lens

TABLE 1–4. Photometric and Radiometric Definitions

	Radiometry	Photometry
Intensity (point source)	Watts/steradian	Candelas
Radiance (area source)	$\frac{\text{Watts/steradian}}{\text{cm}^2}$	Footlamberts
Total flux	Watts	Lumens
Irradiance	Watts/cm^2	Footcandles

Important sources of radiation are the sun, man-made lamps, lasers, and light-emitting diodes (LED). LED devices can be fabricated to emit on wavelengths between about 560 and 910 nm with bandwidths to 30 nm. By comparison, the human eye response peaks at about 555 nm. LEDs fall into two general classifications, emitters and laser diodes, both of which are photodiodes emitting from their valence bands. The principal difference is that laser diodes have higher peak powers and narrower spectral widths than emitters. Emitters are also usually operated continuously, whereas laser diodes only operate in the pulsed mode. The laser is the only source of coherent radiation and is capable of extremely high radiance. Commonly applied types are summarized in Table 1–5. Plastics are replacing glass for optical transmission. However, both glass and plastic are opaque to ultraviolet below about 350 nm, requiring fused quartz or sapphire for low-loss transmission. Far-infrared wavelengths beyond 1 μm require sodium chloride or Irtran.

Light sensors fall into three categories—photoemitters, photodiodes, and photoconductors. Photomultiplier tubes have usable sensitivities down to one photon. Tube gain is expressed by δ^n, which is the ratio of secondary to primary electrons for each of the n dynodes in the tube. Overall gains to 10^6 are common. Photomultipliers are the most sensitive of detectors and require interfacing with low input-bias-current ampli-

TABLE 1–5. Laser Summary

Type	Wavelength (μm)	Peak Power (W)	Feature
Argon	0.49	5/100	Blue–green
He–Ne	0.63	0.1/2	Low-cost red
CO_2	10.6	200/75 KW	High power
HeCd	0.44	0.1/2	Recent blue
Krypton	0.64	5/100	Red or Green

fiers, such as varactor input-stage operational amplifiers, if this sensitivity is to be fully realized. Equation (1-13) expresses photomultiplier output current as a function of tube gain δ^n.

$$I_o = (1.6 \times 10^{-19}) \cdot \delta^n \quad \text{amperes} \tag{1-13}$$

Phototubes are in the same class as photomultipliers and were the first devices to operate by cathode-to-anode electron emission upon exposure to incident light. As indicated in Figure 1–16, phototubes are essentially constant-current devices and a good signal-to-noise ratio is their primary feature. Photovoltaic devices, such as solar cells, provide an output EMF of 0.5 V for silicon and 0.1 V for germanium with efficiency in the 12–15% range (Figure 1–17). Maximum power output is obtained by optimizing load resistance, which typically is about 3 kΩ for silicon devices. Operation is from lowering of the semiconductor potential barrier by incident light resulting in majority carrier current flow.

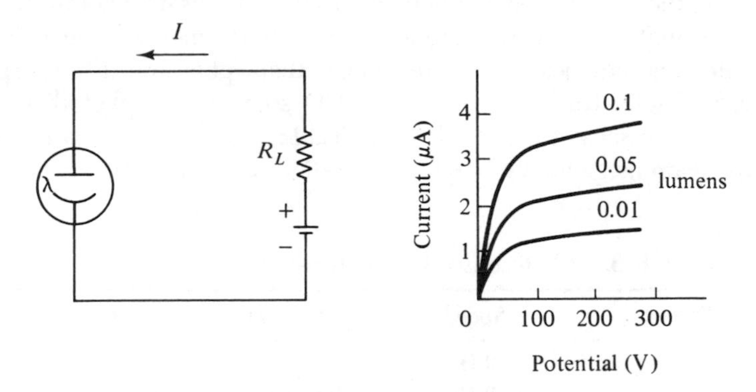

FIGURE 1–16. Phototube Characteristics

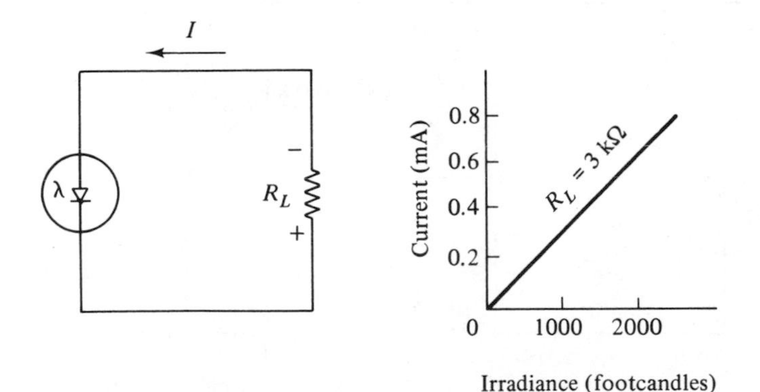

FIGURE 1–17. Photovoltaic Characteristics

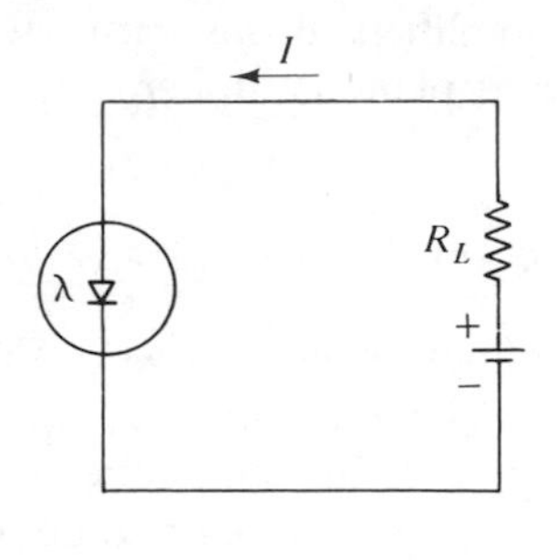

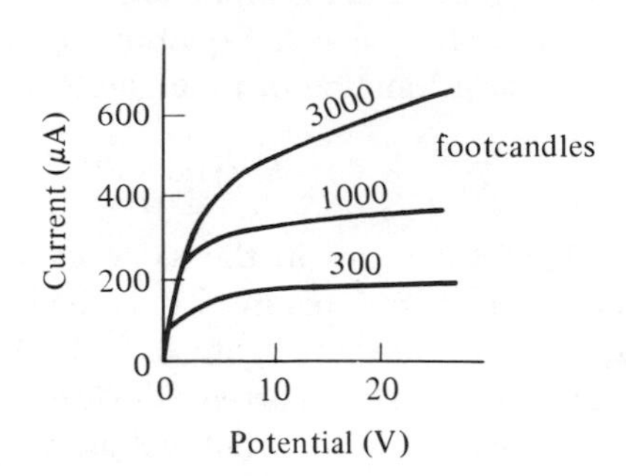

FIGURE 1–18. Photodiode Characteristics

Photodiodes are light-sensitive devices which may either be *pn*-junction diodes or *pnp* and *npn* phototransistors (Figure 1–18). These devices are among the most widely applied electrooptical sensors. Phototransistors in the Darlington connection are also available for increased sensitivities. However, photodiodes are more linear than phototransistors. Speed, power, and gain trade-offs between LED sources and photodiode and phototransistor sensors are tabulated in Table 1–6. Linear signal transmission applications generally employ photodiodes, whereas position sensors

TABLE 1–6. Photosensor Characteristics

Device	Speed	Output	Gain
Darlington	lkHz	lW	1000
Transistor	100kHz	100mW	1
Diode	10MHz	lmW	0.001

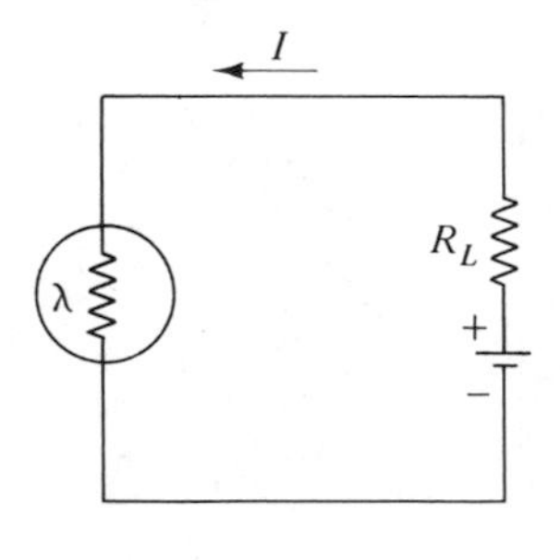

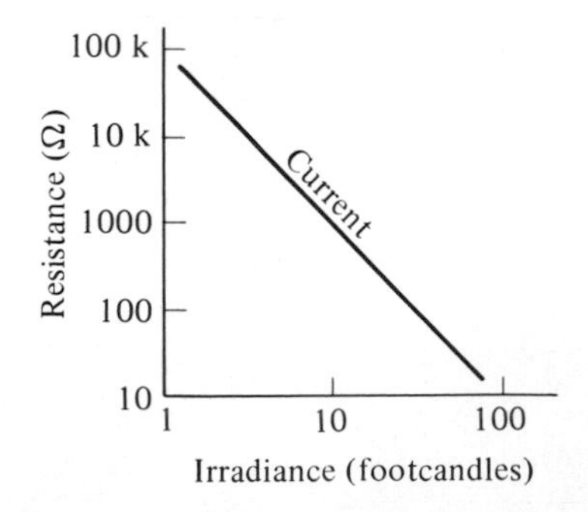

FIGURE 1–19. Photoconductive Characteristics

and optical isolators for digital signals typically use phototransistors. The latter are widely used in industrial applications for voltage isolation purposes. Photoconductive cells are photoresistive devices which exhibit a decreasing resistance with increasing light level (Figure 1–19). They exhibit hysteresis effects and a temperature coefficient which is a function of light level. Power dissipation capability must also be observed when applying these devices.

1-6 GROUNDING PRACTICE

There usually exists a finite resistance in the ground return path between electronic instruments. If there also exists a small difference of potential between these instruments, perhaps due to normal power-supply leakage, a common-mode current may be established which can appear in series with the signal of interest. A single-point ground located at the instrument most susceptable to interference, thereby ensuring the lowest ground impedance at that point, will normally minimize this problem. Figure 1–20 illustrates one procedure for the elimination of this error source.

Noise introduced into an instrumentation system between the transducer and its terminating circuitry may have as its source one or more of the following: (1) inductive coupling of interference to the signal lines; (2) capacitive coupling of interference to the signal lines; and (3) system ground points not at the same potential giving rise to common-mode interference. Prior to the widespread availability of differential amplifiers in the 1950s, the single-point instrumentation ground was employed and implemented with heavy conductors to provide a low impedance path, thereby minimizing common-mode interference (Figure 1–21). However, transducer signals always had to be greater than the common-mode interference for useful system operation. Hence, many applications taken for granted today simply were not possible.

The availability of stable dc differential amplifiers permitted interfering common-mode signals orders of magnitude greater than the transducer signals of interest. Although excellent common-mode rejection was achieved, two independent ground points were now introduced, which limited the ultimate attainable value of rejection due to minute circulating ground currents. A solution to this problem, which permits very high common-mode rejection under difficult interference conditions, is to guard the differential amplifier (Figure 1–22). This technique provides a virtual single-point ground due to the ultra-high impedance introduced between the two grounds. An internal power supply is required with a shielded power transformer plus shielded transducer lines, which are returned to the Faraday box.

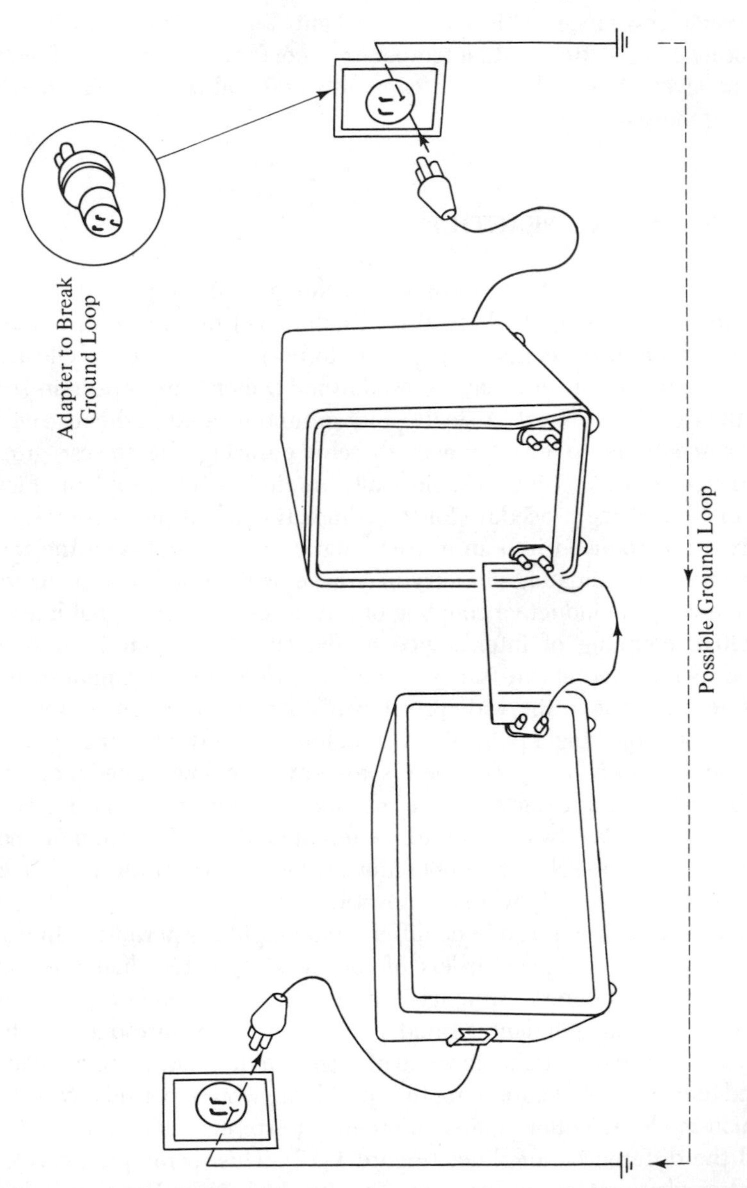

FIGURE 1–20. Ground Loop Prevention

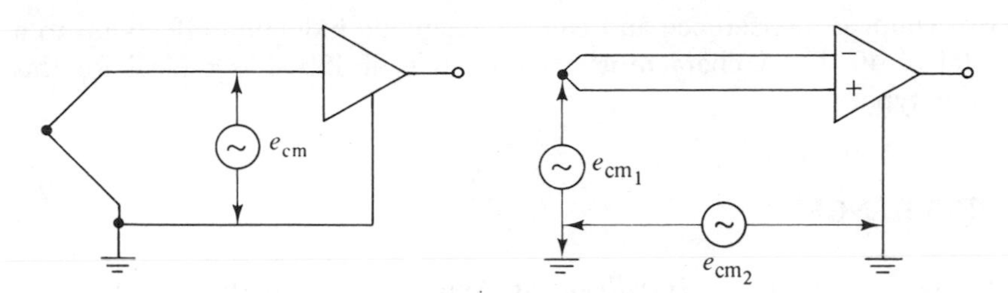

FIGURE 1–21. Single and Differential Input Amplifiers

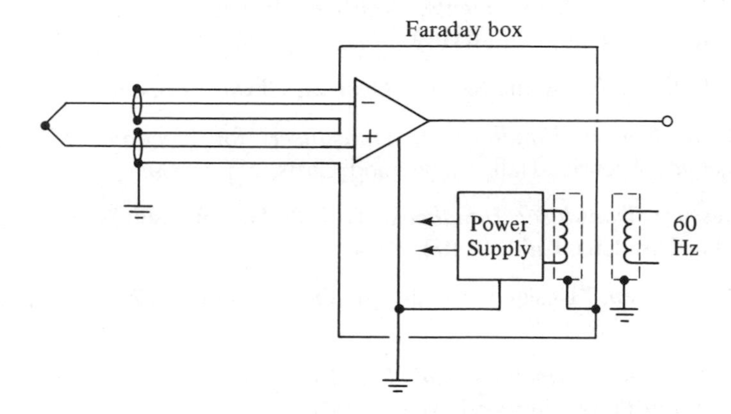

FIGURE 1–22. Guarded Instrumentation Amplifier

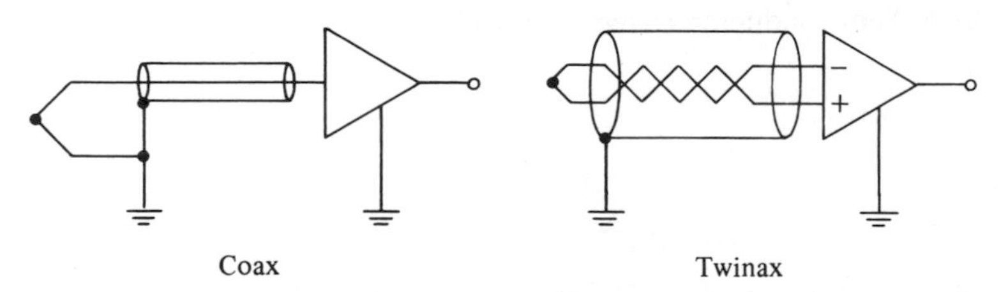

FIGURE 1–23. Shielded Instrumentation Cables

For unshielded signal cables, 1 mV of interference will be coupled per kilowatt of ac load for 1-ft-spaced cables per parallel foot of cable run. Use of a twisted-pair signal cable will reduce the susceptability to inductive interference pickup (Figure 1–23). Also, a coaxial conductive shield will attenuate radiation-induced interference, provided that no current is permitted to flow in the shield. Use of a single-point ground satisfies the latter condition. The rule of thumb is to place this ground at the location of greatest encountered interference, which is usually at the transducer end. A shielded twisted pair, known as twinax, rejects capacitive coupled interference and cancels magnetic induction effects up to a total of 40 dB. A characteristic impedance of 125 Ω is typical for this cable type.

REFERENCES

1. D. M. Considine, *Handbook of Applied Instrumentation*, McGraw-Hill, New York, 1964.
2. *Electrometer Measurements*, Keithley Instruments, 28775 Aurora Road, Cleveland, Ohio 44139, 1972.
3. A. F. Giles, *Electronic Sensing Devices*, Clowes, London, 1966.
4. H. N. Norton, *Handbook of Transducers for Electronic Measuring Systems*, Prentice-Hall, Englewood Cliffs, N.J., 1969.
5. *Pressure Transducer Handbook*, Bell & Howell, 360 Sierra Madre Villa, Pasadena, Calif. 91109, 1974.
6. H. Sorensen, "Designer's Guide to Optoisolators," *Electronic Design News*, April 5, 1976.
7. L. K. Spink, *Principles and Practice of Flow Meter Engineering*, Plimpton Press, Norwood, Mass., 1967.
8. *Transducers: Pressure and Temperature*, National Semiconductor, 2900 Semiconductor Drive, Santa Clara, Calif. 95051, 1974.

2

INSTRUMENTATION AMPLIFIERS

2-0 INTRODUCTION

The forcing function in the application of electronic instrumentation to laboratory and industrial process apparatus is the quest for increased capability and higher performance. This is manifest in many forms from high-resolution and accurate analog data-acquisition systems to reliable analog controllers for the reduction of the variance of controlled variables in automated processes. Electronic instrumentation provides the common denominator of and the signal translation for these components and systems.

Instrumentation amplifiers are generally the first component encountered at the input of analog systems. Their purpose is to interface the transducers of Chapter 1 to the computer inputs or other analog systems developed in subsequent chapters. A basic familiarity is assumed with electronic devices and systems, but a detailed understanding of electronic circuit design is not required. Emphasis is on the development of essential information needed for the design and implementation of analog instrumentation, rather than purely analytical considerations. The principal topics of this chapter include operational amplifier types and their circuit relationships, input and output error contributions, and applications considerations. An error budget is derived for operational amplifiers frequently used in instrumentation service, including determination of the minimum usable input signal levels, plus an evaluation of factors affecting in-circuit rejection of common-mode interference.

2-1 OPERATIONAL AMPLIFIERS

In the decade following introduction of the Fairchild 709 monolithic operational amplifier, improvements in linear integrated-circuit design provided second-generation devices represented by the National LM 108. Advances in fabrication technology permitting mixed devices on a single substrate led to the third-generation devices represented by the RCA 3140. Fortunately, the result of these improvements now permit the realization of nearly ideal operational amplifier performance without need for consideration of earlier concerns, such as the choice of phase compensation to ensure unconditional stability. Present devices are either internally compensated or externally compensated, the latter according to specific instructions by the manufacturer.

All operational amplifiers are similarly constructed, having a differential pair input stage, a high-gain interstage, and a power output stage as depicted by Figure 2–1. Of particular interest is the high-gain interstage with a high impedance current-source active load that is primarily responsible for present operational amplifier technology. Voltage gains of 100,000 can be achieved from a 15-V supply with this circuit technique, whereas a kilovolt power supply would be required to realize the same gain from a single stage with a passive load. Amplifier classification is by the input stage, which largely determines device performance. Table 2–1 delineates this classification.

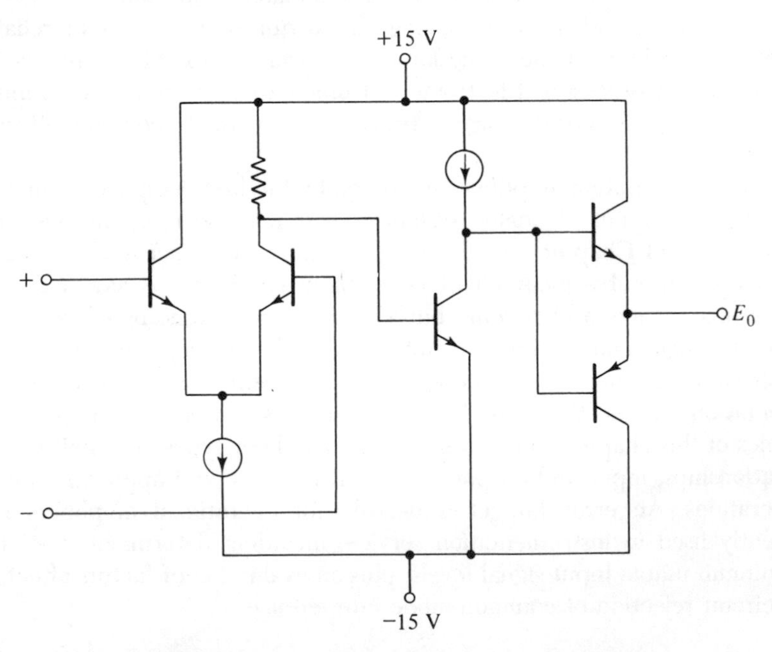

FIGURE 2–1. Basic Operational Amplifier

TABLE 2–1. Operational Amplifier Types

Bipolar	Most prevalent type, used for a wide range of signal-processing applications. Good balance of performance characteristics.
FET	Very high input impedance useful for instrumentation amplifier input. Exhibits larger errors and drift than bipolar devices.
BIMOS	Combined bipolar and FET devices for extended performance. Intended to displace bipolars in general-purpose applications.
Superbeta	A bipolar device approaching FET input impedance with the lower bipolar errors. Disadvantage is lack of device ruggedness.
Isolation	An internal barrier device using modulation or optical methods for very high isolation. Medical and high-voltage industrial applications.
Chopper	A dc–ac–dc circuit with a capacitor-coupled amplifier having very low input errors for applications requiring minimum input uncertainty.
Varactor	A varactor diode input operational amplifier having very low input bias currents for current-amplification applications such as photomultipliers.
Vibrating capacitor	A special input circuit arrangement providing ultra-low input bias currents for current-amplification applications such as electrometers.

The primary utility of the operational amplifier is its ability to amplify dc signals stably and ac signals simultaneously without phase shift due to the direct interstage coupling. The availability of an inverting and noninverting input is of particular interest for instrumentation applications because of the common-mode signal-rejection capability which it affords. However, we shall see later in the chapter that the primary purpose of the differential input stage which provides this rejection is to ensure good dc stability. A single input amplifier provides equal gain to both the signal of interest and interference, with the result that the latter becomes an inseparable error. A differential input amplifier, however, offers equal but opposite polarity amplification to the interference, with a resulting attenuation that is proportional to the amplifier common-mode rejection ratio (CMRR). This is illustrated by Figure 2–2.

Elemental operational amplifier circuits are shown in Figure 2–3 with their respective gains conveniently derived in terms of resistor ratios.

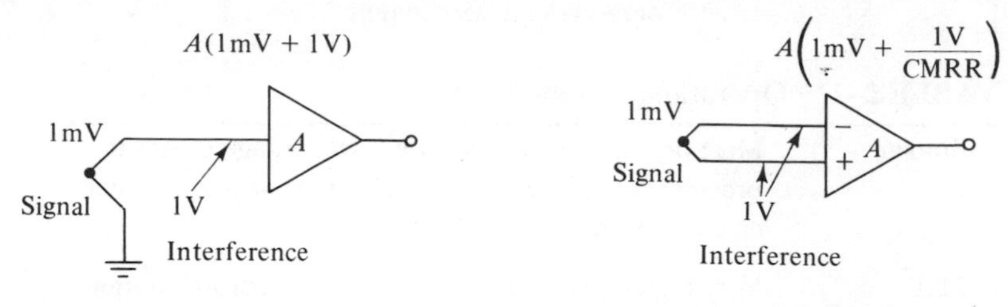

FIGURE 2–2. Common-Mode Interference Rejection

Buffer

$$E_i - \frac{E_o}{A} = E_o$$

$$E_o = E_i \qquad (2\text{-}1)$$

Inverter

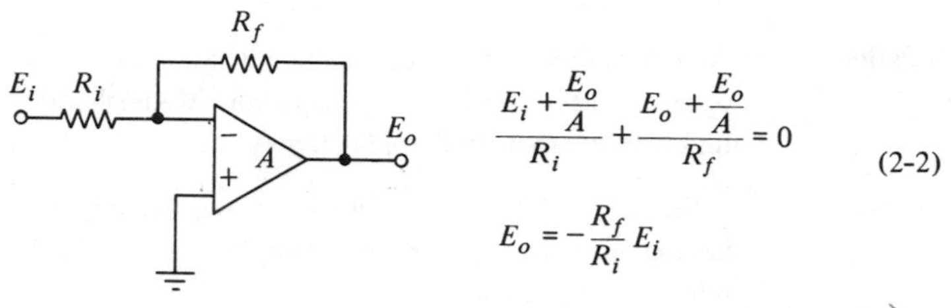

$$\frac{E_i + \frac{E_o}{A}}{R_i} + \frac{E_o + \frac{E_o}{A}}{R_f} = 0 \qquad (2\text{-}2)$$

$$E_o = -\frac{R_f}{R_i} E_i$$

Noninverter

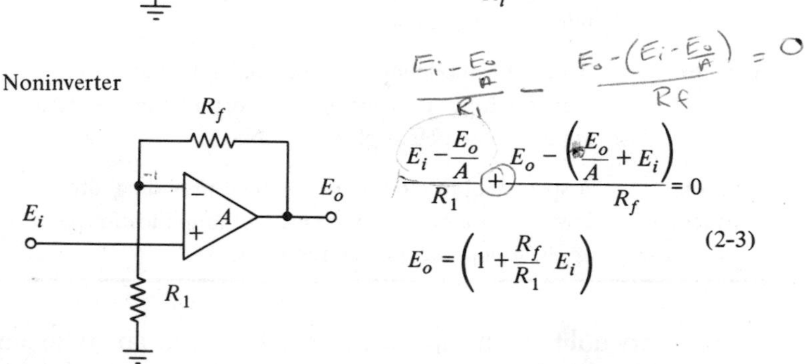

$$\frac{E_i - \frac{E_o}{A}}{R_1} + \frac{E_o - \left(\frac{E_o}{A} + E_i\right)}{R_f} = 0$$

$$E_o = \left(1 + \frac{R_f}{R_1} E_i\right) \qquad (2\text{-}3)$$

Subtractor

$$\frac{R_{f_1}}{R_G} + \frac{R_{f_1}}{R_{i_1}} = \frac{R_{f_2}}{R_G} + \frac{R_{f_2}}{R_{i_2}}$$

Connect R_G for balance:

$$E_o = \frac{R_{f_2}}{R_{i_2}} E_2 - \frac{R_{f_1}}{R_{i_1}} E_1 \qquad (2\text{-}4)$$

FIGURE 2–3. Elemental Amplifier Circuits

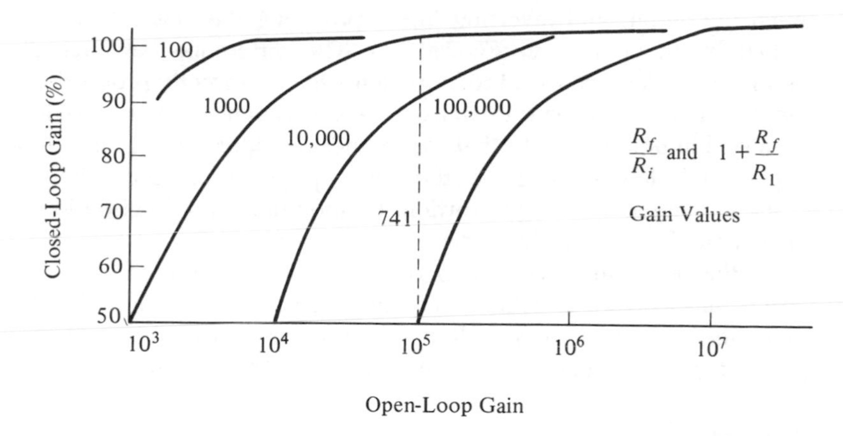

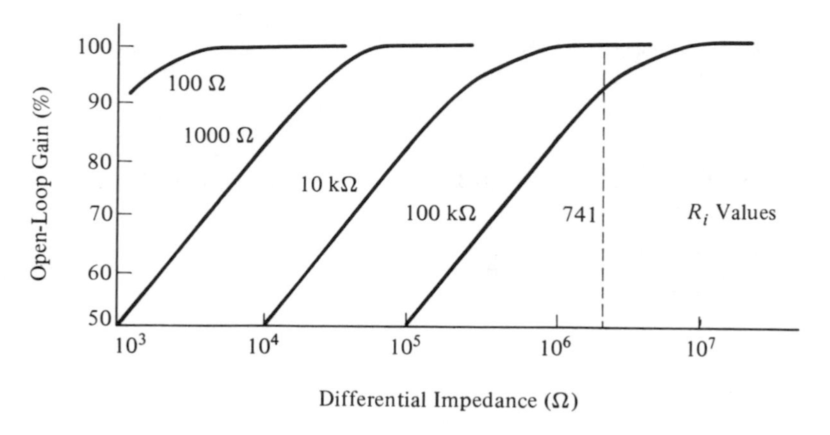

FIGURE 2–4. Device Performance Limitations

The accuracy of these simple gain equations is graphically described by the curves of Figure 2–4 in terms of device open-loop gain and differential input impedance. By way of example, the maximum recommended closed-loop gain and input impedance for the 741 operational amplifier are shown to be 1000 and 20 kΩ, respectively. Note that the differential input voltage is E_o/A in all cases and negligible for large open-loop gain A in Figure 2–3.

Typical operational amplifiers have three internal corner frequencies which can be related to the circuit of Figure 2–1. The lowest may be around 10 Hz and is associated with the high-gain interstage. The second is generally in the vicinity of 1 MHz and is attributable to the input differential stage. The third is perhaps at 50 MHz and is associated with the output stage. However, this composite gain–bandwidth characteristic is not usable for linear amplification until negative feedback is established between the output and inverting input, providing the closed-loop gain described by the curves in Figure 2–5. The difference between the open- and closed-loop gains is the loop gain which is directly proportional to the dc stability, bandwidth extension, and noise and distortion reduction realized in practice. Note that for frequencies approaching closure of the open- and closed-loop gains, the net loop gain diminishes, thereby reducing stability and raising distortion. Caution must be exercised in the amplification of signals in this region.

For the usual large open-loop device gains encountered, negative feedback enhancement is defined according to equations (2-5) and (2-6). Further, the reduction in overall bandwidth for cascaded operational amplifier stages including no inductors is expressed by equation (2-7).

$$\text{BW and dc stability multiplier} = \frac{A_{ol}}{A_{cl}} \tag{2-5}$$

$$\text{distortion and noise reduction} = \frac{A_{cl}}{A_{ol}} \tag{2-6}$$

$$\text{cascaded-stages bandwidth} = \frac{0.35}{1.1\left[(0.35/BW_1)^2 + \cdots + (0.35/BW_N)^2\right]^{1/2}} \tag{2-7}$$

$$\text{voltage gain of cascaded stages} = A_{cl_1} \cdot A_{cl_2} \cdots A_{cl_N} \tag{2-8}$$

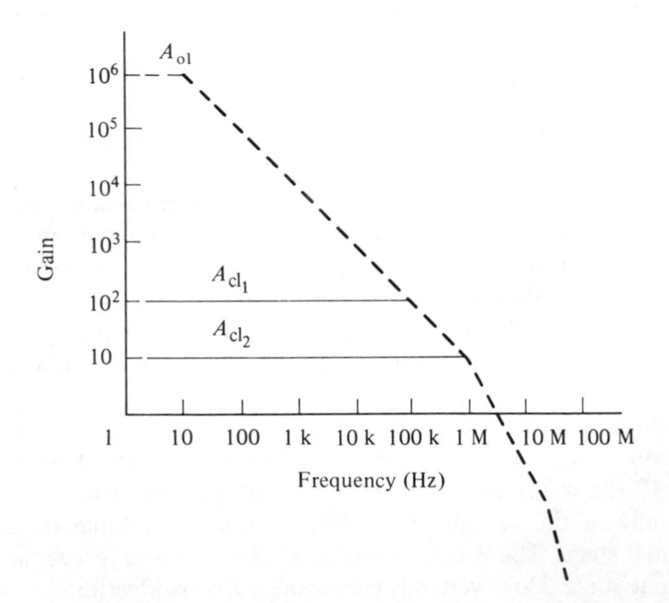

FIGURE 2–5. Gain–Bandwidth Characteristics

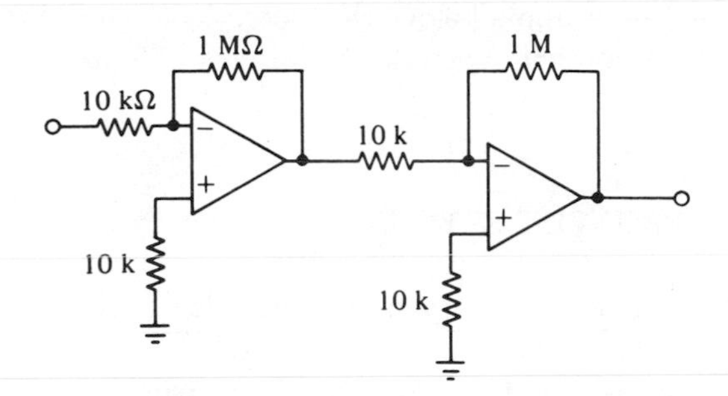

Per stage: $A_{cl_1} = 100$ Overall: gain = 10,000

$BW_1 = 100$ kHz BW = 64 kHz

$THD_1 = 1\%$ THD = 2%

FIGURE 2–6. Gain–Bandwidth Relationships

Consider the example of two inverting amplifiers in cascade, each with a closed-loop gain of 100 and a bandwidth of 100 kHz, and with each amplifier contributing 1% total harmonic distortion. This circuit is characterized by Figure 2–6 with the aid of equation (2-7), observing that distortion is additive. If it is required to reduce distortion by a factor of 10, then equation (2-6) indicates a reduction in closed-loop gain per stage to 10, to obtain a distortion reduction to 0.1%. This modification is described by Figure 2–7. Of course, other criteria, such as bandwidth extension or improved dc stability, may also be of interest. For computa-

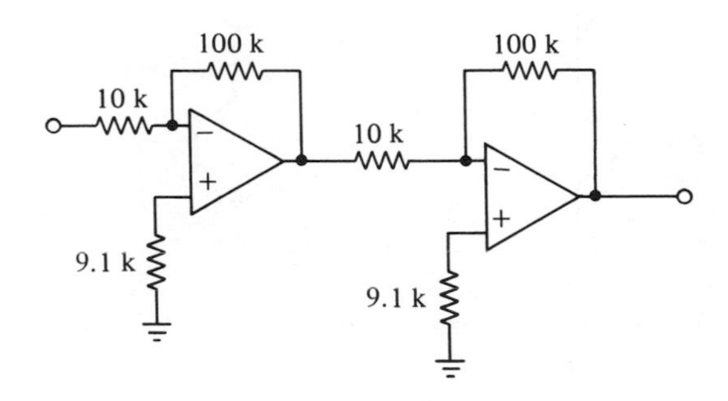

Per stage: $A_{cl_2} = 10$ Overall: gain = 100

$BW_2 = (A_{cl_1}/A_{cl_2})(BW_1)$ BW = 640 kHz

$= 1$ MHz THD = 0.2%

$THD_2 = (A_{cl_2}/A_{cl_1})(THD_1)$

0.1%

FIGURE 2–7. Gain–Bandwidth Modification

tion purposes in the example below, the closed-loop gain of Figure 2–6 is taken as the open-loop gain entry for equations (2-5) and (2-6) of Figure 2–7.

2-2 AMPLIFIER INPUT ERRORS

Three operational amplifier types are of particular interest for instrumentation amplifier applications: the bipolar, JFET, and chopper amplifiers. It is of interest to examine the differential input pair of each because this stage largely determines amplifier performance. The emitter current of a bipolar transistor (Figure 2–8) is described by the classical diode equation of equation (2-9), which is reformulated in terms of its base–emitter voltage in equation (2-10). KT/q is the voltage equivalent of temperature and is equal to 26 mV at $T=300°K$, or room temperature. I_s is the reverse saturation current and is typically near 10^{-15} A, or 1 femtoampere.

The base–emitter voltages of a random group of the same type of bipolar transistors at the same collector current are generally within 20 mV of one another. In practice, selection and operation of a differential pair from a constant-current source permits this V_{be} mismatch, or offset voltage V_{os}, to be maintained within 1 mV. The base–emitter temperature variation for a forward-biased silicon transistor decreases -2.2 mV/°C

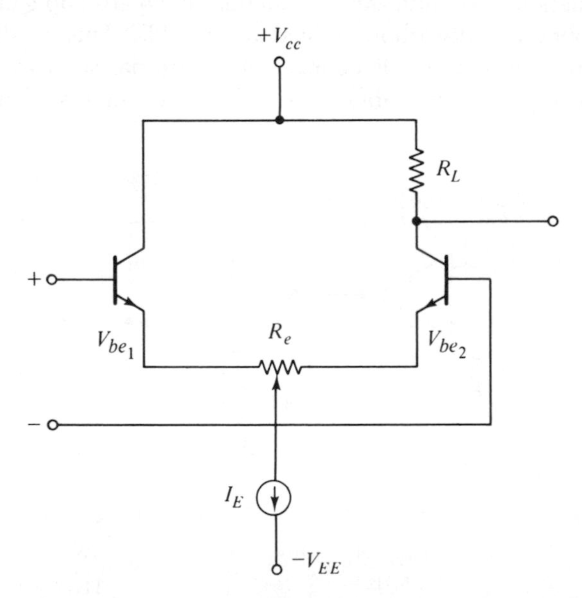

FIGURE 2–8. Bipolar Differential Stage

rise. In a differential configuration, however, the combined temperature drift dV_{os}/dT is reduced by a factor of 1/700 at 300°K, or to 3.3 μV/°C, primarily as a result of the preceding match of the base–emitter voltages.

$$I_E = I_S\left[\exp\left(\frac{qV_{be}}{KT}\right)-1\right] \quad \text{amperes} \qquad (2\text{-}9)$$

$$V_{be} = \frac{KT}{q}\cdot\ln\frac{I_E}{I_S} \quad \text{volts} \qquad (2\text{-}10)$$

$$V_{os} = V_{be_1} - V_{be_2} = 1\,\text{mV} \qquad (2\text{-}11)$$

$$\frac{dV_{os}}{dT} = 3.3\,\mu\text{V}/°\text{C} \qquad (2\text{-}12)$$

Bipolar operational amplifiers require an input bias current to maintain linear circuit operation. This current produces a voltage drop in the input resistors which when multiplied by amplifier gain appears at the output as a voltage error. The input resistor of Figure 2–9 can be balanced by a compensating resistor R_c, with the result that this input bias voltage drop is rejected by the CMRR of the amplifier. Even with matched input resistors, a residual error may remain, resulting from mismatched current gains, β_1 and β_2, of the differential stage. If this offset bias current presents a problem, a better operational amplifier choice is indicated. The temperature dependence of this offset current is a negative factor averaging a $-\frac{1}{2}\%/°\text{C}$. Typical offset current and current drift are shown by equations (2-13) and (2-14). It can now be appreciated that the differential input stage primarily ensures good dc stability, with

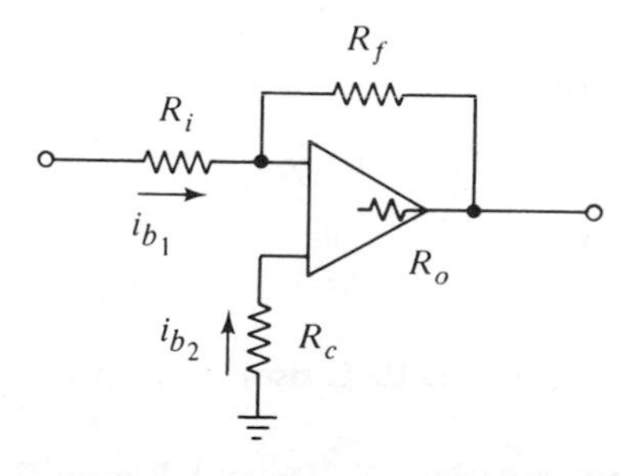

FIGURE 2–9. Bias-Current Compensation

the rejection of common-mode interference an additional dividend.

$$I_{os} = \frac{(\beta_2 - \beta_1) I_c}{\beta_1 \cdot \beta_2} = 50\,\text{nA} \tag{2-13}$$

$$\frac{dI_{os}}{dT} = K \cdot I_{os} \qquad \begin{matrix} K = -0.005/°\text{C} > 25°\text{C} \\ K = -0.015/°\text{C} < 25°\text{C} \end{matrix} \tag{2-14}$$

$$= -0.25\,\text{nA}/°\text{C}$$

$$R_c = R_i \cdot \frac{R_f + R_o}{R_i + R_f + R_o} \qquad \text{ohms} \tag{2-15}$$

Input offset voltage and drift for a JFET differential stage are typically greater than those occurring with a bipolar stage. JFET gate-source voltages for the same type of device may vary by several volts. However, device selection and operation at the same current will permit this V_{gs} offset mismatch to be maintained within about 5 mV. To achieve minimum input offset voltage drift with a JFET differential stage, the devices must be biased at their zero drift drain current point V_{gsz}. Without this biasing, typical offset voltage drifts are near 35 μV/°C. Consequently, the manufacturer trims this current to achieve an offset drift mismatch to within about 5 μV/°C. Insofar as JFET offset current error is concerned, the reverse-biased input gate *pn* junction has only reverse saturation current I_s plus surface leakage current, totaling about 10 pA at room temperature. However, this current doubles for every 10°C rise. Typical JFET device input errors are summarized below.

$$V_{os} = V_{gs_1} - V_{gs_2} \tag{2-16}$$

$$= 5\,\text{mV}$$

$$\frac{dV_{os}}{dT} = 3.5 \times 10^{-3}\left[\left(V_{gsz_1} - V_{gsz_2}\right) - V_{os}\right] \tag{2-17}$$

$$= 5\,\mu\text{V}/°\text{C}$$

$$I_{os} = I_s + \text{surface leakage} \tag{2-18}$$

$$= 10\,\text{pA}$$

$$\frac{dI_{os}}{dT} = (I_{os}) \cdot (\times 2/10°\text{C rise}) \qquad \text{amperes}/°\text{C} \tag{2-19}$$

With reference to equation (2-10) and Figure 2–8, emitter-voltage unbalance may be introduced by R_e to compensate for device I_s variation,

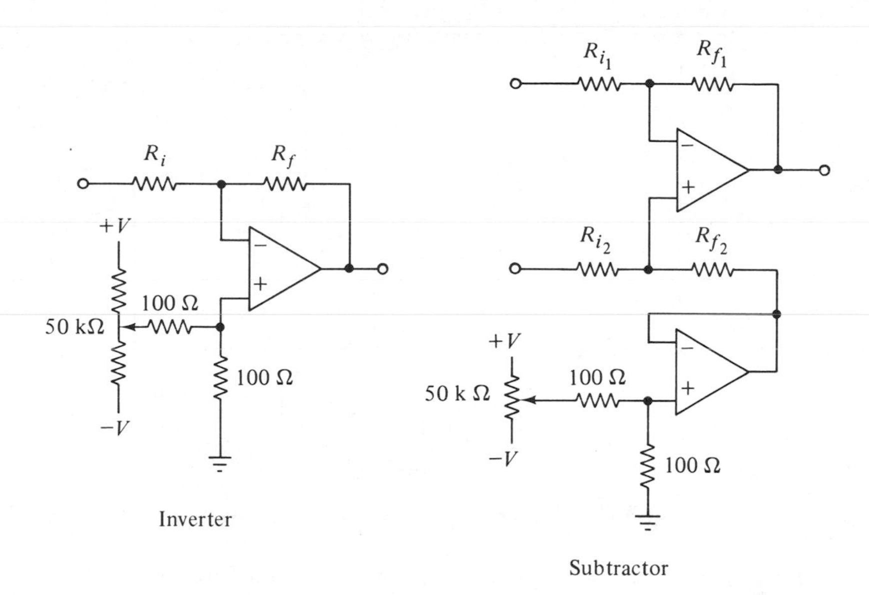

FIGURE 2–10. Preferred Offset Trim Methods

thereby zeroing V_{os}. A collector instead of an emitter trimpot unbalances collector current on one side of the differential pair, permitting dV_{os}/dT minimization. However, this action disturbs V_{os}, possibly requiring an additional trimming operation. Attaching external trimpots to the manufacturer's trim terminals is not the best solution to offset trimming, because of the temperature drift of the trimpot resistance introduced into the tightly matched differential pair. Figure 2–10 presents a preferred external trim method for both bipolar and JFET devices. An additional subtle differential input error occurs in noninverting amplifier service. Since the noninverting terminal may swing above and below zero volts with the input signal in this off-ground connection, the differential pair constant-current source operating point can be driven into a nonlinear region, resulting in amplifier offset voltage. This dynamic error is normally specified by the manufacturer as the peak value of permissible common-mode input voltage.

The chopper-stabilized amplifier uses ac coupling and modulation techniques in its mechanization to minimize dc error voltages and currents referred to its input (Figure 2–11). The most significant improvements are in the reduction of voltage and current thermal drift, which are especially of concern for circuits handling low-level signals unattended over significant periods of time. A disadvantage of the chopper-stabilized amplifier is that it is usually a single input device having no differential capabilities. Nevertheless, the amplifier is particularly useful in applica-

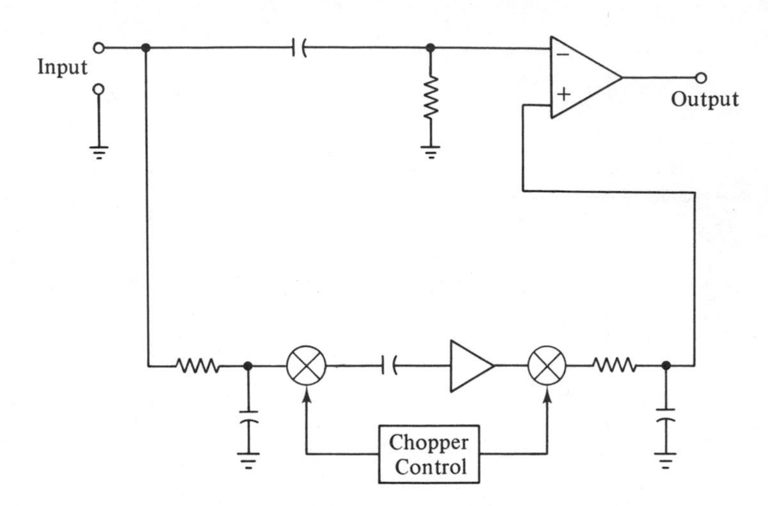

FIGURE 2–11. Chopper-Stabilized Amplifier

tions requiring low input uncertainty, such as null detection circuits. Typical chopper offset and drift specifications are tabulated in Table 2–2.

Electronic noise resulting from semiconductor carrier recombination and surface leakage effects may also be referred to the input of an active device as an error. Passive devices, primarily resistors, connected to operational amplifiers also contribute a noise power as a consequence of electron agitation at temperatures above absolute zero. These active and passive errors referred to the amplifier input may be expressed by equation (2-20), which has a strong dependence on amplifier bandwidth BW and source resistance R_s, where $KT = 0.4 \times 10^{-20}$ W/Hz at 300°K.

$$V_{\text{noise}} = \text{resistor noise} + \text{amplifier noise}$$

$$= \sqrt{4KT \cdot \text{BW} \cdot R_s} + (F-1)\sqrt{4KT \cdot \text{BW} \cdot R_s} \quad \text{volts} \qquad (2\text{-}20)$$

The noise figure, F, is a dimensionless quantity greater than unity, commonly expressed in power dB, which provides a basis for comparison

TABLE 2–2. Typical Amplifier Input Errors

Parameter	Bipolar	JFET	Chopper
V_{os}	1 mV	5 mV	50 μV
dV_{os}/dT	3.3 μV/°C	5 μV/°C	0.5 μV/°C
I_{os}	50 nA	10 pA	30 pA
dI_{os}/dT	−0.25 nA/°C	×2/10°C	1 pA/°C
V_{noise}	1 μV	5 μV	1 μV
R_s	10 kΩ	1 MΩ	500 kΩ

of the noise performance of amplifiers. The noise figure of contemporary operational amplifiers is in the range 1–10 dB, depending upon available amplifier bandwidth and choice of source resistance. If the effective noise voltage referred to the amplifier input is of interest, it may be obtained from equation (2-20) with substitution.

Evaluation with a 10-kΩ source resistance and 10-kHz bandwidth typically yields 1 μV of noise for a bipolar, and 5 μV for an FET amplifier with a 1-MΩ source resistance. The overall noise behavior is described by Figure 2–12, where the $1/f$ flicker noise increases in the vicinity of dc. Beyond the −3-dB bandwidth point, noise again increases, because signal power is decreasing with gain rolloff in relation to a relatively constant noise power. Typical errors referred to the amplifier input are tabulated in Table 2–2, including a nominal source resistance R_s which will maximize the amplifier signal-to-noise ratio.

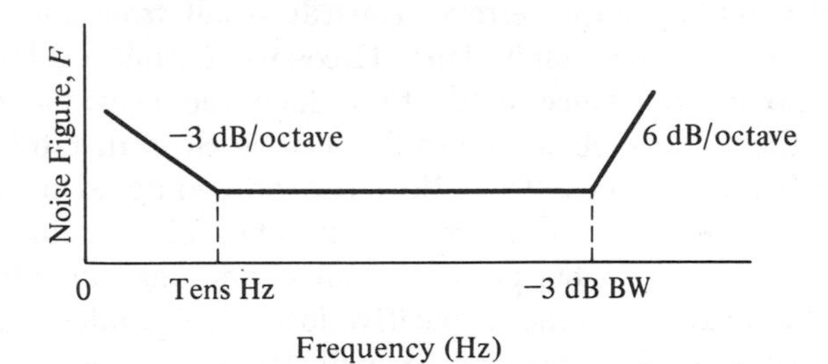

FIGURE 2–12. Operational Amplifier Noise Figure

Consider now an error budget comparison for the bipolar, JFET, and chopper amplifiers of Table 2–2. For this evaluation the recommended source resistance is used for each amplifier; V_{os} is considered to be nulled out, including balancing of the bipolar input resistor bias current voltage drops of Figure 2–9; and a conservative temperature swing of $\Delta T = 20°C$ is assumed. The composite voltage error referred to the amplifier inputs is obtained as the vector sum of the individual error contributions, assumed statistically independent, by equation (2–21). The significance of this

TABLE 2–3. Amplifier Input Uncertainty for $\Delta T = 20°C$

Parameter	Bipolar (μV)	JFET (μV)	Chopper (μV)
dV_{os}/dT	60	100	10
$I_{os} \cdot R_s$	500	10	15
$dI_{os}/dT \cdot R_s$	−50	40	10
V_{noise}	1	5	1
$V_{error_{RTI}}$	506	105	21

evaluation is that the uncertainty at the input of a bipolar operational amplifier is about 500 μV for a 20°C temperature swing (Table 2–3). This decreases to about 20 μV for a chopper amplifier, or better than a 2-orders-of-magnitude improvement. A useful method is therefore defined for determining the minimum level below which input signal levels will be unreliable.

$$V_{\text{error}_{\text{RTI}}}=\sqrt{\left(\frac{dV_{\text{os}}}{dT}\right)^2+(I_{\text{os}}\cdot R_s)^2+\left(\frac{dI_{\text{os}}}{dT}\cdot R_s\right)^2+V_{\text{noise}}^2}\quad \text{volts} \qquad (2\text{-}21)$$

2-3 AMPLIFIER OUTPUT ERRORS

Operational amplifier output errors primarily result from output loading conditions and slew rate limitations. Excessive output loading from a low-driving-point impedance tends to reduce the available open-loop gain. From the Bode plot of Figure 2–13, it is clear that this, in turn, results in a bandwidth loss. This effect can be countered by adding an output power booster available from a number of manufacturers. An alternative is to use a higher-power-output operational amplifier. When driving shielded cables or other capacitive loads, the parallel combination of load resistance and capacitance will form an additional corner frequency described by equation (2-22). Gain peaking or an oscillatory tendency can also occur from excessive capacitive loading. This can be compensated for by the addition of a small feedback capacitor C_f, defined

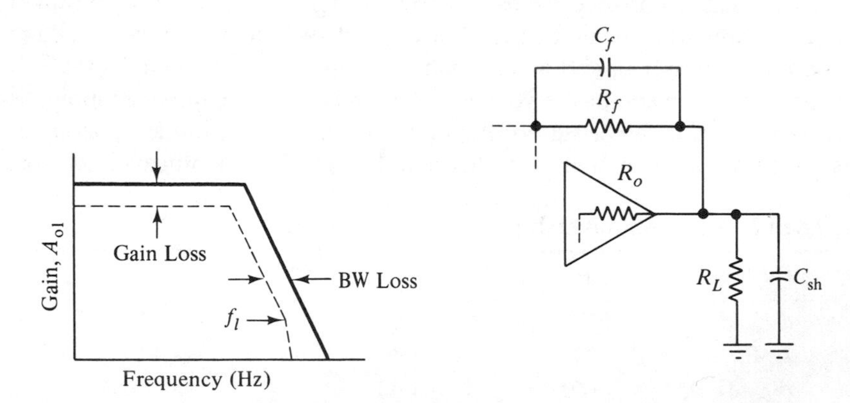

FIGURE 2–13. Output Loading Effects

by equation (2-23).

$$f_l = \frac{1}{2\pi C_{sh}\,(R_f \| R_o \| R_L)} \quad \text{Hertz} \tag{2-22}$$

$$C_f = \frac{1}{2\pi f_l R_f} \quad \text{farads} \tag{2-23}$$

The slew-rate parameter is the rate at which the output voltage is capable of rising in response to an input signal to prevent an undistorted response. Slew rate is defined by the identity of equation (2-24). In practice, the first part is evaluated for slew rate. Then the maximum allowable capacitance for an available output current, or the required current for a given capacitance, is determined by the second part. By way of example, a 1-V peak-to-peak sine-wave signal is required at a signal frequency of 3 MHz. This specifies a slew rate of 9.45 V/μs. If the amplifier is also loaded by 1000 pF of cable capacitance, however, 10 mA of output current capability at 3 MHz is required for a 1-V peak-to-peak output. These considerations are described by Figure 2–14. As another example, the 741 operational amplifier has a slew rate of 0.5 V/μs and a maximum output current of 5 mA. Interpolation of Figure 2–14 indicates that the 741 is capable of driving up to 0.01 μF without distortion.

$$\text{slew rate} = V_{o_{p-p}} \cdot \pi \cdot f_{\text{signal}} \tag{2-24}$$

$$= \frac{I_o}{C_{sh}} \quad \text{volts/second}$$

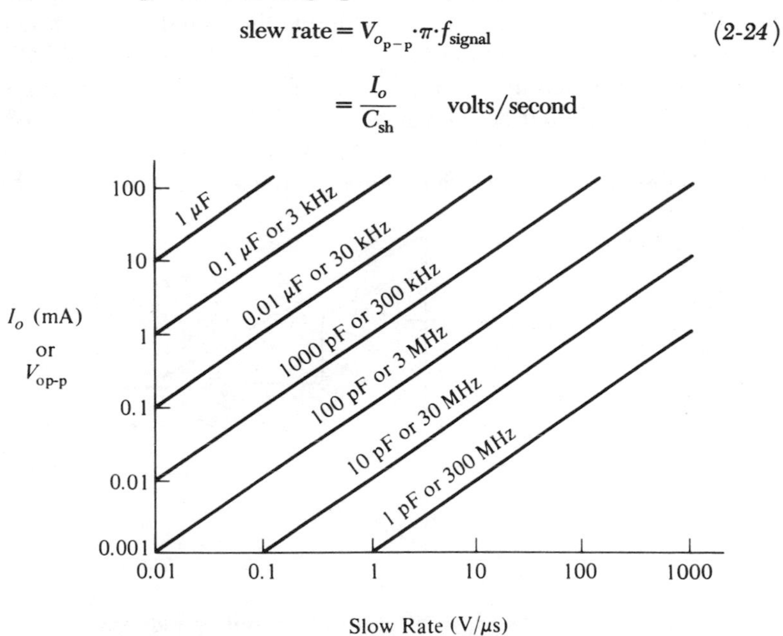

FIGURE 2–14. Slew-Rate Curves

2-4 INSTRUMENTATION APPLICATIONS

The developments of the previous sections culminated in an error-budget comparison of the input errors and determination of the minimum usable input signal levels for operational amplifiers frequently used for instrumentation purposes. This section extends the analysis and examples to considerations that determine the common-mode signal-rejection capability of operational amplifiers and presents recommended amplifier configurations for instrumentation service.

For measuring low-level signals from remote sources, adequate common-mode rejection, gain, input impedance, and stability are required. In a typical industrial situation the signal transducer is 10 or more feet from the input preamplifier. Of principal concern is 60 Hz electrostatically and electromagnetically coupled interference. For unshielded signal cables, a useful rule of thumb is that 1 mV of interference will be coupled per kilowatt of load in a 1-ft-spaced signal cable per parallel foot of cable run. This is derated for shielded signal cables by the attenuation factor, usually expressed in voltage dB, supplied by the cable manufacturer. Common-mode interference is defined as voltage coupled simultaneously to two or more signal lines. In instrumentation applications this is usually taken as the input leads to the inverting and noninverting inputs of an operational amplifier. Equations (2-25) and (2-26) define the amplifier CMRR capability as the ratio of differential to common-mode gain (DMG/CMG) and expresses a common-made error term. These equations are keyed to Figure 2–15. It should be emphasized that CMRR is a function of both amplifier DMG and CMG, which can be set independently as will be shown subsequently. Amplifier closed-loop gain and differential-mode

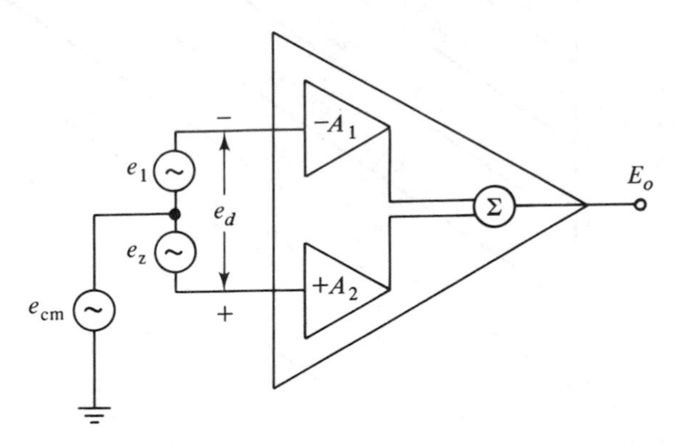

FIGURE 2–15. Differential Amplifier Pictorial

TABLE 2–4. Resistor Tolerance Versus CMG

Resistor Tolerance (%)	5	2	1	$\frac{1}{2}$	0.1
Average CMG	0.1	0.04	0.02	0.01	0.002

gain are the same thing.

$$\text{CMRR} = \frac{\text{DMG}}{\text{CMG}} \tag{2-25}$$

$$= \frac{\frac{1}{2}(|A_2| + |A_1|)}{|A_2| - |A_1|}$$

$$E_o = \text{DMG} \cdot e_d + \text{CMG} \cdot e_{\text{cm}} \tag{2-26}$$

$$= \text{DMG} \cdot e_d \left(1 + \underbrace{\frac{1}{\text{CMRR}} \cdot \frac{e_{\text{cm}}}{e_d}}_{\text{CM error}}\right)$$

Successful common-mode rejection requires that $|A_2| = |-A_1|$. This is closely achieved in practice with the differential pair of Figure 2–8 as a result of the very high impedance constant-current source at the junction of the emitter-coupled pair. Four differential input operational amplifier circuits especially useful for instrumentation applications are shown in Figures 2–16 through 2–18. As a practical matter, the actual CMRR realized by these circuits is primarily dependent upon their operational amplifier intrinsic CMRR, as well as the DMG and CMG of equation (2-25). CMG is primarily determined by the tolerance of the gain-determining resistors associated with each circuit. Table 2–4 presents the average realizable CMG values for various resistance tolerances. Worst-case values, incidentally, are determinable by simply doubling the tabulated CMG entries for each resistor tolerance.

The three-amplifier configuration of Figure 2–16 has the advantage of a higher input impedance at its noninverting inputs, which provides a relaxed tolerance for source impedance unbalance in each input leg of up to 1 kΩ without serious derogation of CMRR. The CMG of the noninverting input section is unity for all values of its DMG, and the CMG of the output subtractor section is dependent on the tolerance of R_1 and R_2. Therefore, the three-amplifier circuit can provide a higher CMRR than the single-amplifier circuit for the same operational amplifier intrinsic CMRR by distributing the closed-loop DMG between the input and subtractor stages. This is illustrated by the following example.

Consider a 2-mV differential signal of interest e_d buried in 1 V of common-mode interference e_{cm}. Equation (2-28) is obtained from the kernel of equation (2-26) and expresses the required CMRR for a specified common-mode error, chosen as 1% for this example. Typical monolithic operational amplifier devices have an intrinsic CMRR of about 86 dB, or 20,000, which is only 40% of the required CMRR of 50,000 and clearly eliminates the single-amplifier circuit. Intrinsic CMRR is specified by the manufacturer's literature. In comparison the three-amplifier circuit with a DMG of 1000 for a 2-V output of the signal of interest does provide adequate CMRR with 1% tolerance resistors. Unity gain is maintained in

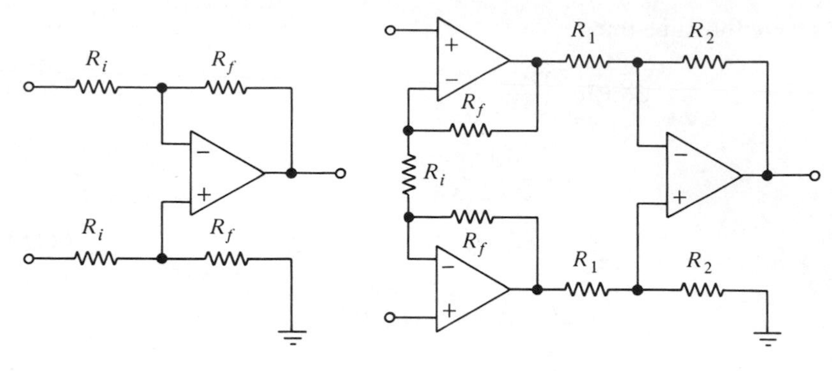

$$\text{DMG} = \frac{R_f}{R_i} \quad (2\text{-}4)$$

$$\text{DMG} = 1 + \left(\frac{2R_f}{R_i}\right)\left(\frac{R_2}{R_1}\right) \quad (2\text{-}28)$$

FIGURE 2–16. Instrumentation Amplifier Circuits

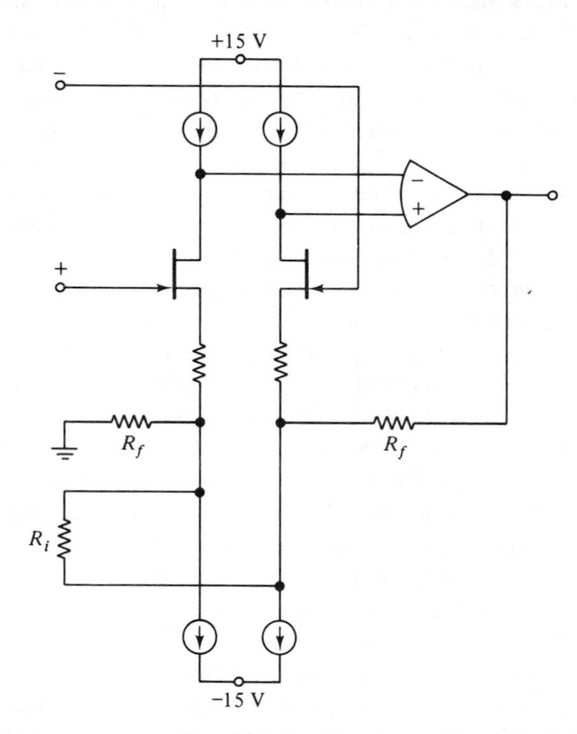

FIGURE 2–17. High-Performance Instrumentation Amplifier

$$\text{DMG} = \left(1 + \frac{2R_f}{R_i}\right) \quad (2\text{-}31)$$

the subtractor stage, so that only the input-stage offset voltages contribute to output offset. The choice of R_f, R_i, R_1, and R_2 in Figure 2–16 and equation (2-27) are 500, 1, 10, and 10 kΩ, respectively. The realizable in-circuit CMRR is shown by equation (2-30).

$$\mathrm{CMRR}_{\mathrm{required}} = \frac{1}{\mathrm{CM}_{\mathrm{error}}} \cdot \frac{e_{\mathrm{cm}}}{e_d} \tag{2-28}$$

$$= \frac{1}{0.01} \cdot \frac{1\mathrm{V}}{2\times 10^{-3}\mathrm{V}}$$

$$= 5\times 10^4$$

$$\mathrm{CMRR}_{\mathrm{input\ section}} = \frac{\mathrm{DMG}}{\mathrm{CMG}} \tag{2-25}$$

$$= \frac{1000}{1}$$

$$= 10^3$$

$$\mathrm{CMRR}_{\mathrm{actual}} = \frac{(\mathrm{CMRR})(\mathrm{CMRR}_{\mathrm{intrinsic}})}{\mathrm{CMRR} + \mathrm{CMRR}_{\mathrm{intrinsic}}} \tag{2-29}$$

$$= \frac{(10^3)(2\times 10^4)}{2.1\times 10^4}$$

$$= 0.95\times 10^3 \qquad \text{for the input section}$$

$$\mathrm{CMRR}_{\mathrm{subtractor\ section}} = \frac{\mathrm{DMG}}{\mathrm{CMG}} \tag{2-25}$$

$$= \frac{1}{0.02}$$

$$= 50$$

$$\mathrm{CMRR}_{\mathrm{actual}} = \frac{(50)(2\times 10^4)}{2.005\times 10^4} \tag{2-29}$$

$$= 49.9 \qquad \text{for the subtractor section}$$

$$\mathrm{CMRR}_{\mathrm{3\text{-}amplifier}} = \mathrm{CMRR}_{\mathrm{input}} \cdot \mathrm{CMRR}_{\mathrm{subtractor}} \tag{2-30}$$

$$= (0.95\times 10^3)(49.9)$$

$$= 4.74\times 10^4$$

Figure 2–17 illustrates what is commonly referred to as a high-performance instrumentation amplifier. This circuit is an extension of the three-amplifier configuration, with the addition of output residual common-mode sensing and feedback to the input-stage current sources for additional common-mode rejection. This circuit can provide in-circuit CMRR values of 10^6 without excessive DMG or tight resistor tolerances for at least a tenfold improvement over the three-amplifier circuit. This extended performance is normally available only in modules trimmed by the manufacturer at a premium price. Other features usually accompany this performance, however, including bootstrapped FET inputs with impedances to $10^{13}\,\Omega$. Table 2–5 provides a comparison of these instrumentation amplifier circuits with practical DMG and CMG values.

TABLE 2–5. Instrumentation Amplifier Comparison

Type	DMG	CMG	CMRR
Single amplifier	10^2	10^{-2}	10^4
Three amplifier	10^3	10^{-2}	10^5
High-performance amplifier	10^3	10^{-3}	10^6

A difficulty frequently encountered in instrumentation systems having shielded differential input leads is the variation in effective capacitance between the cable shield and two input leads. A different capacitance between the shield and inverting and noninverting inputs results in a different capacitive reactance, and hence a common-mode rejection imbalance for ac interference. When this is a problem, a useful solution is to extract the average common-mode signal and drive the shield through a buffer amplifier (Figure 2–18). The shield and inner conductors then track the common-mode interference for realizable CMRR values to 10^6.

The isolation amplifier is a specialized type of instrumentation amplifier which offers the capability of protecting system components from very large voltages such as encountered in industrial applications by virtue of an isolation barrier. This same feature also results in very low leakage currents and ground loop elimination which is of particular importance in biomedical applications. The isolation mode voltage rating is that which exists across the isolation barrier, or between the input and output commons, and the error referred to the output due to the e_{iso} present is determined by the isolation mode rejection ratio (IMRR). Consequently, equation (2-32) provides the relationship for the output signal where DMG and CMRR pertain to the differential input stage illustrated in Figure 2–19. The output stage functionally is a unity gain amplifier.

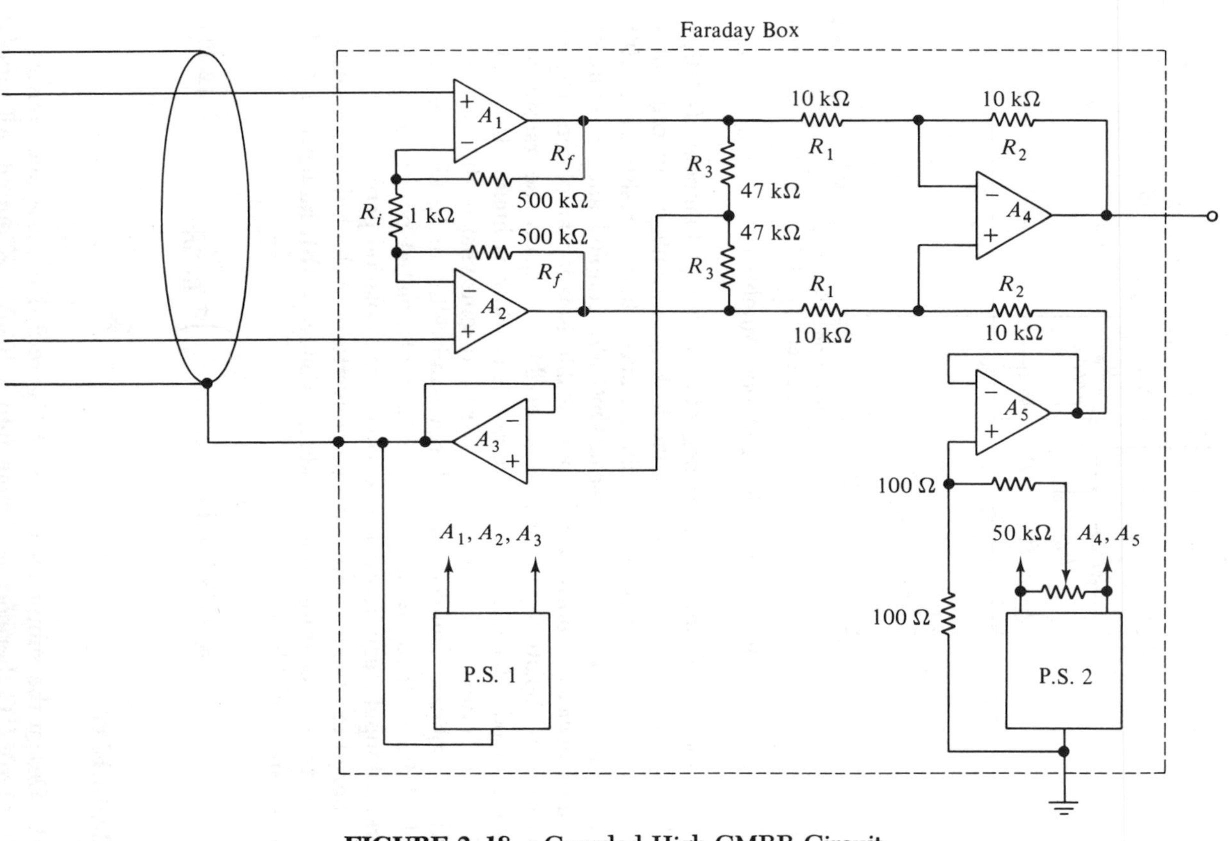

FIGURE 2–18. Guarded High-CMRR Circuit

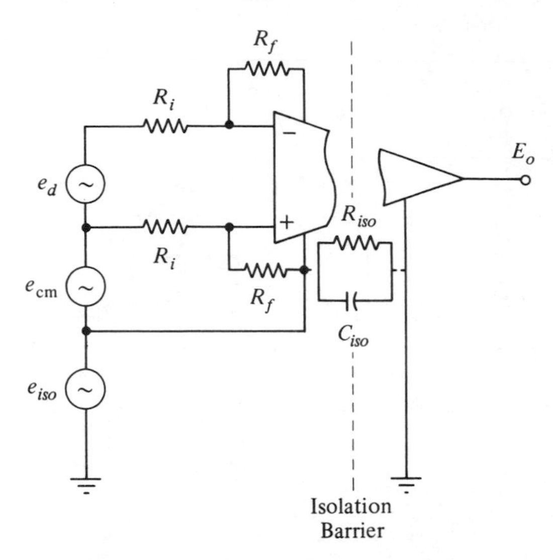

FIGURE 2–19. Isolation Amplifier

In most applications e_{cm} is negligible and e_{iso} dominant. Isolation voltage ratings to 5000 volts peak and leakage currents on the order of a fraction of a microampere are available, and a barrier resistance of 10^{12} ohms shunted by 10 pF is typical. Optically coupled and transformer coupled devices comprise presently available isolation amplifiers. Higher linearity and isolation performance generally accompany the transformer-coupled modulated carrier method, but bandwidth is limited to about 1 kHz. The former specifications are sacrificed somewhat in the LED-photodiode optically coupled method, but bandwidths to 10 kHz are available. Both methods require the provision of isolated power to the differential input stage in order to achieve rated isolation performance. This is realized in practice with a dc/dc converter and the isolation available across its inverter transformer windings. Voltage IMRR ratings to 180 dB or 10^9 are available.

$$E_o = \mathrm{DMG} \cdot e_d \left(1 + \frac{1}{\mathrm{CMRR}} \cdot \frac{e_{\mathrm{cm}}}{e_d}\right) + \frac{e_{\mathrm{iso}}}{\mathrm{IMRR}} \tag{2-32}$$

PROBLEMS

2-1 Design the subtractor circuit of Figure 2–3 to scale and convert a 1 mV/°C thermocouple input into a 10 mV/°K output. All signals are unipolar and of positive polarity, 0°C is equivalent to 273°K, and the feedback resistors are to be 100 kΩ.

2-2 A single operational amplifier instrumentation amplifier has 100 kΩ feedback resistors and 10 kΩ input resistors with an additional 1 kΩ source impedance imbalance in one input leg. Calculate the CMRR for this circuit ignoring the intrinsic CMRR for the device.

2-3 A microprocessor teaching system utilizes multiple CRT displays driven from a master keyboard/terminal over a 75 Ω characteristic-impedance coaxial cable. Determine: (a) the slew rate and output current required to drive this cable to 10 V peak-to-peak, and (b) the maximum cable capacitance which can be driven with this output. The video bandwidth is 3 MHz.

2-4 Determine the optimum number of cascaded identical operational amplifier sections n which maximizes both the overall gain and bandwidth. This may be obtained by plotting curves of the following equations describing cascaded gain and bandwidth relationships versus n for values of n ranging from 1 to 5, and then determining the intercept of the two curves over a common axis of n values.

$$\text{Cascaded Gain} = (\text{Section Gain})^n$$

$$\text{Cascaded BW} = (\text{Section BW}) \cdot (2^{1/n} - 1)^{1/2}$$

2-5 A 10 mV dc signal in 1 V of 60 Hz common-mode interference is to be conditioned so as to exhibit only 1% common-mode error. Determine the required CMRR, the appropriate instrumentation amplifier type, and a representative circuit for a DMG of 100.

2-6 A low input uncertainty differential input null detector is required with an input uncertainty on the order of 1 microvolt under trimmed and constant-temperature conditions. Design a suitable instrumentation preamplifier using a differential-input chopper amplifier connected as shown in Figure 2–3 with the following specifications. Indicate component values and calculate the CMRR and error voltage RTI for a DMG of 1000. The differential source resistance is 50 kΩ.

$V_{os} = \pm 25\,\mu V$ $\qquad I_{os} = \pm 10\,pA$ $\qquad V_{noise} = 1\,\mu V$ RMS

$\dfrac{dV_{os}}{dT} = \pm 0.1\,\mu V/°C$ $\qquad \dfrac{dI_{os}}{dT} = \pm 1\,pA/°C$ $\qquad BW = 100\,Hz$

REFERENCES

1. D. C. Bailey, "An Instrumentation Amplifier Is Not an Op Amp," *Electronic Products*, September 18, 1972.
2. A. P. Brokaw, "Use a Single Op Amp for Many Instrumentation Problems," *Electronic Design News*, April 1, 1972.
3. M. Callahan, "Chopper-Stabilized IC Op Amps Achieve Precision, Speed, Economy," *Electronics*, August 16, 1973.
4. J. W. Jaquay, "Designers Guide to Instrumentation Amplifiers," *Electronic Design News*, May 5, 1973.
5. D. Jones and R. W. Webb, "Chopper-Stabilized Op Amp Combines MOS and Bipolar Elements," *Electronics*, September 27, 1973.
6. J. H. Kollataj, "Reject Common-Mode Noise," *Electronic Design*, April 26, 1973.
7. T. C. Lyerly, "Instrumentation Amplifier Conditions Computer Inputs," *Electronics*, November 6, 1972.
8. F. Poulist, "Simplify Amplifier Selection," *Electronic Design*, August 2, 1973.
9. J. I. Smith, *Modern Operational Amplifier Circuit Design*, John Wiley, New York, 1971.
10. G. Tobey, J. Graeme, and L. Huelsman, *Operational Amplifiers; Design and Applications*, McGraw-Hill, New York, 1971.
11. C. F. Wojslaw, "Use Op Amps with Greater Confidence," *Electronic Design*, March 16, 1972.
12. R. L. Young, "Lift IC Op Amp Performance," *Electronic Design*, February 15, 1973.

3

ACTIVE FILTERS

3-0 INTRODUCTION

Active filter networks using operational amplifiers permit the realization of stable, yet inexpensive frequency-selective networks from dc to about 100 kHz. Filtering at the lower instrumentation frequencies has always been a problem with passive filters because the required L and C values are large and inductor losses appreciable. Although the history of electric wave filters extends well over half a century, the identification of stable active networks and the emphasis on their application has occurred only in the past decade. The excellent behavior and low cost of active filters at lower frequencies makes them especially attractive for instrumentation applications such as high-performance transducer-amplifier-filter signal conditioning implementations.

In 1955 Sallen and Key[1] at MIT published a catalog of 18 filter networks. A proliferation of permutations of these networks subsequently appeared but with the majority suffering high sensitivity to component drift, including most of the original 18 networks. A rigorous analysis by Geffe[2] and others disclosed by 1967 that only four of the original 18 networks exhibited low sensitivity. Of these, the unity gain and multiple feedback networks are particularly useful. Work by Tow and others[3–5] developed the biquad resonator, which provides stable Q values to 200. This chapter presents these optimum networks; develops the mechanizations for lowpass, bandpass, and band-reject realizations for various filter characteristics such as Butterworth and Bessel; and includes illustrative examples. Additional mechanizations are also presented, including the gyrator, stagger tuning for bandpass filters, the very high-Q commutator filter, and a comparison of the analog integrator to the lowpass filter.

3-1 NETWORK SENSITIVITY

The sensitivity of a network can be identified when the change in its Q for a change in its passive element values is evaluated. The active networks to be considered here are second-order systems which provide one complex-conjugate pair of poles from the denominator $D(s)$ of their transfer function with ω_0, the pole frequency.

$$D(s) = s^2 + as + b \qquad \text{for } s = j\omega \tag{3-1}$$

$$Q = \frac{\sqrt{b}}{a} \qquad \sqrt{b} = \omega_0 \tag{3-2}$$

Sensitivity parameters for four frequently applied active networks are presented in Figures 3–1 through 3–5 plus a passive baseline network. To determine the change in Q of a network, the thermal coefficient of the element in question in parts per million per degree centigrade is multiplied by the appropriate sensitivity coefficient. For these stable networks, conventional 50- to 100-ppm components yield good performance. Normally, it is a good procedure to choose standard value resistors of 1% tolerance, such as 10 kΩ, and following network frequency and impedance scaling to parallel a couple of capacitors to obtain the required capacitance values to three significant places.

Unity gain networks have excellent performance for low-Q applications, such as lowpass and highpass filters, and may be cascaded for higher-order filters (Figure 3–2). This is perhaps the most widely applied active filter network. Note that the sensitivity coefficients are typically

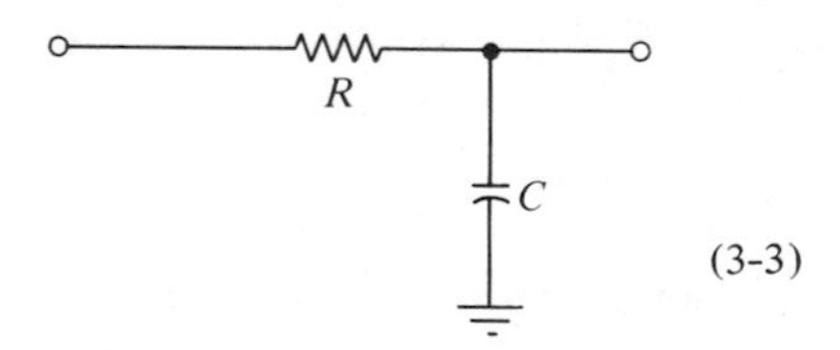

(3-3)

$$S_Z^Q = \pm 1$$
$$S_R^Q = (\pm 1)(100\ \text{ppm}/^\circ\text{C})(100\%)$$
$$= \pm 0.01\%\ Q/^\circ\text{C}$$

FIGURE 3–1. Passive Networks

less than unity—the sensitivity of passive *RC* networks. The advantage of the multiple feedback network is that a bandpass filter can be formed with one operational amplifier (Figure 3–3); however, its Q is limited to 10 for good stability. Owing to its simplicity, this network is efficient for developing special bandpass response shapes through cascading and stagger tuning.

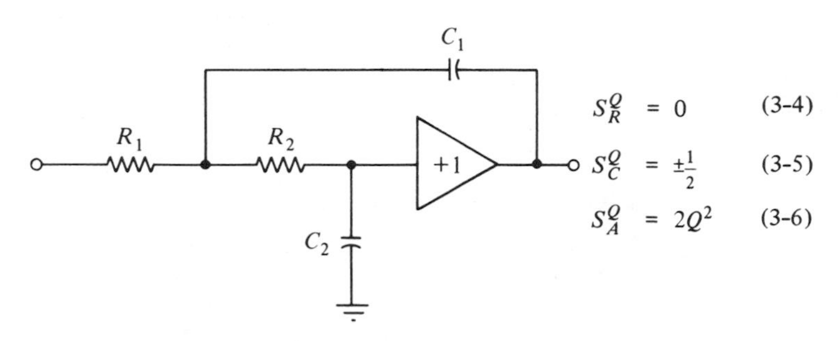

FIGURE 3–2. Unity Gain Network

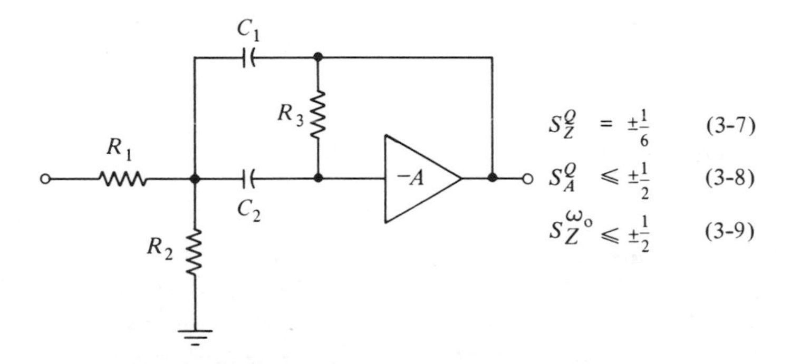

FIGURE 3–3. Multiple Feedback Network

The principal application of the biquadratic network is for bandpass filters with practical Q values up to about 200. The stability of this network at the higher Q values is good with the availability of adequate operational amplifier open-loop gain at the filter center frequency (Figure 3–4). The biquad resonator forms a second-order function by simulating a *RLC* network. The principle of operation of the gyrator is that the conductance $-G$ gyrates a capacitive current to an equivalent inductive current (Figure 3–5). The gyrator is lossless and consequently has excellent stability. Negative impedance converters (NIC) perform the same function, except that they are not lossless and exhibit instability.

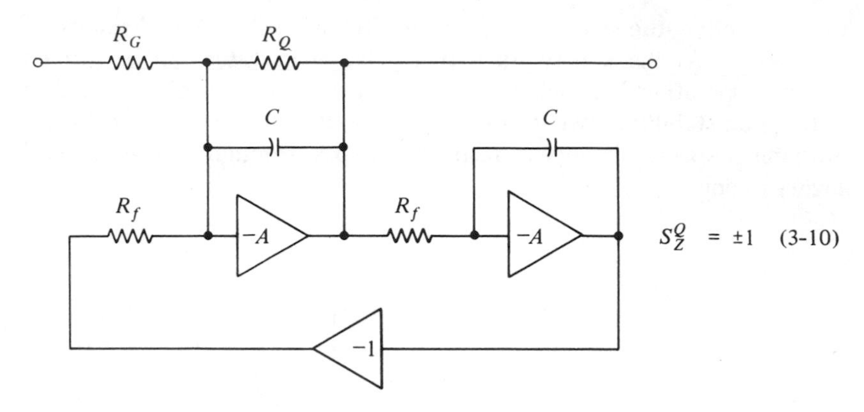

FIGURE 3–4. Biquad Resonator

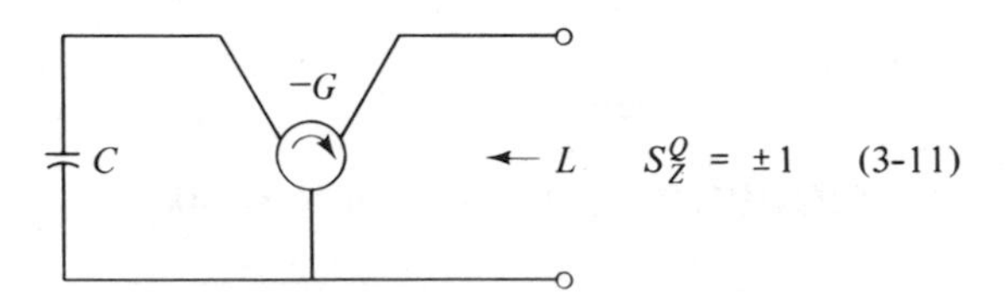

FIGURE 3–5. Gyrator

3-2 FILTER RESPONSE CHARACTERISTICS

The frequency range in which a signal is transmitted through a filter is called the *passband*, and the range in which a signal is rejected is known as the *stopband*. Practical filters are also characterized by a transition band between the passband and stopband, with the exact boundary locations being somewhat arbitrary. Further, it is advantageous to structure the filter transfer function to correspond to certain mathematical functions, for example the Butterworth and Chebyshev polynomials. This provides filter amplitude and phase characteristics which are optimum in one sense or another for specific applications.

It is normal practice to use the lowpass filter as a basis for developing filter approximation functions. Although the simplest expression of filter response is the polar form $A(f)/B(f)$, the alternative amplitude-squared representation $A^2(f)$ is more useful for expressing transfer functions. Butterworth lowpass filters (Figure 3–6) are characterized by the property that their amplitude response is maximally flat in the vicinity of direct current, and hence are optimum in this sense. The Butterworth amplitude-squared response is given by equation (3-12) and is completely specified by the order n of the filter, where n is the number of filter poles and f_c the -3-dB cutoff frequency.

$$A^2(f) = \frac{1}{1+(f/f_c)^{2n}} \tag{3-12}$$

Bessel lowpass filters (Figure 3–9) are characterized by the fact their envelope delay $Tg_{(f)}$, the change in phase per change in frequency, is maximally flat in the vicinity of direct current. Further, the step response of Bessel filters exhibits very low overshoot, making them useful for pulse signal processing, and their amplitude response is Gaussian. However, unlike Butterworth filters, the cutoff frequency varies with the number of filter poles n. The numerator of the Bessel amplitude-squared response is a normalizing constant in equation (3-14).

$$Tg(f) = -\frac{dB(f)}{2\pi df} \tag{3-13}$$

$$A^2(f) = \frac{b^2}{4f^{2n}} \tag{3-14}$$

$$= \frac{1}{4} \quad \text{at } f = f_c$$

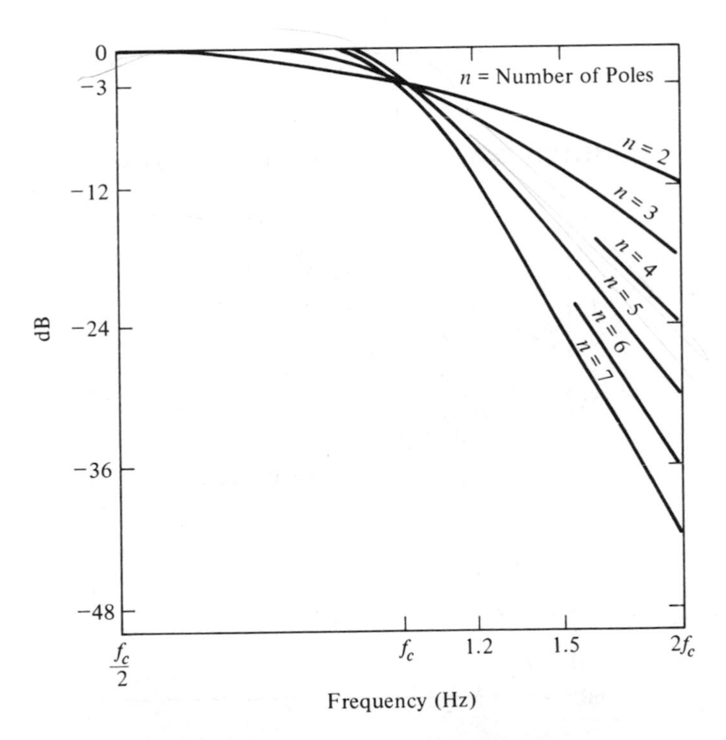

FIGURE 3–6. Butterworth Low Pass

where $b = \dfrac{(2n)!}{2^n n!}$

Chebyshev filters (Figure 3–11) are configured to exhibit equiripple passband behavior and a monotonic stopband response. The optimal property of Chebyshev filters is that they provide the best possible compromise considering both passband and stopband amplitude response. $Tn_{(f/f_c)}$ in the amplitude-squared response is a nth-order Chebyshev polynomial, and ϵ a parameter defining the

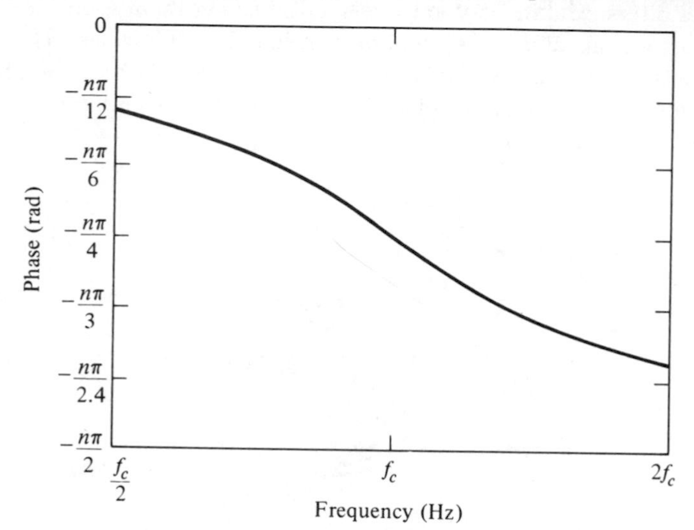

FIGURE 3–7. Butterworth Phase Response

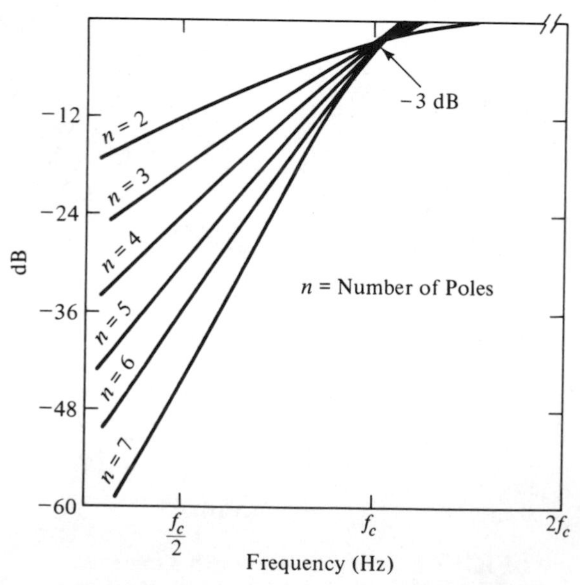

FIGURE 3–8. Butterworth High Pass

passband ripple. The foregoing filter characteristics are presented by Figures 3–6 through 3–13, which were adapted from curves copyrighted by the Burr Brown Research Corporation with permission.

$$A^2(f) = \frac{1}{1 + \epsilon^2 Tn^2\left(\frac{f}{f_c}\right)} \tag{3-15}$$

$$\text{ripple height} = 1 + \epsilon^2 \tag{3-16}$$

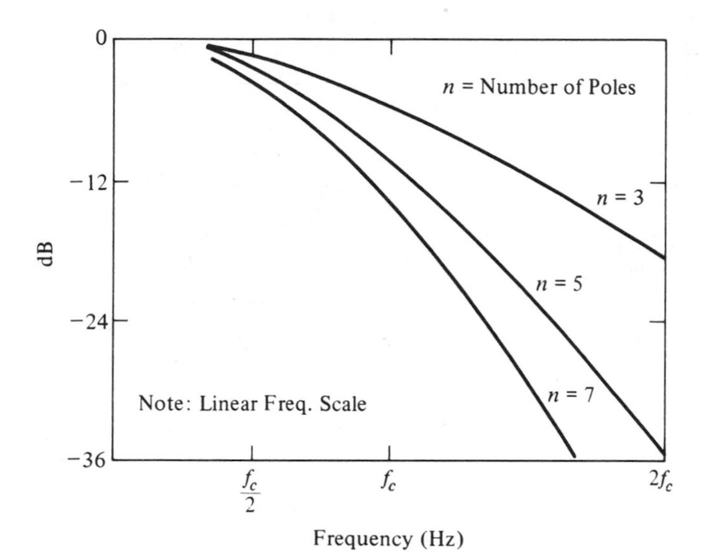

FIGURE 3–9. Bessel Low Pass

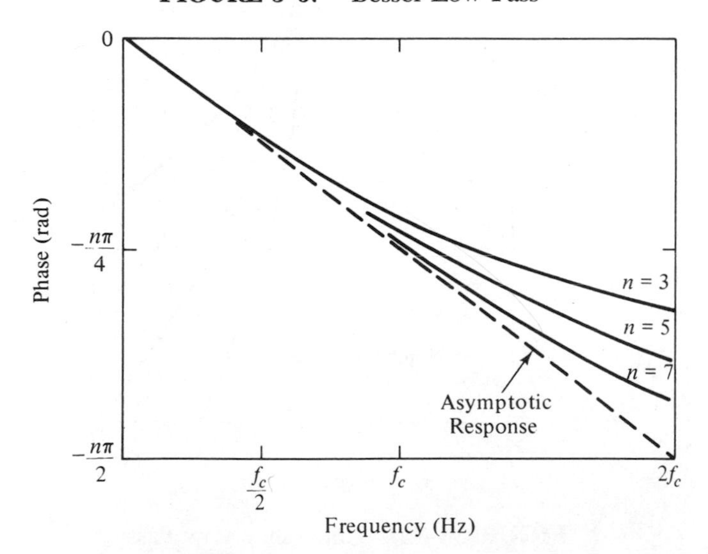

FIGURE 3–10. Bessel Phase Response

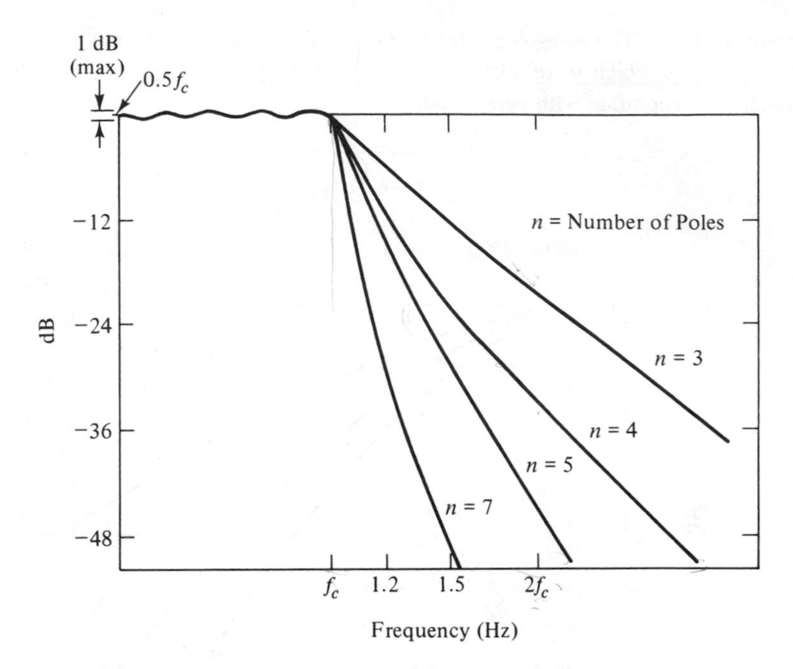

FIGURE 3–11. Chebyshev Low Pass

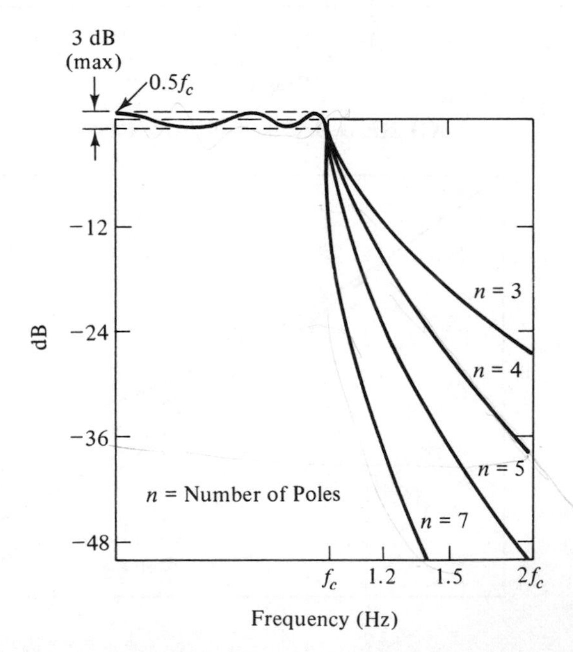

FIGURE 3–12. Chebyshev Low Pass

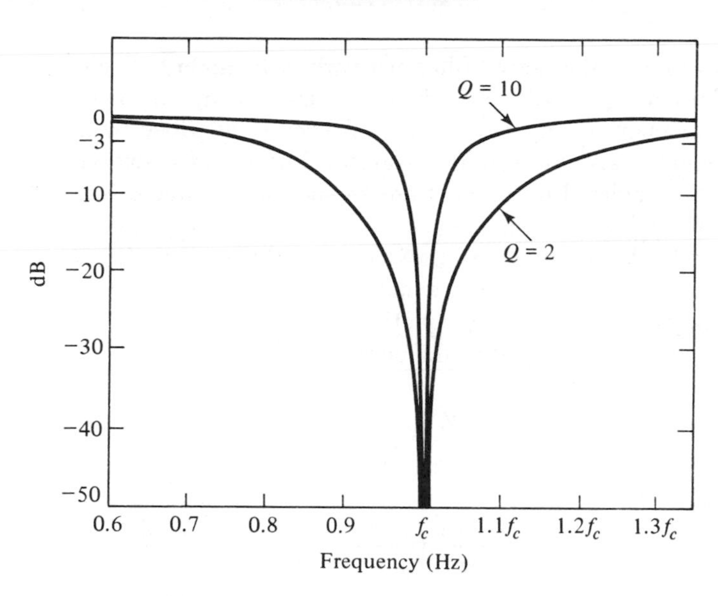

FIGURE 3–13. Band Reject Response

Table 3–1 presents a summary of the preceding filter response characteristics.

TABLE 3–1. Filter Response Summary

Butterworth	A realizable approximation of the ideal filter characterized by very flat amplitude response in the passband and moderate rolloff in the transition band. Has a slightly nonlinear phase response.
Bessel	A minimum-time-delay filter characterized by very linear phase response and Gaussian amplitude response. Especially suited for pulse applications and phase-sensitive signal processing.
Chebyshev	Characterized by a sharp corner frequency with a specifiable passband ripple. A relaxed passband ripple tolerance results in increased transition band attenuation. Exhibits a distorted phase response.

3-3 ACTIVE FILTER DESIGN

The emphasis of this chapter is primarily on the practical implementation of useful active filter designs rather than topics of more theoretical interest. Nervertheless, it is of value to appreciate that the principal contribution of the active filter network is its ability to synthesize one complex-conjugate pole pair which can assume any position in the complex frequency s-plane. How this is achieved is described by the following development, and the resulting transfer function of equation (3-19) may then be formulated in terms of any of the filter characteristics described in the preceding section.

Kirchhoff's current law provides that the sum of the currents into any node is zero. Therefore, a nodal analysis of the unity gain lowpass network yields the following equations, which include the assumption that the current in C_2 is equal to the current in R_2.

$$\frac{V_i - V_x}{R_1} = \frac{V_x - V_o}{1/j\omega C_1} + \frac{V_x - V_o}{R_2} \tag{3-17}$$

$$\frac{V_x - V_o}{R_2} = \frac{V_o}{1/j\omega c_2} \tag{3-18}$$

Rearranging,

$$V_x = V_o \cdot \frac{R_2 + 1/j\omega c_2}{1/j\omega c_2}$$

The realization of this requires the use of a low input bias current operational amplifier for proper filter performance. The transfer function is obtained upon substitution for V_x in equation (3-17), which is then rearranged into the standard form for a second-order system in equation (3-19). The coefficient δ is the damping factor, which is set by capacitor

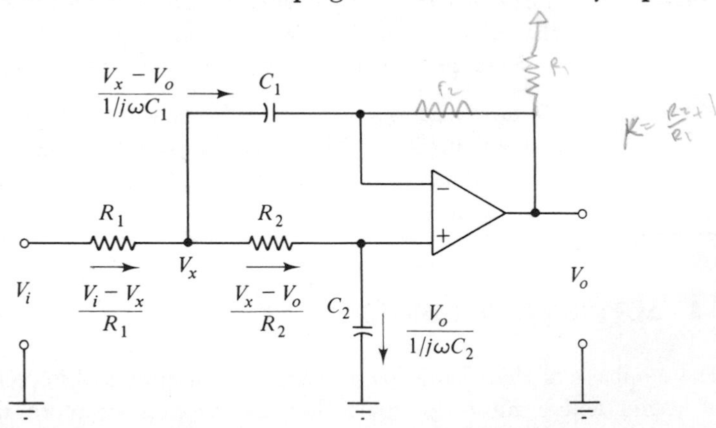

FIGURE 3–14. Unity Gain Network Nodal Analysis

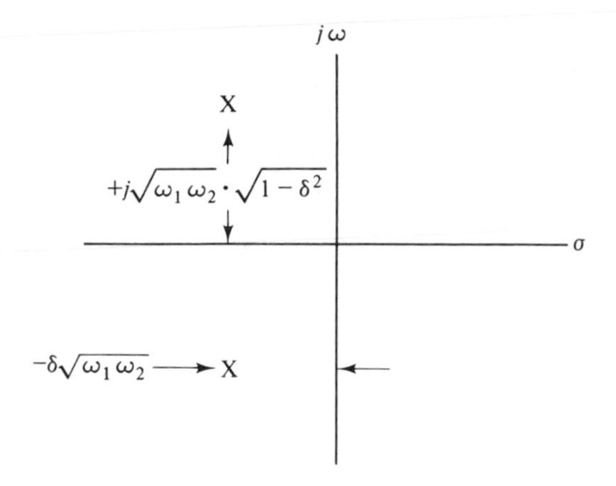

FIGURE 3–15. *s*-Plane Pole Locations

C_2. The amplifier, of course, provides a noninverting unity gain.

$$\frac{V_o}{V_i}=\frac{1}{\omega^2 R_1 R_2 C_1 C_2+\omega C_2(R_1+R_2)+1} \tag{3-19}$$

$$=\frac{1}{\dfrac{s^2}{\omega_1\omega_2}+2sC_2\left(\dfrac{R_1+R_2}{2}\right)+1}$$

$$=\frac{\omega_1\omega_2}{s^2+2s\delta+\omega_1\omega_2}$$

$$\delta=\frac{C_2}{2}(R_1+R_2) \tag{3-20}$$

$$S_1=-\delta\sqrt{\omega_1\omega_2}+j\sqrt{\omega_1\omega_2}\cdot\sqrt{1-\delta^2} \tag{3-21}$$

$$S_2=-\delta\sqrt{\omega_1\omega_2}-j\sqrt{\omega_1\omega_2}\cdot\sqrt{1-\delta^2} \tag{3-22}$$

A useful approach to the design of active filters can be summarized as follows:

1. Select an acceptable filter characteristic from the curves of Figures 3–6 through 3–13 and determine the number of poles required to provide the necessary attenuation.
2. Choose the appropriate filter network from the circuits of Figures 3–2 through 3–5.
3. Perform the necessary component frequency and impedance scaling such as from the values in Table 3–2.

TABLE 3–2a. Capacitor Values In Farads

	Bessel		Butterworth	
Poles	C_1	C_2	C_1	C_2
2	0.9066	0.6799	1.414	0.7071
4	0.7351	0.6746	1.082	0.9241
	1.0120	0.3900	2.613	0.3825
6	0.6352	0.6098	1.035	0.9660
	0.7225	0.4835	1.414	0.7071
	1.0730	0.2561	3.863	0.2588
8	0.5673	0.5539	1.091	0.9809
	0.6090	0.4861	1.202	0.8313
	0.7257	0.3590	1.800	0.5557
	1.1160	0.1857	5.125	0.1950
10	0.5172	0.5092	1.012	0.9874
	0.5412	0.4682	1.122	0.8908
	0.5999	0.3896	1.414	0.7071
	0.7326	0.2792	2.202	0.4540
	1.1510	0.1437	6.389	0.1563

TABLE 3–2b. Capacitor Values In Farads

	Chebyshev					
	0.1-dB Ripple		1-dB Ripple		3-dB Ripple	
Poles	C_1	C_2	C_1	C_2	C_1	C_2
2	1.638	0.6955	2.218	0.6061	3.103	0.4458
4	1.901	1.2410	3.125	1.2690	4.863	1.0490
	4.592	0.2409	7.546	0.1489	11.740	0.0943
6	2.553	1.7760	4.410	1.9040	7.012	1.6070
	3.487	0.4917	6.024	0.3117	9.572	0.2002
	9.531	0.1110	16.460	0.0642	26.150	0.0400
8	3.270	2.3230	5.756	2.5380	9.217	2.1560
	3.857	0.6890	6.792	0.4435	10.870	0.2866
	5.773	0.2398	10.150	0.1395	16.270	0.0873
	16.440	0.0629	28.940	0.0357	46.340	0.0222
10	4.011	2.8770	7.125	3.1700	11.440	2.7040
	4.447	0.8756	7.897	0.5680	12.690	0.3681
	5.603	0.3353	9.952	0.1962	15.990	0.1231
	8.727	0.1419	15.500	0.0805	24.910	0.0501
	25.320	0.0404	44.980	0.0227	72.310	0.0141

Table 3–2 provides the capacitor values in farads for the unity gain network tabulated according to the number of filter poles. Note that higher-order filters are formed by a cascade of these networks, each of which is different (i.e., not a cascade of 2-pole networks with identical component values). Figures 3–16 and 3–17 illustrate the design procedure for unity gain networks with examples of two-pole Butterworth lowpass and highpass filters having a 1-kHz cutoff frequency.

A gyrator realization with operational amplifiers is adaptable to providing a stable band-reject or notch filter (Figure 3–18). Frequency

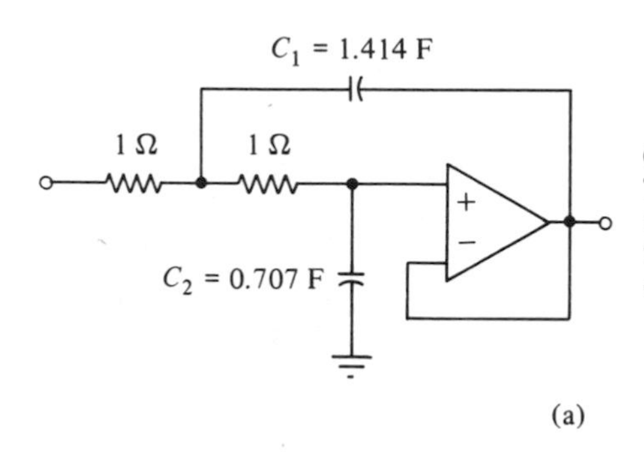

Component values from Table 3-2a are normalized to 1 rad/s with resistors taken as 1 Ω and capacitors in farads.

(a)

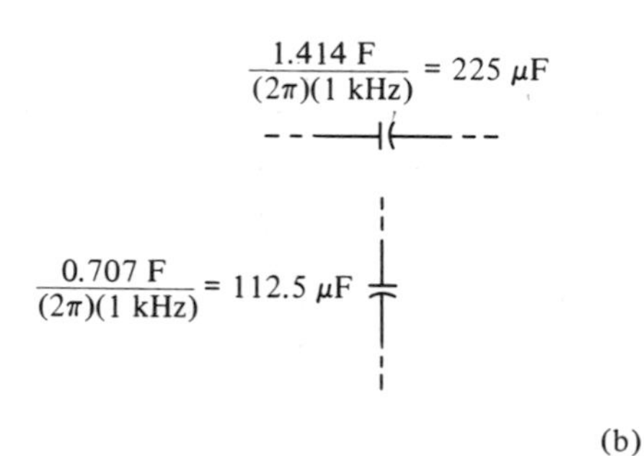

The filter is then frequency-scaled by dividing the capacitor values from the table by the cutoff frequency in radians ($2\pi \times 1$ kHz).

(b)

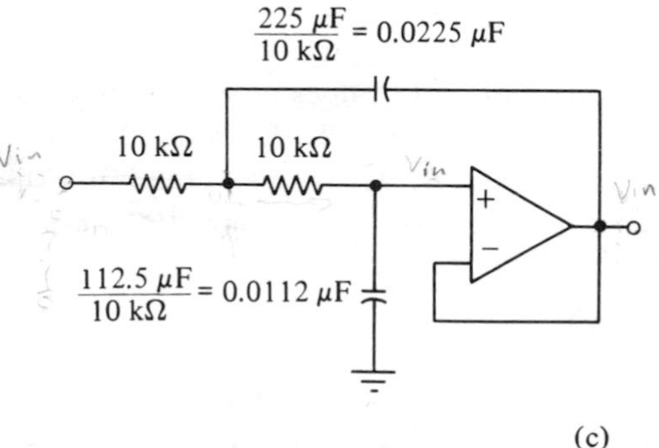

The filter is finally impedance-scaled by multiplying the resistor values by a convenient value (10 kΩ) and dividing the capacitor values by the same value.

(c)

FIGURE 3–16. Butterworth Unity Gain Lowpass Filter

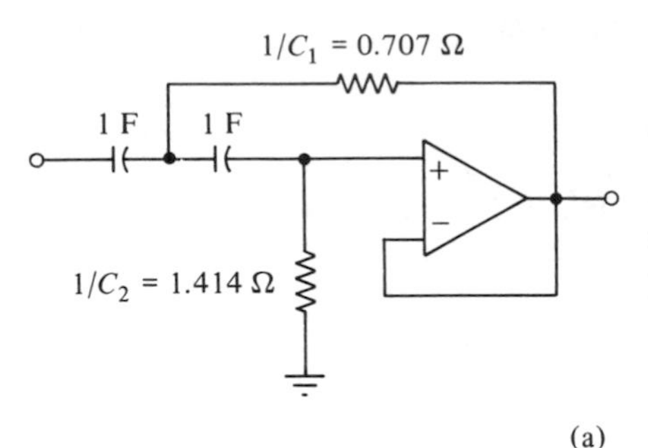

Component values from Table 3-2a are normalized to 1 rad/s with capacitors taken as 1 F and resistors the inverse capacitor values from the table in ohms.

(a)

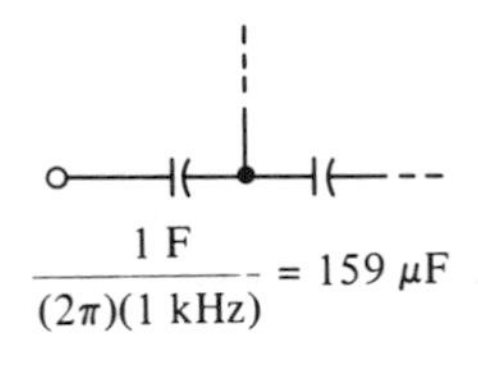

The filter is then frequency-scaled by dividing the capacitor values by the cutoff frequency in radians of value ($2\pi \times 1$ kHz).

(b)

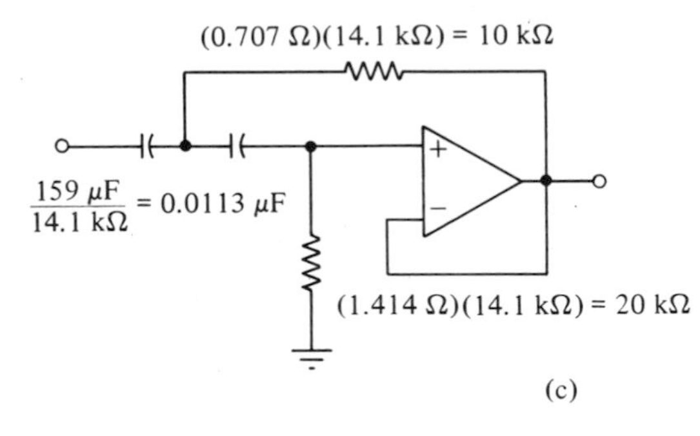

The filter is finally impedance-scaled by multiplying the resistor values by a convenient value (14.1 kΩ) and dividing the capacitor values by the same coefficient.

(c)

FIGURE 3–17. Butterworth Unity Gain Highpass Filter

stability is very good, but the realization of Q values greater than about 5 requires amplifier open-loop gain in excess of 60 dB at the notch frequency f_c. Also, at higher Q values the signal input amplitude may have to be attenuated in order to preserve gyrator linearity. A notch depth to about −40 dB is possible with this circuit.

$$c = \frac{400}{f_c^2} \qquad \text{microfarads} \tag{3-23}$$

A more flexible but complicated approach to the design of band-reject filters is to sum the parallel outputs of unity gain highpass and

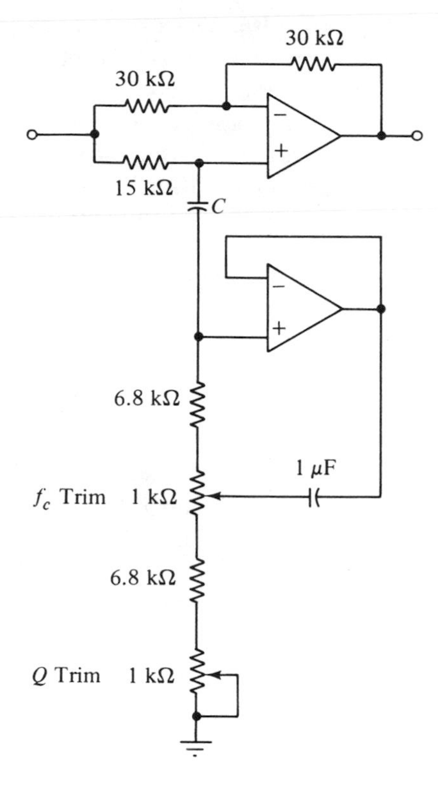

FIGURE 3–18. Gyrator Notch Filter

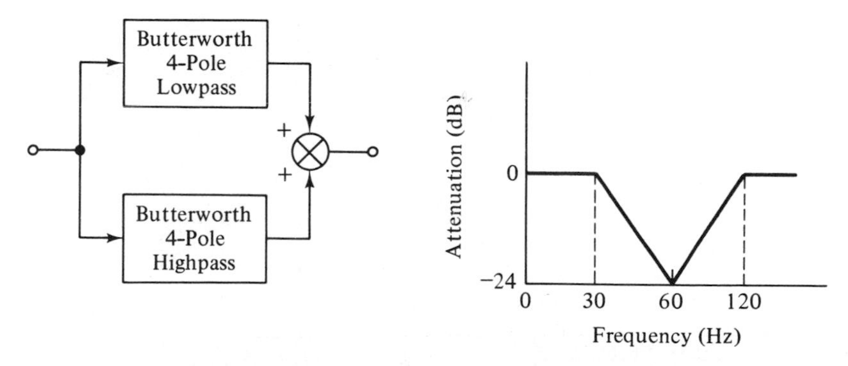

FIGURE 3–19. Lowpass Plus Highpass Notch Filter

lowpass active filters (Figure 3–19). The Q of the resultant band-reject realization is a function of the number of sections of lowpass and highpass networks used. The notch depth is a function of the choice of the lowpass and highpass cutoff frequencies. Consider the design of a $Q=5$ band-reject filter centered at $f_c = 60\,\mathrm{Hz}$. For a Butterworth response, each branch requires a four-pole filter, determined from Figures 3–6 and 3–8, with the lowpass cutoff frequency at 30 Hz and the high pass cutoff at 120 Hz. Notch depth is $-24\,\mathrm{dB}$ at 60 Hz. The advantage of this filter is the excellent passband flatness maintained below 30 Hz and above 120 Hz.

3-4 BANDPASS FILTERS

Three bandpass filter networks are of interest for instrumentation purposes. The *multiple feedback network* is useful for Q values up to 10 and has the advantage of requiring only one operational amplifier. The *biquad resonator* is a more complicated three-amplifier mechanization but provides Q values to 200 with the stability of passive filter designs. And commutative filters can provide Q values to 1000 for very selective signal separation requirements with stability directly proportional to the

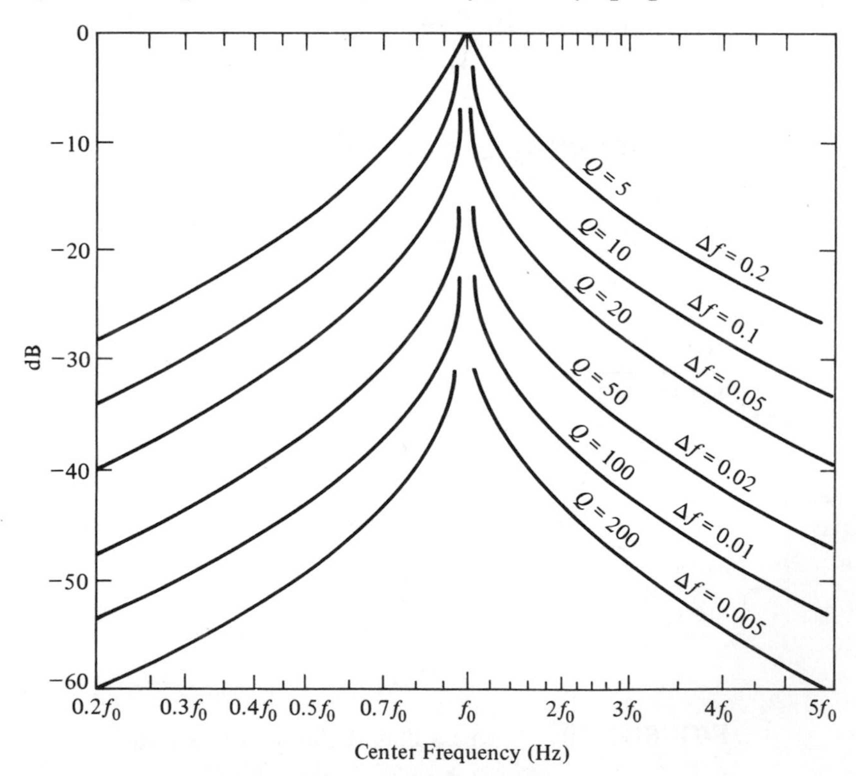

FIGURE 3–20. Quality Factor Curves

frequency drift of its associated clock. Designs are developed in this section with these filters, including the application of stagger tuning. Quality factor Q is defined in all cases by equation (3-24) and is plotted for a range of Q values by Figure 3–20.

$$Q = \frac{f_o}{\Delta f} \quad \frac{\text{center frequency}}{-3\text{-dB bandwidth}} \tag{3-24}$$

Equations (3-25) through (3-28) define the component values for the multiple feedback bandpass filter (MFBF) in terms of Q and center frequency f_o (Figure 3–21). This design provides for unity gain at f_o to maximize the stability of the network. Normally, standard capacitor values are chosen and the required resistors calculated. Consider a $Q = 10$ design at an $f_o = 1\,\text{Hz}$, choosing 5% tolerance $1\,\mu\text{F}$ capacitors and 1% tolerance metal film resistors. It should be noted that this circuit produces an inversion.

$$k = 2\pi f_o C \tag{3-25}$$

$$= (6.28)(1\,\text{Hz})(1\,\mu\text{F})$$

$$= 6.28 \times 10^{-6}\ \text{mho}$$

$$R_1 = \frac{Q}{k} \tag{3-27}$$

$$= \frac{10}{6.28 \times 10^{-6}}$$

$$= 1.6\text{M}\Omega$$

$$R_2 = \frac{1}{(2Q - 1/Q)k} \tag{3-26}$$

$$= \frac{1}{(20 - 0.1)(6.28 \times 10^{-6})}$$

$$= 8\ \text{k}\Omega$$

$$R_3 = \frac{2Q}{k} \tag{3-28}$$

$$= \frac{20}{6.28 \times 10^{-6}}$$

$$= 3.2\,\text{M}\Omega$$

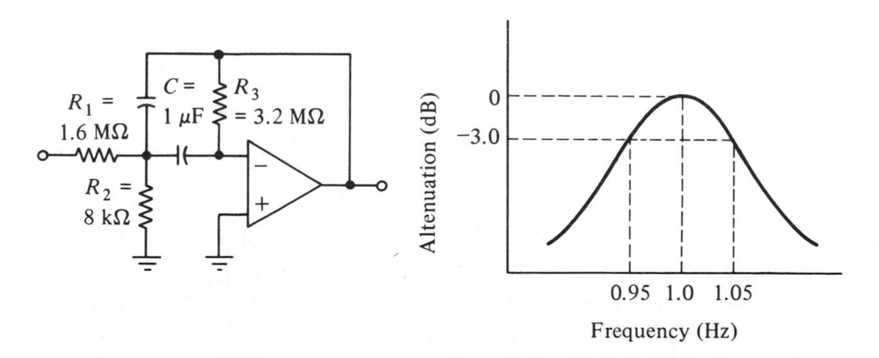

FIGURE 3–21. Multiple Feedback Bandpass Filter

The multiple feedback bandpass filter may also be used to form a band-reject or notch filter (Figure 3–13) with the addition of an output subtractor as shown in Figure 3–22. For example, the preceding $f_o = 1\,\text{kHz}$ $Q = 10$ bandpass design will provide a 1-Hz notch filter having the characteristics shown by Figure 3–13 using the circuit of Figure 3–22. In this realization, the unity gain all-pass throughput has subtracted from it the frequency selective output of the inverting MFBF.

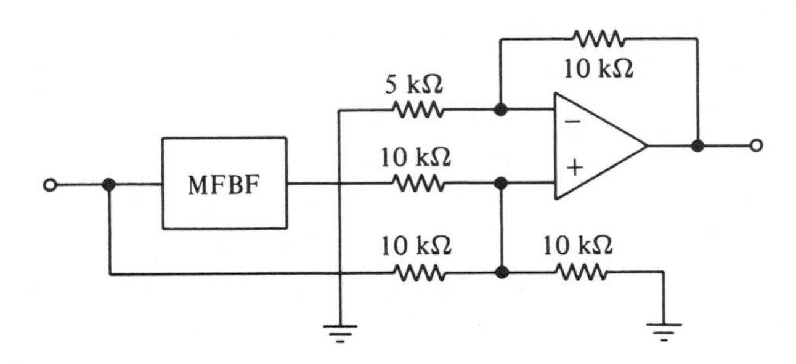

FIGURE 3–22. MFBF Notch Filter

A practical approach to the design of biquad resonator bandpass filters is to fix R_{fo} at a convenient standard value and then calculate the component values to independently set filter center frequency f_o, Q, and gain at the center frequency A_{fo} (Figure 3–23). These equations are shown in Table 3–3, including a tabulation of some representative values spanning instrumentation applications.

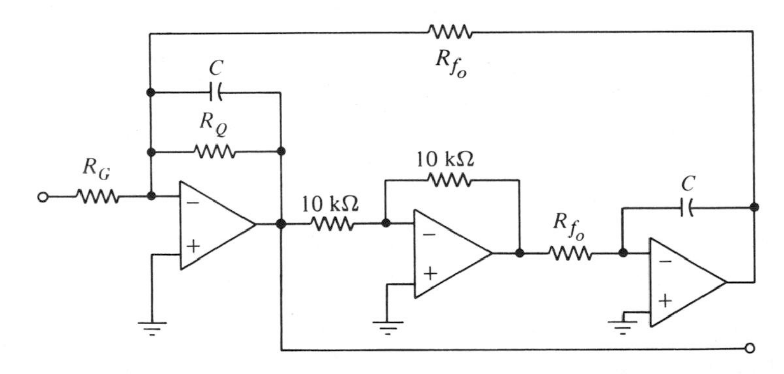

FIGURE 3–23. Biquad Bandpass Filter Network

Since most instrumentation systems involve amplitude measurements of transducer outputs, it is of interest to maintain amplitude flatness in the passband of the signal. In the case of single-tuned bandpass filters, such as a biquad resonator, the amplitude rolls off immediately on both sides of the center frequency. However, a stagger tuning scheme for multiple

TABLE 3–3. Biquad Component Values for $R_{f_o} = 10\,\mathrm{k\Omega}$

f_o	$C=\sqrt{\dfrac{1}{(2\pi f_o R_{f_o})^2}}$ (3-29)	Q	$R_q=\dfrac{Q}{2\pi f_o C}$ (3-30)	A_{f_o}	$R_g=\dfrac{R_q}{A_{f_o}}$ (3-31)
10 Hz	1.6 μF	10	100 kΩ	$Q/100$	1 MΩ
100 Hz	0.16 μF	50	500 kΩ	$Q/50$	500 kΩ
1 kHz	0.016 μF	100	1 MΩ	$Q/10$	100 kΩ
10 kHz	0.0016 μF	200	2 MΩ	Q	10 kΩ

single-tuned bandpass filters can produce a maximally flat passband with additional skirt selectivity.[6–8] Table 3–4 presents optimum single-tuned bandpass filter −3-dB bandwidths Δf_r and center frequencies f_r in terms of the overall −3-dB filter bandwidth Δf and center frequency f_o. Passband flatness and skirt selectivity both improve, of course, as the number of cascaded single-tuned bandpass filters is increased.

TABLE 3–4. Stagger-Tuning Parameters

Single-Tuned Filters	Δf_r	f_r
2	$0.71\Delta f$	$f_o+0.35\Delta f$
	$0.71\Delta f$	$f_o-0.35\Delta f$
3	$0.5\Delta f$	$f_o+0.43\Delta f$
	$0.5\Delta f$	$f_o-0.43\Delta f$
	$1.0\Delta f$	f_o
4	$0.38\Delta f$	$f_o+0.46\Delta f$
	$0.38\Delta f$	$f_o-0.46\Delta f$
	$0.93\Delta f$	$f_o+0.19\Delta f$
	$0.93\Delta f$	$f_o-0.19\Delta f$

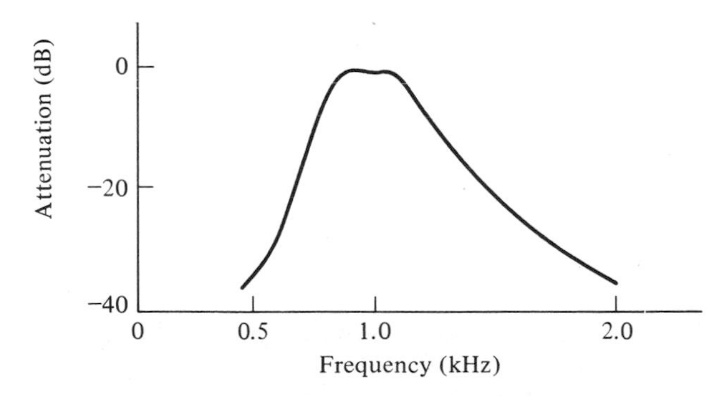

FIGURE 3–24. Composite Filter Characteristic

In the design of all active filters, it is useful to bracket the filter requirement with both overdesigned and austere solutions in order to realize an efficient mechanization. Consider, for example, a bandpass filter requirement having a $\Delta f = 200$-Hz bandwidth, flat to 1 dB, and centered at 1 kHz (Figure 3–24). The filter is also to achieve −35-dB attentuation at ±1 octave on both sides of the center frequency. Two designs are considered which illustrate this suggestion. A cascaded four-pole 1-dB ripple Chebyshev lowpass followed by a four-pole 1-dB ripple Chebyshev highpass filter satisfies these requirements with a four-operational-amplifier design (Figure 3–25). Alternately, two stagger-tuned multiple feedback bandpass filters are able to meet the same specifications with two operational amplifiers (Figure 3–26). Reference to the capacitor tabulations of Table 3–2b for the Chebyshev characteristic provides component values which are then frequency- and impedance-scaled for the unity gain networks. The cutoff frequency for the lowpass filter is 1100 Hz; for the highpass, 900 Hz. The impedance scaling values were chosen so as to result in resistor values as close to standard values as practicable. This is demonstrated in the examples associated with Figures 3–16 and 3–17.

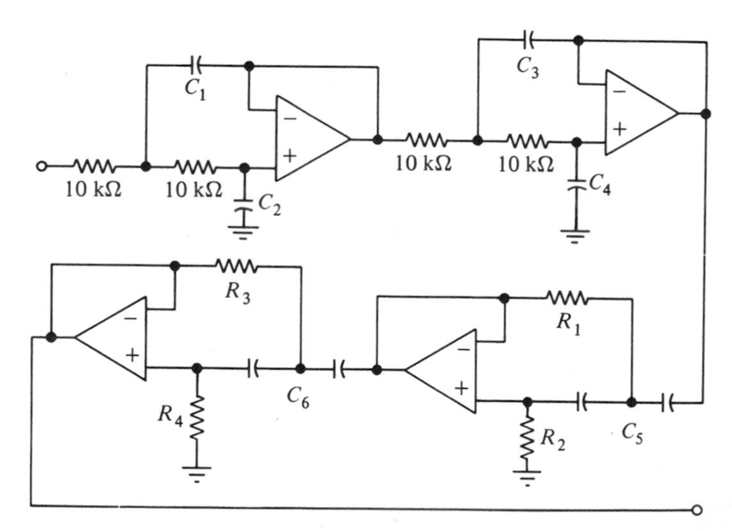

FIGURE 3–25. Chebyshev Lowpass and Highpass Cascade

$$C_1 = \frac{3.125 \text{ F}}{(2\pi)(1100 \text{ Hz})(10 \text{ k})}$$

$$= 0.045 \ \mu\text{F}$$

$$C_2 = \frac{1.269 \text{ F}}{(2\pi)(1100 \text{ Hz})(10 \text{ k})}$$

$$= 0.02 \ \mu\text{F}$$

$$C_3 = \frac{7.546 \text{ F}}{(2\pi)(1100 \text{ Hz})(10 \text{ k})}$$

$$= 0.11 \ \mu\text{F}$$

$$R_1 = \left(\frac{1}{3.125}\right) \cdot (31.25 \text{ k})$$

$$= 10 \text{ k}$$

$$R_2 = \left(\frac{1}{1.269}\right) \cdot (31.25 \text{ k})$$

$$= 20 \text{ k}$$

$$C_4 = \frac{0.1489 \text{ F}}{(2\pi)(1100 \text{ Hz})(10 \text{ k})}$$

$$= 0.0022 \ \mu\text{F}$$

$$C_5 = \frac{1 \text{ F}}{(2\pi)(900 \text{ Hz})(31.25 \text{ k})}$$

$$= 0.005 \ \mu\text{F}$$

$$C_6 = \frac{1 \text{ F}}{(2\pi)(900 \text{ Hz})(75.4 \text{ k})}$$

$$= 0.002 \ \mu\text{F}$$

$$R_3 = \left(\frac{1}{7.546}\right) \cdot (75.4 \text{ k})$$

$$= 10 \ k$$

$$R_4 = \left(\frac{1}{0.1489}\right) \cdot (75.4 \ k)$$

$$= 506 \ k$$

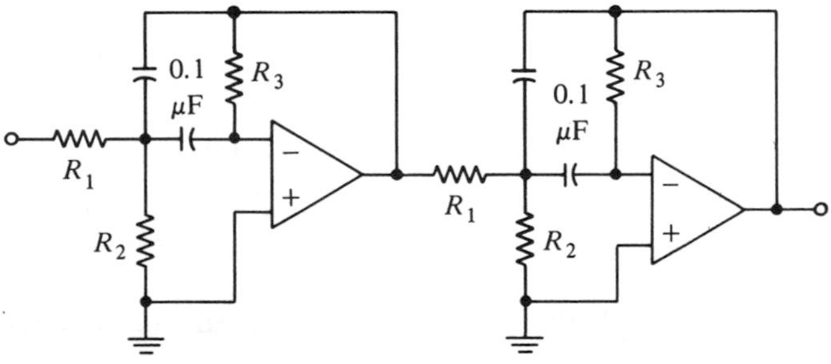

FIGURE 3–26. Stagger-Tuned Multiple Feedback Realization

The multiple feedback bandpass filter sections in the stagger-tuned approach are implemented as in the example associated with Figure 3–21. The tuning parameters are obtained from Table 3–4 and the capacitors chosen as 0.1 μF. Each section center frequency is determined by R_2, the Q by R_3, and the gain by R_1 if final tuning adjustments are required. A minor penalty of the stagger-tuning arrangement is a gain loss which is a result of the algebraic addition of the individual bandpass section skirts.

However, the loss per section can be calculated by the equations shown below, and compensated for by increasing the gain of each network above unity by correcting the values of two of the resistors in each section. This procedure is included in the implementation of the stagger-tuned example, where f_g is the geometric center of the overall filter response and f_U and f_L the upper and lower passband frequencies, respectively.

$$\text{gain loss}_r = \frac{A_r}{\sqrt{A_r^2 + B_r^2}} \qquad (3\text{-}32)$$

$$A_r = \frac{(2\pi f_r)(2\pi f_g)}{Q_r} \qquad (3\text{-}33)$$

$$B_r = (2\pi f_r)^2 - (2\pi f_g)^2 \qquad (3\text{-}34)$$

$$f_g = \sqrt{f_u \cdot f_L} \qquad (3\text{-}35)$$

$$= \sqrt{(1100\,\text{Hz})(900\,\text{Hz})}$$

$$= 995\,\text{Hz}$$

First Section:

$$\Delta f_{r_1} = 0.71\Delta f$$

$$= (0.71)(200\,\text{Hz})$$

$$= 141\,\text{Hz}$$

$$f_{r_1} = f_o + 0.35\Delta f$$

$$= 1\,\text{kHz} + (0.35)(200\,\text{Hz})$$

$$= 1.07\,\text{kHz}$$

$$Q_1 = \frac{f_{r_1}}{\Delta f_{r_1}} \qquad (3\text{-}24)$$

$$= \frac{1.07\,\text{kHz}}{141\,\text{Hz}}$$

$$= 7.6$$

Second Section:

$$\Delta f_{r_2} = 0.71\Delta f$$

$$= (0.71)(200\,\text{Hz})$$

$$= 141\,\text{Hz}$$

$$f_{r_2} = f_o - 0.35\Delta f$$

$$= 1\,\text{kHz} - (0.35)(200\,\text{Hz})$$

$$= 930\,\text{Hz}$$

$$Q_2 = \frac{f_{r_2}}{\Delta f_{r_2}} \qquad (3\text{-}24)$$

$$= \frac{930\,\text{Hz}}{141\,\text{Hz}}$$

$$= 6.6$$

First Section:

$$k_1 = 2\pi f_{r1} C \qquad (3\text{-}25)$$

$$= (2\pi)(1.07\,\text{kHz})(0.1\,\mu\text{F})$$

$$= 6.72 \times 10^{-4}\,\text{mho}$$

$$A_1 = \frac{(2\pi f_{r_1})(2\pi f_g)}{Q_1} \qquad (3\text{-}33)$$

$$= \frac{(2\pi \cdot 1.07\,\text{kHz})(2\pi \cdot 995\,\text{Hz})}{7.6}$$

$$= 5.53 \times 10^6$$

$$B_1 = (2\pi f_{r_1})^2 - (2\pi f_g)^2 \qquad (3\text{-}34)$$

$$= (2\pi \cdot 1.07\,\text{kHz})^2 - (2\pi \cdot 995\,\text{Hz})^2$$

$$= 6.15 \times 10^6$$

$$\text{gain loss}_1 = \frac{A_1}{\sqrt{A_1^2 + B_1^2}} \qquad (3\text{-}32)$$

$$= \frac{5.53 \times 10^6}{\sqrt{(5.53 \times 10^6)^2 + (6.15 \times 10^6)^2}}$$

$$= 0.669$$

Second Section:

$$k_2 = 2\pi f_{r_2} C \qquad (3\text{-}25)$$

$$= (2\pi)(930\,\text{Hz})(0.1\,\mu\text{F})$$

$$= 5.85 \times 10^{-4}\,\text{mho}$$

$$A_2 = \frac{(2\pi f_{r_2})(2\pi f_g)}{Q_2} \qquad (3\text{-}33)$$

$$= \frac{(2\pi \cdot 930\,\text{Hz})(2\pi \cdot 995\,\text{Hz})}{6.6}$$

$$= 5.53 \times 10^6$$

$$B_2 = (2\pi f_{r_2})^2 - (2\pi f_g)^2 \qquad (3\text{-}34)$$

$$= (2\pi \cdot 930\,\text{Hz})^2 - (2\pi \cdot 995\,\text{Hz})^2$$

$$= -4.9 \times 10^6$$

$$\text{gain loss}_2 = \frac{A_2}{\sqrt{A_2^2 + B_2^2}} \qquad (3\text{-}32)$$

$$= \frac{5.53 \times 10^6}{\sqrt{(5.53 \times 10^6)^2 + (-4.9 \times 10^6)^2}}$$

$$= 0.75$$

First Section:

$$R_1 = \frac{Q_1 \cdot \text{gain loss}_1}{K_1} \quad (3\text{-}36)$$

$$= \frac{(7.6)(0.669)}{6.72 \times 10^{-4} \text{ mho}}$$

$$= 7.55\,\text{k}\Omega$$

$$R_2 = \frac{1}{\left(2Q_1 - \frac{1}{Q_1 \cdot \text{gain loss}_1}\right) k_1} \quad (3\text{-}37)$$

$$= \frac{1}{\left(15.2 - \frac{1}{(7.6)(0.669)}\right)(6.72 \times 10^{-4}) \text{ mho}}$$

$$= 99\,\Omega$$

$$R_3 = \frac{2Q_1}{K_1} \quad (3\text{-}28)$$

$$= \frac{15.2}{6.72 \times 10^{-4} \text{ mho}}$$

$$= 22.6\,\text{k}\Omega$$

Second Section:

$$R_1 = \frac{Q_2 \cdot \text{gain loss}_2}{K_2} \quad (3\text{-}36)$$

$$= \frac{(6.6)(0.75)}{5.85 \times 10^{-4} \text{ mho}}$$

$$= 8.47\,\text{k}\Omega$$

$$R_2 = \frac{1}{\left(2Q_2 - \frac{1}{Q_2 \cdot \text{gain loss}_2}\right) k_2} \quad (3\text{-}$$

$$= \frac{1}{\left(13.2 - \frac{1}{(6.6)(0.75)}\right)(5.85 \times 10^{-4}) \text{ mho}}$$

$$= 132\,\Omega$$

$$R_3 = \frac{2Q_2}{K_2} \quad (3\text{-}28)$$

$$= \frac{13.2}{5.85 \times 10^{-4} \text{ mho}}$$

$$= 22.6\,\text{k}\Omega$$

3-5 SPECIAL FILTER MECHANIZATIONS

Occasionally it is required to provide very high Q values, even beyond the capability of the biquad resonator. Stable Q values to 1000 are available with the commutator filter by synthesizing a frequency sampling spectrum and then selecting the first bandpass-shaped spectrum beyond the baseband. The Q of this filter is determined by equation (3-38), where N is the number of multiplexer channels and Nf_o the required commutator clock frequency. The cutoff frequency of the baseband-elimination highpass filter is specified by equation (3-39), and the lowpass filter cutoff frequency by equation (3-40) for eliminating aliasing and the repeated frequency spectrum responses. Two-pole Butterworth highpass and eight-pole Butterworth lowpass filters provide adequate attenuation for

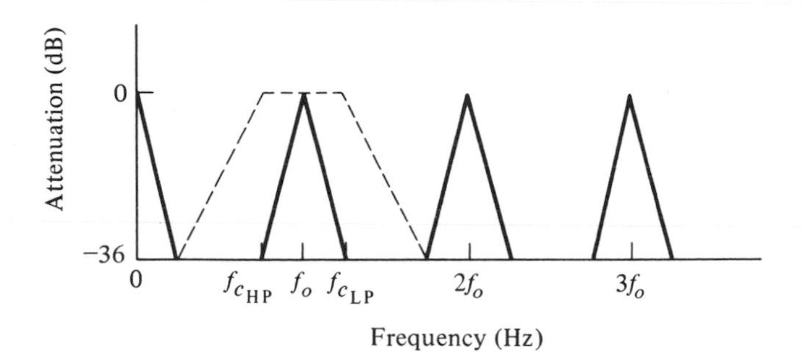

FIGURE 3–27. Commutator Frequency-Sampling Spectrum

these purposes. The frequency-sampling spectrum is described by Figure 3–27.

$$Q = \pi N f_o RC \tag{3-38}$$

$$f_{C_{HP}} = 0.8 f_o \tag{3-39}$$

$$f_{C_{LP}} = 1.2 f_o \tag{3-40}$$

$$\text{clock} = N f_o \tag{3-41}$$

Consider the design of a bandpass commutator filter at an $f_o = 1\,\text{kHz}$ and $Q = 1000$. This specifies a -3-dB bandwidth $\Delta f = 1\,\text{Hz}$ by equation (3-24). In order to provide an adequate sampling rate, a Fairchild 3705 eight-channel analog multiplexer is chosen as the commutator, which requires a clock frequency of $Nf_o = 8\,\text{kHz}$. Equation (3-38) is then rearranged to determine the RC product, which is equal to 0.04 s. This is satisfied by 0.1-μF commutating capacitors and a 400-kΩ multiplexer input resistor. For very good performance a crystal oscillator is required with a stability of about 1 part in 10^{-5}. Figure 3–28 shows the completed circuit having highpass and lowpass active filter cutoff frequencies of $f_{c_{HP}} = 800\,\text{Hz}$ and $f_{c_{LP}} = 1.2\,\text{kHz}$. The active filters were designed by application of the data from Table 3–2a.

There are applications where the analog integrator is used as a lowpass filter, and it is of interest to compare its performance with that of a simple RC lowpass filter. To accomplish this, the two networks will be compared on a normalized basis using the one-sided noise equivalent bandwidth B_n (Figure 3–29). To obtain a transfer function in the frequency domain for the integrator, we assume an impulsive input whose time-domain representation may be Fourier-transformed to the frequency domain, resulting in a $\sin X/X$ response. The frequency-domain transfer function for the RC filter may be simply expressed in terms of its cutoff

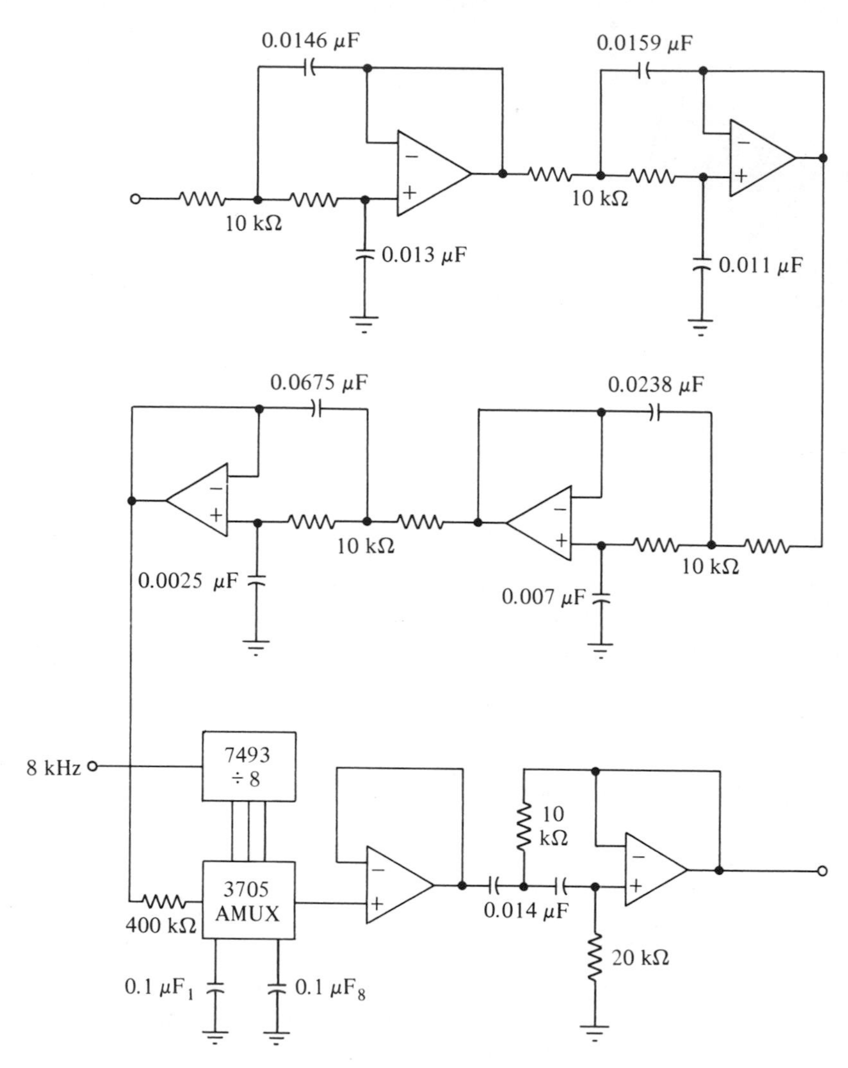

FIGURE 3–28. Commutator Bandpass Filter: $f_o = 1$ kHz; $Q = 1000$

frequency $\omega_C = 1/RC$ rad/s. The noise-equivalent bandwidth can then be calculated for both transfer functions, as shown by equation (3-44).

The results indicate that the RC filter has one half the B_n as the integrator for the same RC product. The significance of this is that the RC filter will provide twice the processing gain against random noise, or a 3-dB processing gain over the analog integrator. Aside from this result, however, a dumping integrator will eliminate all signal past history, such as transients, with each reset. The *RC* filter carries along this history or memory, which diminishes as a direct function of its *RC* time constant. Table 3–5 presents a compendium of the results developed in this chapter for active filter applications.

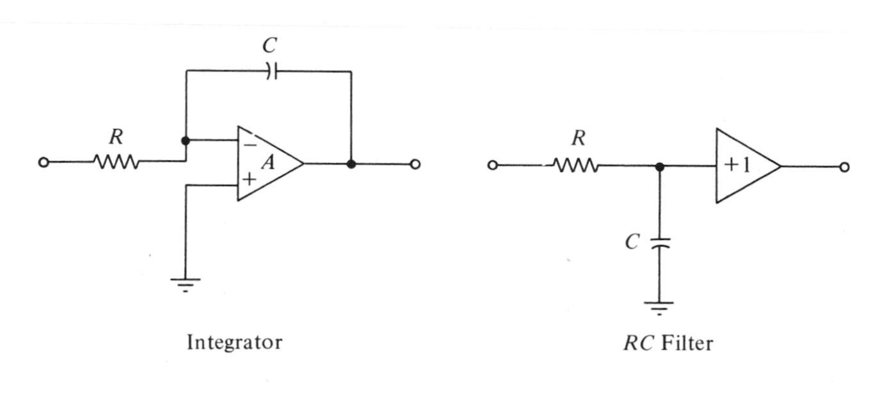

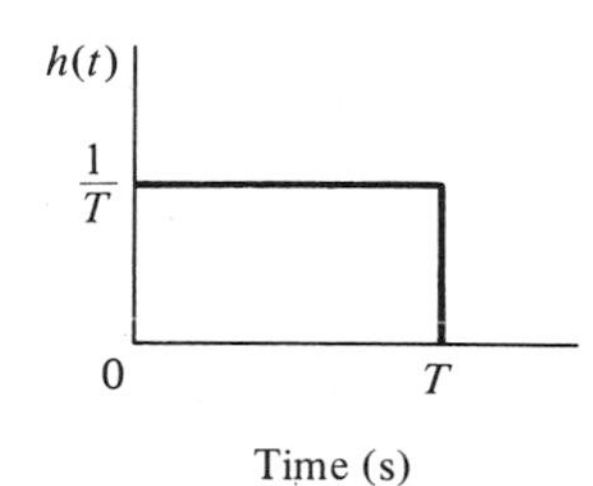

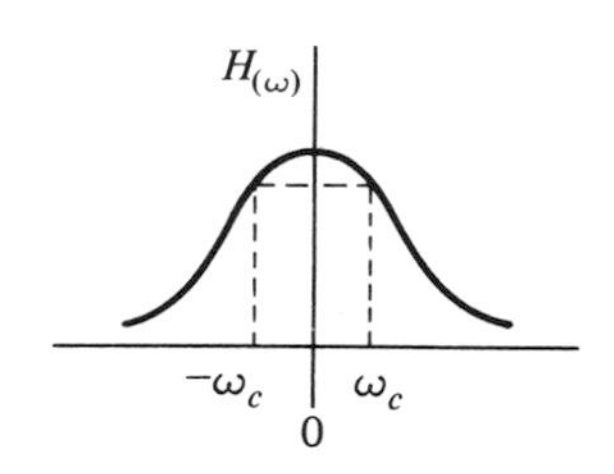

$$H_{(\omega)} = \int^{\infty} h(t)\cdot e^{-j\omega t}\cdot dt \qquad (3.42)$$

$$= e^{-j\omega T/2} \cdot \frac{\sin(\omega T/2)}{\omega T/2}$$

$$H_{(\omega)} = \frac{\omega_c}{\omega + \omega_c} \qquad (3.43)$$

$$B_{n_I} = \frac{1}{2\pi}\int_{o}^{\infty} H^2_{(\omega)}\cdot d\omega \qquad (3.44)$$

$$= \frac{1}{2\pi}\int_{o}^{\infty} \frac{\sin^2(\omega T/2)}{(\omega T/2)^2}\cdot d\omega$$

$$= \frac{\omega}{2}\ \text{rad/s}$$

$$B_{n_{RC}} = \frac{1}{2\pi}\int_{o}^{\infty} H^2_{(\omega)_c}\cdot d\omega \qquad (3.44)$$

$$= \frac{1}{2\pi}\int_{o}^{\infty} \left(\frac{\omega_c}{\omega + \omega_c}\right)^2 \cdot d\omega$$

$$= \frac{\omega_c}{4}\ \text{rad/s}$$

FIGURE 3–29. Integrator Versus *RC* Filter Comparison

TABLE 3–5. Active Filter Selector

Function	Network	Feature
Lowpass	Unity gain	−100 db/Octave Practical
Highpass	Unity gain	−100 db/Octave Practical
Low-Q bandpass	MFBF	Requires 1 op amp
High accuracy	Unity gain	Lowpass + highpass
Maximally flat	MFBF	Stagger-tuned
High-Q bandpass	Biquad	Only choice $Q > 10$
Very high Q	Commutator	Q to 1000
Maximally flat	Biquad	Stagger-tuned
Band-reject	Gyrator	−40 db notch
Alternative	Inverted MFBF	Q to 10

PROBLEMS

3-1 Design a 10-pole Butterworth lowpass filter having a 1 kHz cutoff frequency. Use unity gain active filter networks, 1 MΩ resistors, and show the circuit including all component values and a plot of expected frequency response.

3-2 A band-reject filter is required in the conditioning of a slowly varying dc signal that provides 60 dB of attenuation at 60 Hz. Choose a suitable network, design a filter using two operational amplifiers, and show the complete circuit including a sketch of its frequency response.

3-3 Repeat the solution of Problem 3–2 using an alternate network, and again determine the circuit values and frequency response using two operational amplifiers.

3-4 Design the circuit described by Problem 4–2 and show all component values. The presampling filter is to be a 6-pole Bessel type implemented with unity gain networks. Label the switching arrangement for the selectable amplifier DMG and filter cutoff frequency values.

3-5 An elementary spectrum analyzer can be mechanized with a voltage-tuned bandpass filter and an X-Y oscilloscope. Design a Q of 200 biquad bandpass filter at a center frequency of 1 kHz and with a gain of unity. Use analog multipliers in series with the frequency determining resistors as variable conductance tuning elements, and scale the input signal and tuning voltages for 60 dB of amplitude and 2-decades of frequency between 10 Hz and 1 kHz. Determine the final filter circuit including all component values.

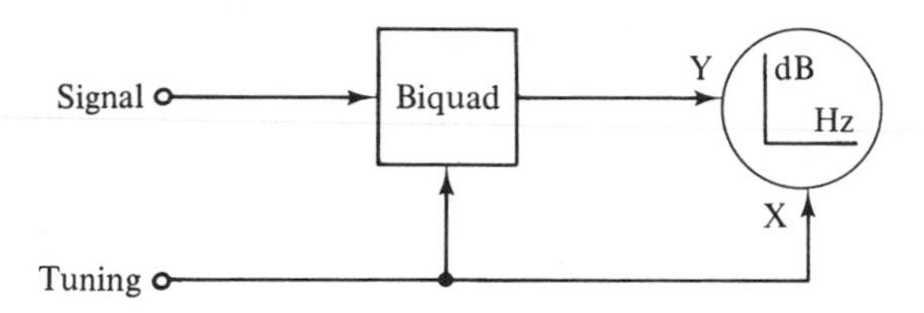

3-6 The discrete FM quadracast system proposed by General Electric includes a vestigal sideband signal between 60 kHz and 90 kHz of the detected composite signal. Design a cascade of multiple feedback bandpass filters to select this signal component while preserving passband flatness and the minimum stopband attenuation shown at 53 kHz. Use 0.001 μF capacitors, show all calculations leading to the final component values, and plot the expected frequency response including the attenuation at 53 kHz and 90 kHz.

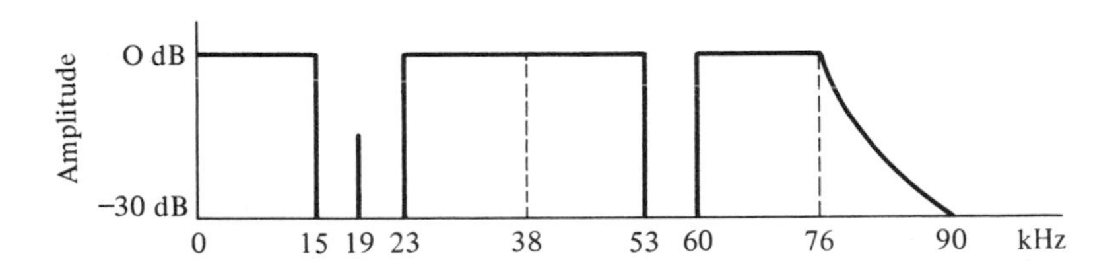

REFERENCES

1. R. P. Sallen and E. L. Key, "A Practical Method Of Designing *RC* Active Filters," *IRE Transactions on Circuit Theory*, Vol. CT-2, March 1955.

2. P. R. Geffe, "Toward High Stability in Active Filters," *IEEE Spectrum*, Vol. 7, May 1970.

3. J. Tow, "A Step-by-Step Active Filter Design," *IEEE Spectrum*, Vol. 6, December 1969.

4. L. C. Thomas, "The Biquad: Part 1—Some Practical Design Considerations," *IEEE Circuit Theory Transactions*, Vol. CT-18, May 1971.

5. S. K. Mitra, "Synthesizing Active Filters," *IEEE Spectrum*, Vol. 6, January 1969.

6. R. Brandt, "Active Resonators Save Steps in Designing Active Filters," Electronics, April 24, 1972.

7. B. Zeines, *Introduction to Network Analysis*, Prentice-Hall, Englewood Cliffs, N. J., 1967.

8. C. Mitra, *Analysis And Synthesis of Linear Active Networks*, John Wiley, New York, 1969.

4

SIGNAL CONDITIONING OPERATIONS

4-0 INTRODUCTION

The design of data-acquisition systems between measurement transducers and a computer input requires the convergence of several considerations in order to obtain an optimum implementation. Of usual concern is the achievement of required performance within some framework of imposed error, cost, and timing budgets, with confidence in this performance even under difficult signal conditions. This chapter presents a unified approach to the design of signal conditioning circuits through an adaptation of matched filter methods to process against additive noise and includes the effect of systematic error resulting from preamplifier input uncertainty.

The basic data-acquisition channel consists of a preamplifier, presampling filter, and analog-to-digital (A/D) converter. Signal quality can be compactly expressed as a signal-to-noise ratio (SNR) from analog input to digital output word, which provides a unified figure of merit for evaluating system performance. Although a number of input options and signal conditioning functions may be provided by a data-acquisition system, we shall focus on the essential considerations of raising the input signal quality to the level of interest, presampling filter criteria, and sample rate selection. Of primary concern is that each transducer-to-computer channel of the data-acquisition system upgrade the SNR as the signal progresses to the A/D converter so that the number of required binary bits delivered to the computer are valid data. The considerations that determine this, together with associated trade-offs, are developed in this chapter, and practical examples are given.

4-1 SIGNAL QUALITY CONSIDERATIONS

A useful starting point is to evaluate the characteristics of each analog input signal plus noise to determine the input SNR. This is acquired at the input of the data-acquisition system as the dc or rms signal level squared over the rms interference voltage squared, with the resulting ratio having the dimensions of watts over watts. The interference measurement may be obtained with the aid of an oscilloscope or true rms voltmeter with the signal cable terminated in the transducer source impedance but the transducer disconnected. The oscilloscope is not an accurate method if the interference is predominantly Gaussian noise, for example, rather than 60 Hz. This is so because of the varying crest factor of Gaussian noise, which precludes a simple peak voltage measurement-to-rms mathematical relationship. However, an approximate rms value can be obtained with an average responding voltmeter calibrated for sine waves, where $\text{rms}_{\text{noise}} =$ (reading)(1.127).

Since the transducer output amplitude normally corresponds to some measurement of interest, such as temperature or pressure, of primary concern is the acquisition of a true amplitude measurement. The probability that the signal corrupted by additive interference is within a specified Δ region centered about the true value can be determined from well-known probability relationships. For matched filter processing of the signal plus noise, a particularly useful expression is available for the confidence in the measurement of an amplitude a as a function of SNR[1,2]. The use of this formula, given by equation (4-2), is shown to be valid because of the connection demonstrated by Fano[3,4] between linear filters used for signal conditioning and correlator matched filters for SNRs $\geqslant 100$. Also, a sinusoidal phase measurement is occasionally required, such as from a resolver or radio navigation system, which is correspondingly described in terms of SNR by equation (4-3), where ϕ is in degrees. Accordingly, Table 4–1 presents a tabulation of the required SNR for specified amplitude and phase errors for 68% confidence in the measurement, or one standard deviation (1σ). For 95% (2σ) confidence, simply double the error values for each entry.

$$\text{input SNR} = \left(\frac{\text{rms signal}}{\text{rms interference}}\right)^2 \tag{4-1}$$

$$P(\Delta a; a) = \text{erf}\left(\frac{1}{2} \cdot \frac{\Delta a}{a} \cdot \sqrt{\text{SNR}}\right) \tag{4-2}$$

$$P(\Delta\phi; \phi) = \text{erf}\left(\frac{1}{2} \cdot \frac{\Delta\phi}{57.3°/\text{rad}} \cdot \sqrt{\text{SNR}}\right) \tag{4-3}$$

TABLE 4–1. SNR Versus Amplitude and Phase Errors

SNR	Amplitude Error (%)	Phase Error (deg)	Confidence (%)
10^1	44.0	22.5	68
10^2	14.0	7.5	68
10^3	4.4	2.5	68
10^4	1.4	0.82	68
10^5	0.44	0.27	68
10^6	0.14	0.09	68
10^7	0.044	0.027	68
10^8	0.014	0.009	68
10^9	0.0044	0.003	68
10^{10}	0.0014	0.001	68

Equations (4-2) and (4-3) are exact for sinusoidal signals in Gaussian interference and asymptotically correct depending upon how well the signal plus noise conforms to the exact case. Nevertheless, the results are conservative and generally applicable since most signals can be decomposed into sinusoidal components and even though some interference is more coherent in nature, such as 60 Hz. The latter is so because the majority of the signal conditioning SNR improvement is obtained from the preamplifier common-mode rejection ratio, which is generally more effective against the typical lower frequency coherent interference than wideband random noise. This will result in a preamplifier noise output having largely Gaussian statistical properties, for which linear filtering is effective in providing additional SNR improvement.

The preamplifier will be either an operational, instrumentation, or isolation amplifier, depending upon the application requirements. Of interest here is the in-circuit common-mode rejection ratio (CMRR) exhibited by the preamplifier, which is equal to the ratio of differential-mode gain (DMG) to common-mode gain (CMG) as developed in Chapter 2. CMRR is also equivalent to the square root of the ratio of SNRs shown in equation (4-4), which can be rearranged to provide the preamp output SNR quantity. Note that CMRR is a voltage relationship, whereas SNR is a power ratio.

$$\mathrm{CMRR} = \frac{\mathrm{DMG}}{\mathrm{CMG}} \tag{2-25}$$

$$= \sqrt{\frac{\text{preamp output SNR}}{\text{input SNR}}} \tag{4-4}$$

$$\text{preamp output SNR} = \text{input SNR} \cdot \mathrm{CMRR}^2 \tag{4-5}$$

Between the output of the preamplifier and the input to the A/D converter, the presampling filter must provide any additional signal quality improvement needed. Fano demonstrated for filter input SNRs ⩾ 100 that linear filtering methods asymptotically approach the same efficiency as the correlator matched filter. An interpretation of the matched filter is that its frequency response function is shaped like the complex conjugate of the signal, which maximizes the power extracted from the signal while minimizing the contribution by the noise. Later work[5] has shown that linear filtering has an efficiency only about 3 dB less than matched filtering for high-input SNRs. In terms of the basic system shown by Figure 4–1, therefore, the processing gain is closely approximated by the identity of equation (4-6).

$$\text{processing gain} = \frac{\text{filter output SNR}}{\text{preamp output SNR}} = \frac{1}{2} \cdot \frac{\text{preamp BW}}{\text{filter BW}} \tag{4-6}$$

This identity may be rearranged in terms of f_{c_1}, the presampling filter cutoff frequency required to provide the additional signal quality improvement between the preamplifier output and the A/D converter input. The necessary signal quality at the A/D input in terms of an adequate filter output SNR is equated to binary bit quality in Table 4–2 for a 10-V full-scale (FS) converter analog input amplitude. Other full-scale values, such as 5 V, would change only the $\frac{1}{2}$LSB entries. Equation (4-8) provides the percentage of the full-scale amplitude represented by A/D converter one-half least-significant-bit amplitudes which is applicable to any converter bit length. It is interesting to note that although the converter minimum output error is generally specified as 1 LSB, the use of the uniform quantizing algorithm discussed in detail in Chapter 6 specifies the minimum allowable input amplitude error as $\pm\frac{1}{2}$LSB. Con-

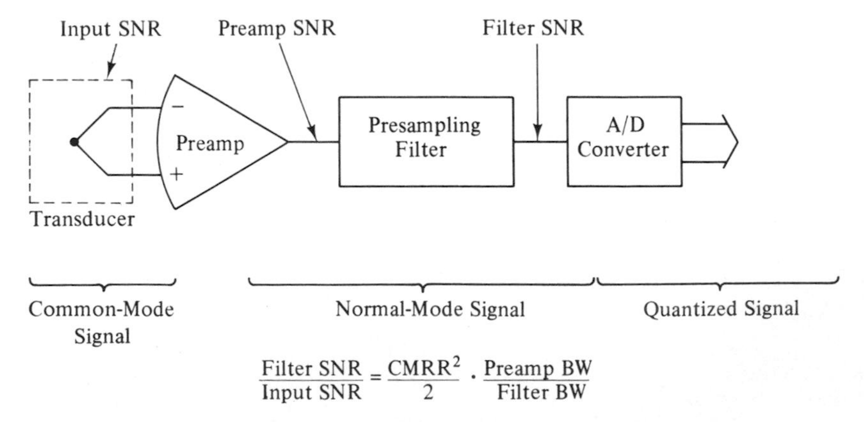

FIGURE 4–1. Basic Data-Acquisition Channel

sequently, the quantization loss across the converter is a constant 6 dB in SNR regardless of the fact that longer bit-length converters have a smaller separation between their levels. In addition, the essential difference between quantization noise and Gaussian noise is that the former can assume values only between $\pm\frac{1}{2}$LSB, whereas the latter can assume any value in theory.[6] The argument of equation (4-9) is squared because it represents a voltage ratio.

TABLE 4–2. Equivalent Binary 1σ Signal Quality

Binary Quality	$\frac{1}{2}$ LSB (10 V FS)	$\frac{1}{2}$ LSB % of FS	Filter Output SNR	
4 (bits)	625 mV/2	3.2	2.0×10^{3}	33 (dB)
5	312 mV/2	1.6	8.0×10^{3}	39
6	156 mV/2	0.8	3.2×10^{4}	45
7	78.1 mV/2	0.4	1.3×10^{5}	51
8	39.0 mV/2	0.2	5.0×10^{5}	57
9	19.6 mV/2	0.1	2.0×10^{6}	63
10	9.8 mV/2	0.05	8.0×10^{6}	69
11	4.9 mV/2	0.025	3.2×10^{7}	75
12	2.45 mV/2	0.012	1.3×10^{8}	81
13	1.22 mV/2	0.006	5.0×10^{8}	87
14	610 μV/2	0.003	2.0×10^{9}	93
15	305 μV/2	0.0015	8.0×10^{9}	99
16	153 μV/2	0.00075	3.2×10^{10}	105

$$\text{filter cutoff } f_{c_1} = \frac{1}{2}\cdot\frac{(\text{preamp BW})(\text{preamp output SNR})}{\text{filter output SNR}} \tag{4-7}$$

$$\%\text{ of FS amplitude} = \frac{\pm\frac{1}{2}\text{LSB}}{\text{FS value}}\cdot 100\% \tag{4-8}$$

$$\text{A/D quantization loss} = 10\log\left(\frac{1\text{LSB}}{\pm\frac{1}{2}\text{LSB}}\right)^2 \tag{4-9}$$

$$= 6\text{ dB}$$

4-2 SAMPLE RATE SELECTION

Selection of an A/D sample rate f_s requires knowledge of both the highest significant signal frequency component and the final signal reconstruction or representation method[7]. The final signal representation method considered here is the step interpolator, which is the way data are handled internally in digital computers, whereby a value remains that of the previous sample until a new sample is taken. The presampling filter cutoff frequency can also be determined from the consideration of ensuring adequate spectral occupancy for the signal. For example, for arbitrary complex signals, this cutoff frequency may be determined from the signal fundamental period with the expectation that the amplitudes of the harmonics decrease approximately as $1/n$. Accordingly, a presampling filter chosen to accommodate harmonics of at least 5% amplitude will have a cutoff frequency $f_{c_2} = 20/\text{fundamental period}$. Of course, dc and sinusoidal-type signals require proportionally less bandwidth. The fundamental period of periodic signals and the width at the half-power points of single events can usually be obtained with the aid of an oscilloscope.

A presampling filter is always desirable to prevent conversion of noise above the highest significant signal frequency component. An ambiguity can exist in the choice of the presampling filter cutoff, however, because it is specified both by the required processing gain and signal spectral occupancy requirements shown by Table 4-3. Difficulty arises only when the cutoff frequency required to provide the necessary processing gain is lower than that necessary for adequate spectral occupancy, or $f_{c_1} < f_{c_2}$. Values of $f_{c_1} \geqslant f_{c_2}$ present no problem, because both processing gain and spectral occupancy are satisfied, and either value may be used. The smaller frequency is usually chosen, however, because it minimizes the sample rate f_s.

TABLE 4–3. Presampling Filter Cutoff Frequency

Signal Type	Filter Cutoff f_{c_2} (Hz)
Dc	1/rate change
Sinusoidal	1/period
Complex periodic	20/fundamental period
Single events	1/width

In situations where the initial design iteration yields $f_{c_1} < f_{c_2}$, the f_{c_1} of equation (4-7) must be increased to equal or exceed f_{c_2} of Table 4–3 while simultaneously realizing the processing gain required for signal quality improvement expressed by equation (4-6). The available action for achieving this is by increasing the preamplifier bandwidth common to equations (4-6) and (4-7). This can normally be done, where required, by lead compensating the preamplifier to provide the required bandwidth at the closed-loop gain of interest.[8] Many instrumentation amplifiers provide terminals for lead compensation. Alternatively, it can be implemented by modifying the feedback network to add a network zero near the amplifier unity-loop-gain crossover frequency.

An additional concern is the frequency-domain overlap at the folding frequency $f_o = f_s/2$ shown in Figure 4–2. Aliasing may result if this overlap is not suppressed due to interpolation errors between the spectral components of the signal. This error is a complicated function of the ratio of signal plus noise in the overlap area to that in the remainder of the sampled signal spectrum. Overlap suppression at f_o is increased with an increasing sample rate and increasing presampling filter rolloff rate. In the interest of avoiding an excessive sample rate, however, it is more efficient to utilize a higher-order presampling filter. An overlap amplitude on the order of 1% or so of the passband amplitude at f_o is a conservative value. Table 4–4 provides a tabulation of sample rates for this value of overlap amplitude.

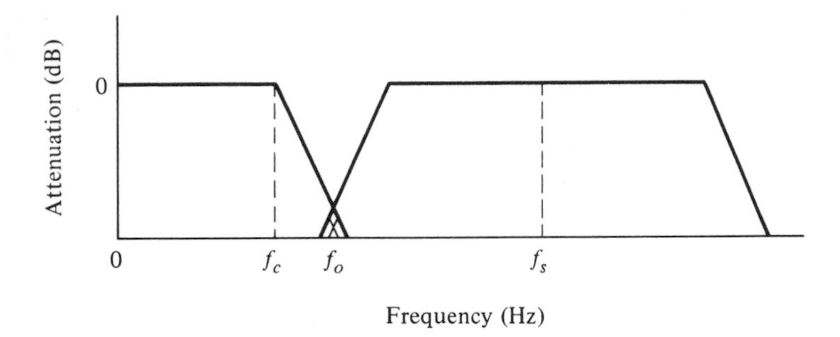

FIGURE 4–2. Sampled Data Frequency Spectrum

TABLE 4–4. Sample Rate Versus Overlap Amplitude at f_o

	Overlap Amplitude		Butterworth	Bessel
Sample Rate f_s	**%**	**dB**	**(poles)**	**(poles)**
$3f_c$	1.6	−36	10	
	0.8	−44		10
$4f_c$	1.6	−36	6	
	1.6	−36		6
$5f_c$	1.0	−40	4	
	1.2	−38		4
$8f_c$	1.6	−36	2	
	3.1	−30		2
$14f_c$	1.6	−36	1	

TABLE 4–5. Signal Conditioning Design Guide

1.	Identify input signal and common-mode interference voltage levels and resulting input SNR.
2.	Establish the required A/D bit length per signal sample and relate this to a presampling filter output SNR requirement.
3.	Determine the realizable preamplifier CMRR and select components to realize this CMRR.
4.	Design the preamplifier to provide enough gain to raise its output SNR ≥ 100.
5.	Calculate the presampling filter bandwidth required to provide the filter output SNR above and compare this with the filter cutoff frequency necessary for adequate signal spectral occupancy.
6.	Select the A/D sample rate and presampling filter order to minimize sampling spectrum overlap at f_o.
7.	Evaluate the preamplifier input uncertainty and compare with the calculated input threshold value to determine possible output bit quality reduction. This is primarily of consequence for direct coupled inputs.

Since typical instrumentation signals extend from dc into the audio-frequency range, a good facsimile of a presampling filter for signal types described by Table 4–3 can be provided by a sharp-cutoff lowpass characteristic. If the delay through the presampling filter is not constant throughout the passband, a complex periodic signal will undergo delay distortion such that the frequency components of the signal will have their phase relationship with the fundamental frequency altered. If these properties are more important than flatness of the signal amplitude, then a linear-phase Bessel presampling filter should be used instead of a maximally flat amplitude Butterworth design. The Bessel characteristic does have reduced flatness in the passband, and a 1-dB variation corresponds to an 11% amplitude change. Both of these filter characteristics are described in Chapter 3. Table 4–5 provides a condensed seven-step signal conditioning design guide.

4-3 SINGLE AMPLIFIER EXAMPLE

Consider a 2-mV rms input signal of the complex periodic type and a 0.5-s period from a transducer having a 100-Ω source impedance R_s. This signal is transmitted to the signal conditioning circuit over a twisted pair upon which 1 V rms of common-mode interference is induced. This corresponds to a low-level industrial or biomedical signal that is to be conditioned and raised to an 8-bit binary quality signal which specifies a filter output SNR of 5×10^5 from Table 4–2. Designing for a preamp output SNR of 100 imposes a CMRR requirement described by equation (4-4), which, in turn, defines the minimum preamp gain. One percent tolerance resistors are chosen, which sets the average expected common-mode gain at 0.02 from Table 2–3. Although the single amplifier circuit offers simplicity, it has the disadvantage of poor source impedance unbalance characteristics and resulting CMRR degradation due to the low input impedance provided by its input resistors.

$$\text{input SNR} = \left(\frac{\text{RMS signal}}{\text{RMS interference}}\right)^2 \tag{4-1}$$

$$= \left(\frac{2 \times 10^{-3} V}{1 V}\right)^2$$

$$= 4 \times 10^{-6}$$

$$\text{CMRR} = \sqrt{\frac{\text{preamp output SNR}}{\text{input SNR}}} \tag{4-4}$$

$$= \sqrt{\frac{100}{4 \times 10^{-6}}}$$

$$= 5 \times 10^3$$

$$\text{DMG} = \text{CMG} \cdot \text{CMRR} \tag{2-25}$$

$$= (0.02)(5 \times 10^3)$$

$$= 100$$

$$\text{preamp output SNR} = \text{input SNR} \cdot \text{CMRR}^2 \tag{4-5}$$

$$= (4 \times 10^{-6})(5 \times 10^3)^2$$

$$= 10^2$$

It is apparent that a single operational amplifier such as the Fairchild 741 is capable of meeting both the required CMRR and gain requirements. Examination of the manufacturer's literature for the open-loop gain of this device provides a -3-dB bandwidth of about 9 kHz at the closed-loop gain of 100 intersection. The difference between the preamp output SNR and required filter output SNR for 8-bit quality is 5×10^3.

This deficiency is to be provided by the processing gain defined by equation (4-6), which is primarily influenced by the presampling filter bandwidth. The required presampling filter cutoff frequency f_{c_1} is defined both by equation (4-7) for signal quality improvement and as a function of the input signal fundamental period from Table 4–3, which specifies f_{c_2} for adequate signal spectral occupancy. Trial values for f_{c_1} and f_{c_2} are pursued, and difficulty is immediately apparent because $f_{c_1} \ll f_{c_2}$ and adequate spectral occupancy cannot be realized while simultaneously providing the necessary processing gain. The difference is too great to correct by preamplifier bandwidth widening methods.

An 8-bit-quality binary signal is clearly not available from this signal conditioning approach with the severe input SNR of this example. Of course, with a less severe input SNR, this austere mechanization could be satisfactory for providing the signal quality of interest. Consequently, the design will be pursued to a circuit realization including evaluation of the signal quality possible with the present input signal. Rearrangement of equation (4-7) yields the realizable filter output SNR, which is found to be equivalent to a 5-bit-quality binary signal. A 2-pole Butterworth active filter of unity gain and 40-Hz cutoff frequency is used which requires a sample rate f_s from Table 4–4 of $8f_c$, or 320 Hz, for a 1.6% overlap amplitude at the folding frequency. Although this is inefficient from the

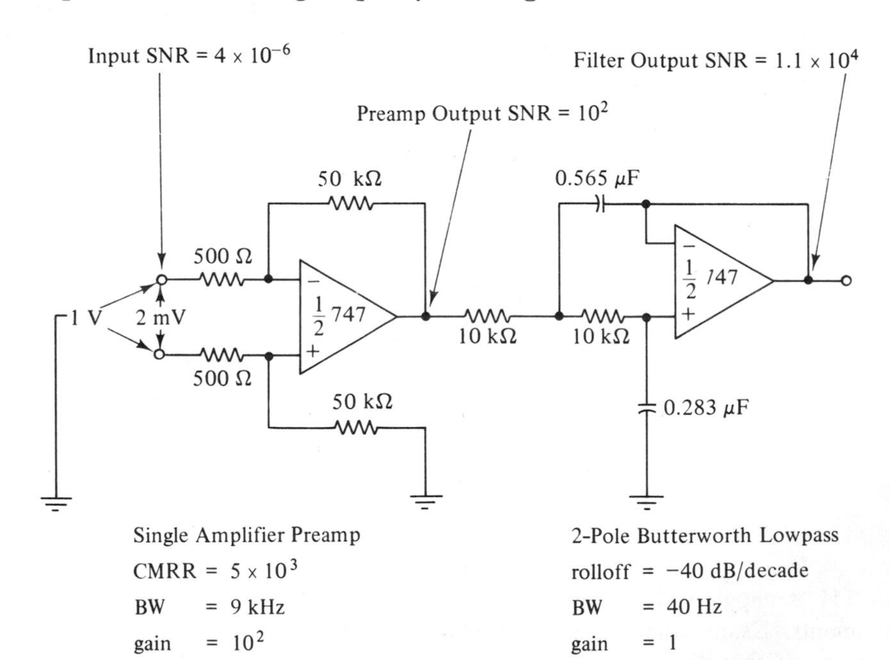

FIGURE 4–3. Austere Signal Conditioning Channel

viewpoint of conserving sample rate, it is justifiable for low-data-rate computer interfaces. A dual-741, or 747 device, is used in the circuit implementation of Figure 4–3.

$$f_{c2} = \frac{20}{\textit{fundamental period}} \tag{4-10}$$

$$= \frac{20}{0.5\,\mathrm{s}}$$

$$= 40\,\mathrm{Hz}$$

$$f_{c_1} = \frac{1}{2} \cdot \frac{(\text{preamp BW})(\text{preamp output SNR})}{\text{filter output SNR}} \tag{4-7}$$

$$= \frac{1}{2} \cdot \frac{(9\,\mathrm{kHz})(10^2)}{5 \times 10^5}$$

$$= 0.9\,\mathrm{Hz}$$

$$\text{filter output SNR} = \frac{1}{2} \cdot \frac{(\text{preamp BW})(\text{preamp output SNR})}{f_{c_2}}$$

$$= \frac{1}{2} \cdot \frac{(9\,\mathrm{kHz})(10^2)}{40\,\mathrm{Hz}}$$

$$= 1.12 \times 10^4$$

4-4 THREE-AMPLIFIER APPROACH

A three-amplifier instrumentation preamplifier circuit design will now be developed using 1% tolerance resistors, higher closed-loop gain of 10^3, and L144 operational amplifiers. Equations (4-11) and (4-5) show an improved CMRR and preamp output SNR, and overall preamp bandwidth is determined from equation (4-12), which is valid for *n* identical sections. If the gain is partitioned by distributing the value of DMG of 10^3 equally between the preamplifier input and subtractor sections, which yields a per-section gain of 30 dB, a per-section bandwidth of approximately 14 kHz is obtained from Figure 4–4. Equation (4-12) then converts this to the overall preamp bandwidth. Recall that $\mathrm{CMG_I}$ is unity regardless of the preamplifier input section closed-loop gain or resistor tolerances. And assume that amplifier intrinsic CMRR is adequate to prevent appreciable degradation of the calculated values. Further, the high input impedance provided by the noninverting differential inputs relaxes the sensitivity to

CMRR degradation as a result of source impedance unbalance up to a few hundred ohms. This unbalance primarily comes about as a result of the difference in capacitive reactance to ground of the two input conductors. Only the CMRR to ac interference is affected by this, such as at 60 Hz.

$$\text{CMRR} = \frac{1+2R_2/R_1}{\text{CMG}_I} \cdot \frac{R_4/R_3}{\text{CMG}_S} \qquad (4\text{-}11)$$

$$= \frac{1+(2)(75\,\text{k}\Omega)/5\,\text{k}\Omega}{1} \cdot \frac{160\,\text{k}\Omega/5\,\text{k}\Omega}{0.02}$$

$$= (31)(32)(50)$$

$$= 5 \times 10^4$$

$$\text{preamp output SNR} = \text{input SNR} \cdot \text{CMRR}^2 \qquad (4\text{-}5)$$

$$= (4 \times 10^{-6})(5 \times 10^4)^2$$

$$= 10^4$$

$$\text{preamp BW} = \text{section BW} \cdot \sqrt{2^{1/n} - 1} \qquad (4\text{-}12)$$

$$= 14\,\text{kHz} \cdot \sqrt{2^{1/2} - 1}$$

$$= (14\,\text{kHz}) \cdot (0.64)$$

$$= 9\,\text{kHz}$$

Solution of equation (4-7) yields the presampling filter cutoff frequency f_{c_1} value that provides the processing gain for an 8-bit-quality output signal. Since the value of f_{c_1} is greater than f_{c_2} of equation (4-10), no further iteration of the design is required. The lower cutoff frequency of f_{c_2} from equation (4-10) is selected for the filter design primarily because it minimizes the required sample rate and provides additional filter output SNR. The preamplifier–filter signal conditioning channel is implemented with a pair of micropower L144 triple operational amplifiers which will operate from a ± 3-V supply and dissipate 600 μW. A sharp-rolloff 120-dB/decade six-pole Butterworth active filter is selected as the presampling filter.[9] This design yields an 8-bit-quality output signal and requires a sample rate of $4f_c$, or 160 Hz. The complete circuit is shown in

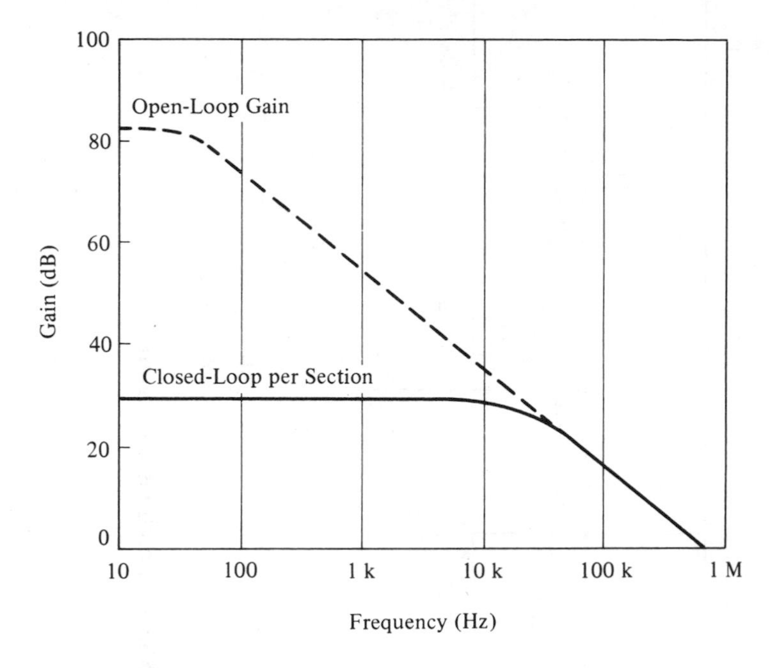

FIGURE 4–4. Siliconix L144 Gain Versus Frequency

Figure 4–5 and uses standard value resistors, with the nonstandard capacitor values for the filter selected by paralleling a couple of standard units.

$$f_{c_1} = \frac{1}{2} \cdot \frac{(\text{preamp BW})(\text{preamp output SNR})}{\text{filter output SNR}} \tag{4-7}$$

$$= \frac{1}{2} \cdot \frac{(9\,\text{kHz})(10^4)}{5 \times 10^5}$$

$$= 90\,\text{Hz}$$

$$\text{filter output SNR} = \frac{1}{2} \cdot \frac{(\text{preamp BW})(\text{preamp output SNR})}{f_{c_2}}$$

$$= \frac{1}{2} \cdot \frac{(9\,\text{kHz})(10^4)}{40\,\text{Hz}}$$

$$= 1.12 \times 10^6$$

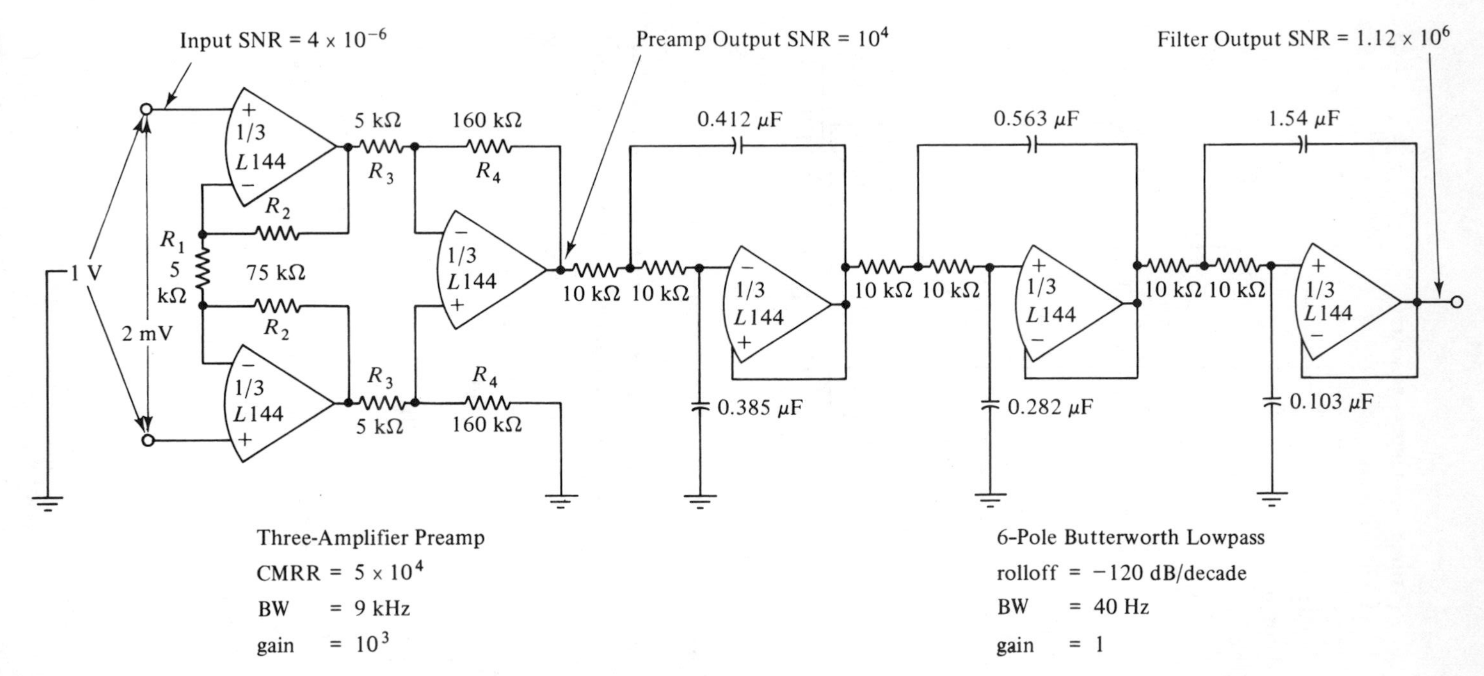

FIGURE 4–5. Micropower Signal Conditioning Channel

4-5 HIGH-PERFORMANCE SOLUTION

Application of a high-performance instrumentation amplifier to the preceding input signal can provide a higher CMRR and preamp output SNR with the trade-off of increased cost. The 4253 JFET-input instrumentation amplifier by Teledyne Philbrick is a representative example (Figure 4–6). This device offers a CMRR of 10^6 up to 100 Hz and a gain of 10^3 at a bandwidth of 5 kHz, while allowing a 1-kΩ source impedance unbalance. Equation (4-5) shows the preamp output SNR to be more than adequate for providing the signal quality necessary for an 8-bit binary output. An additional benefit of the high-performance amplifier is its considerably reduced input uncertainty, which is increasingly important as the output binary bit quality and resolution increase. This consideration will be explored in the following section.

Since the signal requires a spectral occupancy of 40 Hz, this is the lowest allowable presampling filter cutoff frequency. Accordingly, equation (4-7) is rearranged to solve for the available filter output SNR from the processing gain relationship of equation (4-6) again. Reference to Table 4–2 shows this to be equivalent to a 12-bit-quality signal. The sampling frequency and presampling filter design used are identical to

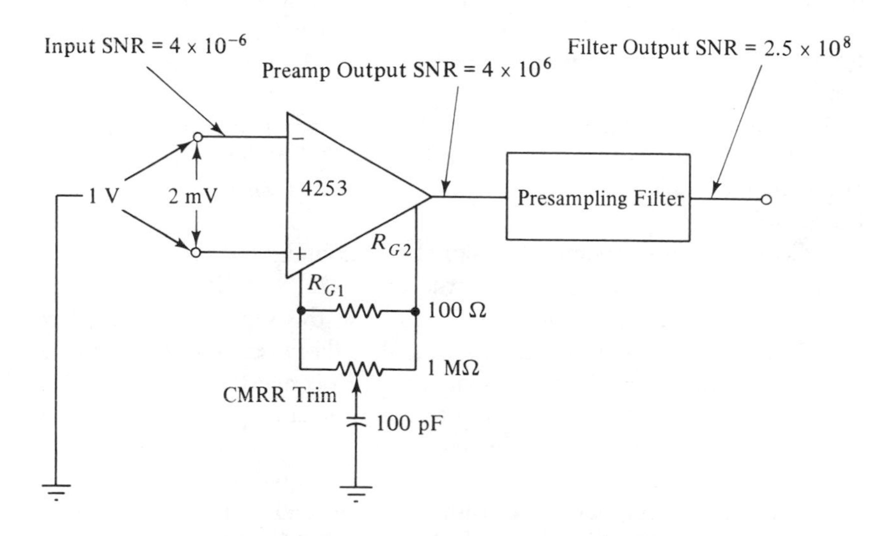

FIGURE 4–6. High-Performance Signal Conditioning Channel

those of the previous three-amplifier approach.

$$\text{preamp output SNR} = \text{input SNR} \cdot \text{CMRR}^2 \tag{4-5}$$

$$= (4 \times 10^{-6})(10^6)^2$$

$$= 4 \times 10^6$$

$$\text{filter output SNR} = \frac{1}{2} \cdot \frac{(\text{preamp BW})(\text{preamp output SNR})}{f_{c_2}} \tag{4-7}$$

$$= \frac{1}{2} \cdot \frac{(5\,\text{kHz})(4 \times 10^6)}{40\,\text{Hz}}$$

$$= 2.5 \times 10^8$$

4-6 INPUT ERROR AND SCALING CONSIDERATIONS

Practical considerations require that the full signal excursion range be carefully evaluated in scaling the signal conditioning circuit gains in order to ensure an appropriate output. The preceding signal quality development is based upon SNR calculations of relative signal to noise amplitudes. Consequently, although the conditioned output signals of the examples indeed possess the bit quality arrived at in each case, their amplitudes must additionally be raised to the full-scale value associated with the A/D converter chosen, in this case 10V. Other full-scale values are available, such as 2.5 and 5V, and can just as easily be worked into this development.

Consider the three-amplifier signal conditioning channel, which provides a 2-V rms output signal by virtue of its DMG of 10^3. An additional normal-mode gain (NMG) of $5/\sqrt{2}$ will raise this signal to the required 10V full scale if it is essentially sinusoidal. Otherwise, the peak value of an ac signal must be raised to equal the A/D converter full-scale value. This can be provided by an additional operational amplifier at the signal conditioning channel output. The signal quality is not further improved, of course, but the efficiency of matching an 8-bit-quality signal to an 8-bit A/D converter is realized, where for 10 V full scale the LSB is approximately equal to 39mV. Alternatively, if the 2-V signal is converted without the additional amplification, valid data will exist between bits 1 and 8 of a 10-bit converter, where the LSB will correspond to about 10mV. The 8-bit quality is unchanged, but the output format is awkward. Therefore, the maximum signal level must equal the A/D converter full-scale analog value in order to match the equivalent signal bit quality and the converter bit length.

When the input signal exists over a range of amplitude values of interest, the signal conditioning calculations are carried out for the largest expected amplitude value. A check should also be made to ensure that the minimum input amplitude is at least as large as the input threshold value specified by equation (4-13), where $\frac{1}{2}$ LSB is determined from the actual signal conditioning bit quality realized. If it is not as large, the output signal quality must be improved, such as by the use of a higher-performance instrumentation amplifier, until the minimum input signal of interest equals or exceeds the calculated threshold value. Note that the product of the DMG and NMG is chosen to just raise the largest input signal to the 10-V full-scale A/D converter input value. An 8-bit quality signal, therefore, is capable of resolving an input signal to the threshold level shown in equation (4-13) for the three-amplifier example.

$$\text{input threshold} = \frac{\frac{1}{2}\,\text{LSB}}{(\text{DMG})(\text{NMG})} \tag{4-13}$$

$$= \frac{19.6\,\text{mV}}{(10^3)(5/\sqrt{2}\,)}$$

$$\simeq 5.5\,\mu\text{V}$$

A final important consideration is the effect of the preamplifier input uncertainty on the signal conditioning channel performance. This is a systematic or bias error which was developed in detail in Chapter 2 and has the result of reducing the A/D converter resolution. This differs from the random error defined by the signal quality calculations of the previous

TABLE 4–6. Preamplifier Input Errors

Parameter	741	L144	4253
I_{os}	50 nA	50 nA	10 pA
dV_{os}/dT	3.3 μV/°C	3.3 μV/°C	0.5 μV/°C
dI_{os}/dT	−0.25 nA/C	−0.25 nA/C	1 pA/°C
V_{noise}	1 μV	1 μV	0.5 μV
$V_{os_{drift}}$	—	—	10 μV/month
R_s	1.1 kΩ	100 Ω	100 Ω
V_{error} 25°C	55 μV	5 μV	0.5 μV
V_{error} 25 ± 10°C	64 μV	34 μV	5.1 μV

TABLE 4–7. Signal Conditioning Design Summary

Circuit			Input			Channel			Output		
Method	Device	Temperature (°C)	Error (μV)	Threshold (μV)	SNR	Preamp SNR	Filter f_c (Hz)	Filter SNR	Quality	Resolution	Sample Rate
Single	747	25	55	88	4×10^{-6}	10^2	40	1.1×10^4	4 bits	$\frac{625\,mV}{10\,V}$	$8f_c$
amplifier		25±10	64	88	4×10^{-6}	10^2	40	1.1×10^4	4 bits	$\frac{625\,mV}{10\,V}$	$8f_c$
Three	L144	25	5	5.5	4×10^{-6}	10^4	40	1.1×10^6	8 bits	$\frac{39.0\,mV}{10\,V}$	$4f_c$
amplifier		25±10	34	44	4×10^{-6}	10^4	40	1.1×10^6	5 bits	$\frac{312\,mV}{10\,V}$	$4f_c$
High-	4253	25	0.5	0.7	4×10^{-6}	4×10^6	40	2.5×10^8	12 bits	$\frac{2.45\,mV}{10\,V}$	$4f_c$
performance amplifier		25±10	5.1	5.5	4×10^{-6}	4×10^6	40	2.5×10^8	8 bits	$\frac{39.0\,mV}{10\,V}$	$4f_c$

sections, which was caused by induced interference. Table 4–6 presents an error budget for the three preamplifiers utilized in the examples, which is evaluated for input uncertainty both at a constant 25°C with output offsets nulled out, and for a ±10°C temperature variation about 25°C without further adjustment. This is essentially a dc error, which can be ignored only in the case of a bandpass presampling filter or ac coupling. Offset voltage drift with temperature variation dV_{os}/dT is the primary contributor to this error. The result of this uncertainty is a degradation in output resolution depending upon the amount by which the uncertainty exceeds the input threshold value. Note that the output bit quality is adjusted as required until the calculated input threshold value closely approximates the expected input uncertainty error.

$$V_{error_{RTI}} = \sqrt{(I_{os} \cdot R_s)^2 + (dV_{os}/dT)^2 + (dI_{os}/dT \cdot R_s)^2 + (V_{noise})^2} \quad \text{volts} \quad (2\text{-}21)$$

In conclusion, for identical input signals and accommodation of the various trade-offs encountered in the design of a signal conditioning channel, it is apparent from Table 4–7 that a nominal 4-bit spread exists in output signal quality between each of the three basic preamplifier-filter channels. This is primarily due to the CMRR differences of Table 2–5 and their effect on equation (4-5). The drop in output bit quality produced by the increase in preamplifier uncertainty for the worst-case ±10°C change in temperature is severe considering the signal conditioning effort required to raise the quality initially. However, the input SNR is very small, which tends to magnify the effects of this error, but serves to illustrate where the system sensitivities are located.

PROBLEMS

4-1 The output of a non-differential input signal conditioning circuit having a gain of 100 is to provide an amplitude accuracy of 1%. For a 0 dB input SNR and a preamplifier gain-bandwidth product of 10^6, determine: (a) the necessary presampling filter output SNR for a 68% confidence, (b) the required processing gain, and (c) the filter bandwidth required to realize this processing gain.

4-2 A signal conditioning channel is to accommodate input signals ranging from 1 V to 1 mV rms with common-mode interference ranging from 1 mV up to 1 volt rms, and provide a minimum 8-bit quality output signal. The L144 three-amplifier preamplifier has selectable DMG values of 1, 10 and 100 by switching R_i in the input section, and a fixed DMG of 10 in the subtractor section. The presampling filter has selectable cutoff frequencies f_c of 10 Hz, 100 Hz and 1 kHz, and the total circuit is implemented with $\frac{1}{2}$%

tolerance resistors. Determine: (a) the maximum and minimum expected input SNR, (b) the preamplifier CMRR and bandwidth for each of the DMG values, (c) the preamplifier output SNR values for the preceding input SNR values and CMRR possibilities, (d) the processing gains for the preamplifier bandwidth and presampling filter bandwidth values, and (e) a table of filter output SNR values at the minimum input SNR to determine which DMG and presampling filter f_c bandwidth values preclude achieving an 8-bit quality output signal.

4-3 For the input uncertainty associated with the chopper preamplifier of Problem 2–6 and a 1 mV rms sinusoidal input signal of interest, determine the equivalent maximum binary resolution available at the output of this preamplifier. Assume a 10 V full-scale amplitude level.

4-4 The DD693 class destroyer has a turbine conversion efficiency monitor which senses inlet and outlet steam temperatures with thermocouples and implements the equation shown. Design signal conditioning circuits for 1 to 100 mV thermocouple signals, provide for 60 dB of CMRR, and allow maximum divider input voltages of 10 volts. Use the multifunction module described in Chapter 5 and by equation 5–9 for the division operation with the constant $Y = 0.1$ and $M = 1$. Sketch the circuit implementation including the component values and voltage scaling.

$$\text{Efficiency} = 1 - \frac{T_{\text{outlet}}}{T_{\text{inlet}}}$$

4-5 The differential-lag signal conditioning circuit below provides preamplification and lowpass filtering with a single operational amplifier. Practical CMG values are limited to about 0.1 due to the necessity to match feedback resistors and capacitors. Determine: (a) the transfer function for this circuit using nodal analysis, (b) expressions for the DMG and filter f_c, and (c) the practically realizable CMRR.

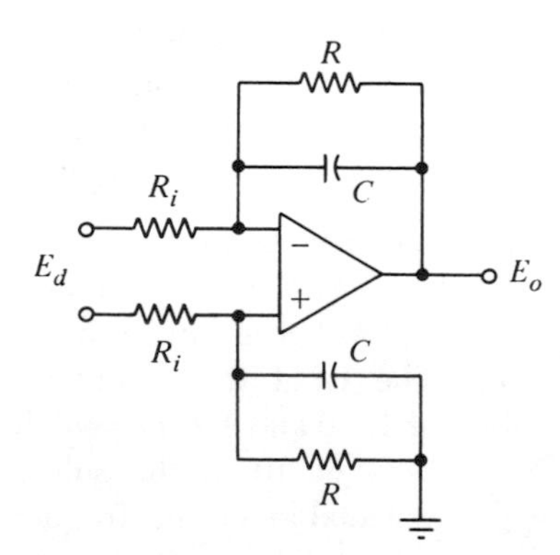

4-6 A color television video signal is to be digitally encoded to provide for a resolution of 525 lines by 800 picture elements (pixels) per frame. For 64 discrete brightness levels per pixel and 30 frames per second, determine: (a) the appropriate A/D converter bit length and minimum signal input SNR, (b) the signal bandwidth necessary, and (c) the required sampling rate and presampling filter type. Each pixel is considered an independent signal component in the time domain.

REFERENCES

1. H. R. Raemer, *Statistical Communications Theory And Applications*, Prentice-Hall, Englewood Cliffs, N.J., 1969, p. 254.
2. Raemer, op. cit., p. 255.
3. M. Schwartz, W. Bennett, and S. Stein, *Communications Systems and Techniques*, McGraw-Hill, New York, 1966, p. 310.
4. R. M. Fano, "Signal to Noise Ratio in Correlation Detectors," *MIT Technical Report 186*, February 19, 1951.
5. Raemer, op. cit., p. 190.
6. M. Schwartz, *Information Transmission Modulation and Noise*, 2nd ed., McGraw-Hill, New York, 1970, p. 255.
7. L. W. Gardenshire, "Selecting Sample Rates," *ISA Journal Reprint*, April 1964.
8. J. Millman, and C. Halkias, *Integrated Electronics*, McGraw-Hill, New York, 1972, p. 532.
9. P. Garrett, "Optimize Transducer/Computer Interfaces," *Electronic Design*, May 24, 1977.

5

ANALOG SIGNAL PROCESSING

5-0 INTRODUCTION

A distinction is made between signal conditioning and signal processing in analog instrumentation and data-acquisition systems. The former relates to those operations concerned with improving signal quality, developed in Chapter 4. This chapter is concerned with analog signal processing, which involves manipulations of the signal, usually following improvement of its quality. Topics include linearization of transducer signals, logarithmic operations such as signal compression and expansion for bit-length reduction in data-conversion systems, analog computation methods and applications for efficient data reduction of sensor signals prior to digital conversion, and programmable functions. The availability of capable and low-cost devices for performing linear and nonlinear operations continues to promote the usefulness of analog signal processing.

5-1 FUNCTION FITTING AND LINEARIZATION

It is well known that some sensor outputs, such as thermocouples and bridge elements, often depart significantly from a linear characteristic. It is common practice to compensate such measurements by applying an additional nonlinearity to correct for the transducer signal. To generate a successful fit, with the understanding that there is almost always a residual error, the function to be fit must be defined over a finite range and be single-valued in terms of its input values. For typically encountered functions, the accuracy and reasonable cost of linear ICs and function modules results in the analog approach being a viable one.

Two approaches are available for empirical function fitting: (1) continuous functions and (2) piecewise-linear segments. The former technique requires more mathematics to implement, but its error function is smooth and continuous. The latter technique is quicker to set up, but its error function consists of a series of discontinuous cusps which can cause problems if later signal differentiation is required or it undergoes nonlinear signal processing operations. For these reasons, continuous function fitting is preferred and offers the additional advantage of easier visualization of the final result.

Continuous function fitting permits the translation of an empirical relationship between an independent input variable and dependent output variable. A practical approach consists of (1) formulation of a close approximation in terms of a theoretical model in building-block form and (2) the implementation of a specific circuit to mechanize the model to the accuracy, frequency response, and scaling of interest. It is helpful to begin with the data in normalized form and to select a function that is likely to approximate the function to be fit. Useful functions include natural laws, such as $1/X$, X^m, and $\log X$, and polynomials, such as the cubic equation $AX+BX^3$. Both integral and nonintegral powers are useful for function fitting. Integral-power polynomials, efficiently realizable by means of analog multipliers and operational amplifiers, are described in the following example. Nonintegral powers, realizable with logarithmic multifunction modules, will be discussed in a later section.

Consider a type J iron–constantan thermocouple with the response shown by Figure 5–1. The device has a linear output of 40 μV/°C to about 400°C. It is required to double the linear response range by means of continuous function fitting. The task, therefore, is to convert the thermocouple output to the linear straight-line response shown in Figure 5–1 and described by equation (5-1). The curvilinear thermocouple characteristic is amenable to a quadratic fit by equation (5-2). These two independent expressions may then be equated and solved for the required linearization function $X-f(X)$. Trial coefficients are obtained for A and B at the intermediate points of 250°C and 750°C, as follows.

$$y=(\text{slope})(\text{input})+\text{intercept}-\text{correction} \tag{5-1}$$

$$=\left(25\frac{°\text{C}}{\text{mV}}\right)(X_{\text{mV}})+0-\left(25\frac{°\text{C}}{\text{mV}}\right)f(X_{\text{mV}})$$

$$=\left(25\frac{°\text{C}}{\text{mV}}\right)[X_{\text{mV}}-f(X_{\text{mV}})]$$

$$=\left(A\frac{°\text{C}}{\text{mV}}\right)(X_{\text{mV}})+\left(B\frac{°\text{C}}{\text{mV}^2}\right)(X_{\text{mV}})^2 \tag{5-2}$$

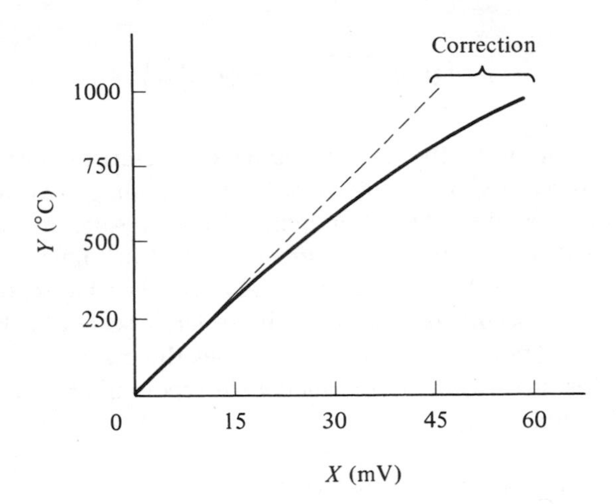

FIGURE 5–1. Type J Thermocouple Linearization

Rearranging for the linearized signal,

$$X - f(X) = \frac{AX + BX^2}{25} \qquad \text{millivolts}$$

Trial 1:

$$X = 13.5\,\text{mV} \qquad y = 250°\text{C}$$

$$y = AX + BX^2 \tag{5-2}$$

$$250°\text{C} = A(13.5\,\text{mV}) + B(182.25\,\text{mV}^2)$$

$$A = 18.5\frac{°\text{C}}{\text{mV}} - B(13.5\,\text{mV})$$

Trial 2:

$$X = 42.3\,\text{mV} \qquad y = 750°\text{C}$$

$$750°\text{C} = \left[\left(18.5\frac{°\text{C}}{\text{mV}}\right) - B(13.5\,\text{mV})\right](42.3\,\text{mV}) + B(1799\,\text{mV}^2)$$

$$B = -0.026\frac{°\text{C}}{\text{mV}^2}$$

Substituting,

$$A = 18.5\frac{°\text{C}}{\text{mV}} - \left(-0.026\frac{°\text{C}}{\text{mV}^2}\right)(13.5\,\text{mV})$$

$$= 18.85\frac{°\text{C}}{\text{mV}}$$

This yields

$$y = \left(18.85\frac{°\mathrm{C}}{\mathrm{mV}}\right)X - \left(0.026\frac{°\mathrm{C}}{\mathrm{mV}^2}\right)X^2 \tag{5-2}$$

An excellent fit to the thermocouple characteristic resulting in its linearization is realized up to 800°C, with an increasing error to 4% of the full-scale output at the 1000°C endpoint. These results are tabulated in Table 5–1, with the approximation error graphed in Figure 5–2. Figures 5–3 and 5–4 describe the linearizer model in building-block form, including one posssible circuit realization, with the latter scaled for the conventional output of 1 mV/°C. Table 5–2 provides the quadratic linearization coefficients for three common thermocouple types, all of which assume a 0°C reference junction.

TABLE 5-1. Linearization Tabulation

X(mV)	Y(°C)	$X-f(X)$(mV)	y(°C)	%FS$_{\text{error}}$(%)
0	0	0	0	0
13.5	250	10.0	250	0
27.4	500	19.9	498	−0.2
42.3	750	30.0	750	0
59.8	1000	41.6	1040	+4.0

The analog multiplier is a device that produces an output voltage proportional to the product of two independent input voltages, V_x and V_y, with a proportionality constant K usually fixed at 10 V. The operating range of a multiplier is normally defined in terms of its inputs. For the usual two inputs, each having a possibility of two polarities, there exist four combinations of polarity. Multipliers that can accept these four combinations and provide outputs of correct polarity are referred to as four-quadrant multipliers. One-quadrant multipliers, such as the logarith-

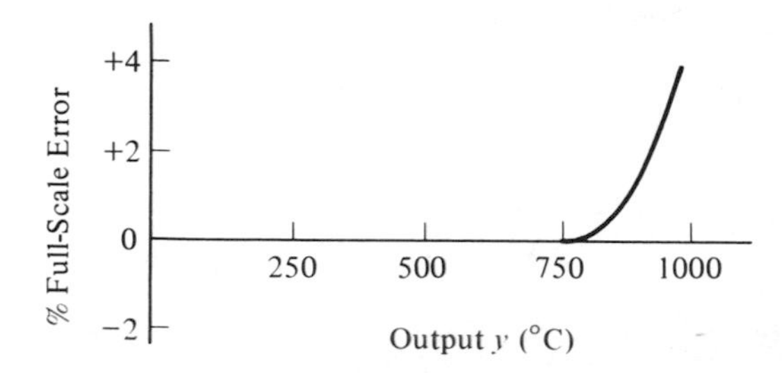

FIGURE 5–2. Approximation Error

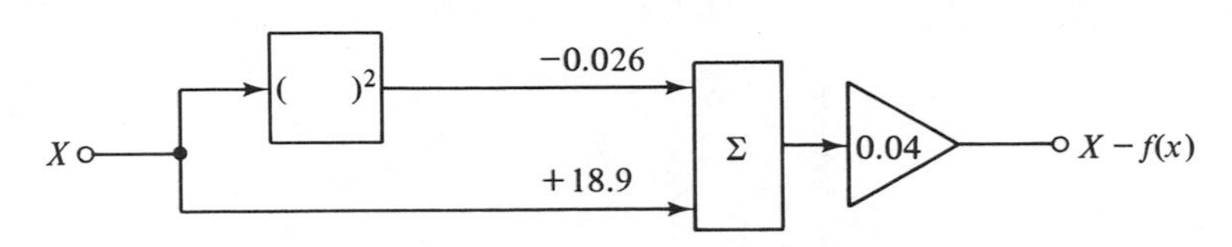

FIGURE 5–3. Building-Block Model

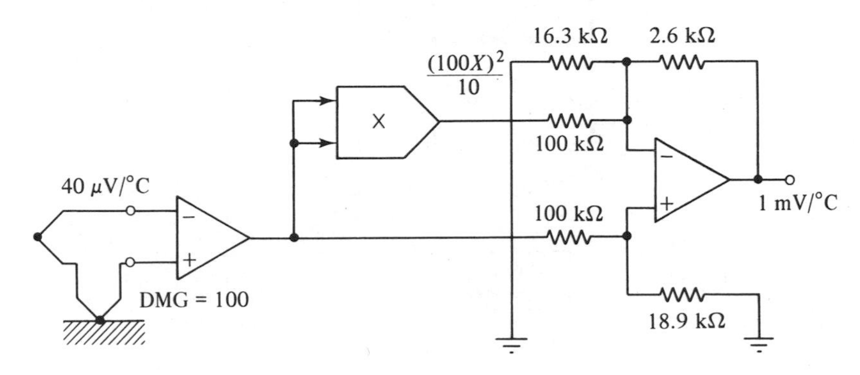

FIGURE 5-4. Linearizer Circuit Implementation

mic multifunction modules considered later, respond to unipolar inputs in a single quadrant only.

At present the most commonly encountered method of performing electronic analog multiplication is with the variable-transconductance Gilbert cell, in which one input variable directly drives the emitters of diode-connected transistors and the other input varies a controlled current source attached to the same emitters (Figure 5–5). An exacting square-law transfer characteristic can be obtained in this manner with bandwidths extending from DC to 1 MHz. Multiplier accuracy can best be described by a three-dimensional surface representing the error components (Figure 5–6). Careful device matching and on-chip laser trimming methods can provide low offset, feedthrough, and nonlinearity errors such that 0.5% accuracy of the full-scale output is typically available. For demanding precision multiplier applications, pulse height–pulse width multipliers are available with 0.1% accuracy and bandwidths from DC to 1 kHz. Equation (5-3) describes the primary multiplier errors referred to

TABLE 5–2. Thermocouple Linearization Coefficients

Thermocouple	A	B	Range (°C)
J	18.9	−0.026	0 to 800
K	24.4	−0.022	−50 to 1200
T	32.3	−0.630	−150 to 400

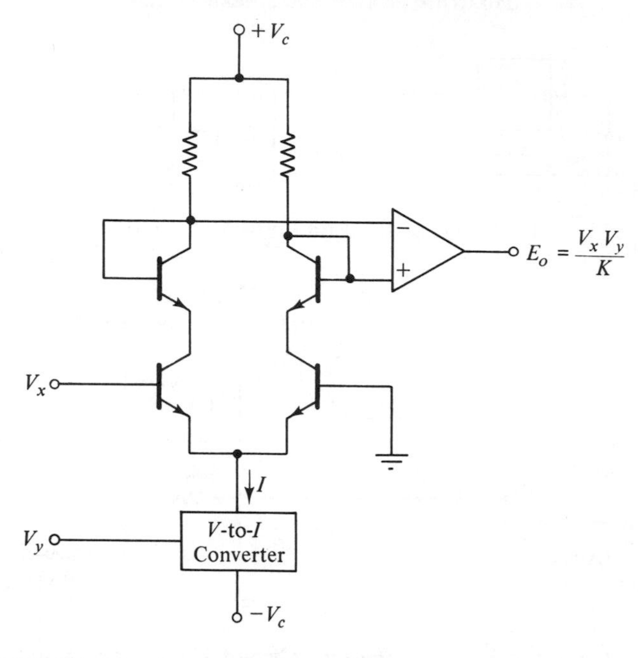

FIGURE 5–5. Representative Transconductance Multiplier

the output.

$$V_{error} = \underset{\substack{(scale)\\(factor)}}{\Delta K V_X V_Y} + \underset{(feed\,through)}{V_{FX} + V_{FY}} + \underset{\substack{(dc)\\(offset)}}{V_{os}} + \underset{(nonlinearity)}{f(X, Y)} \quad \text{volts} \qquad (5\text{-}3)$$

Wheatstone bridges, used in a variety of force, strain, and electrical measurements, normally exhibit a nonlinearity that increases with sensitiv-

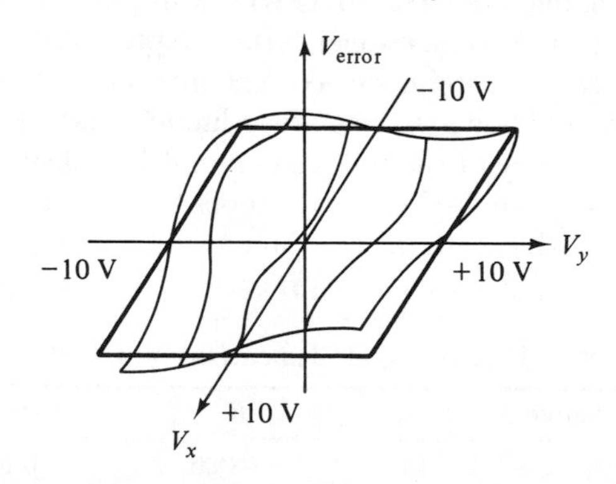

FIGURE 5-6. Analog Multiplier Error Surface

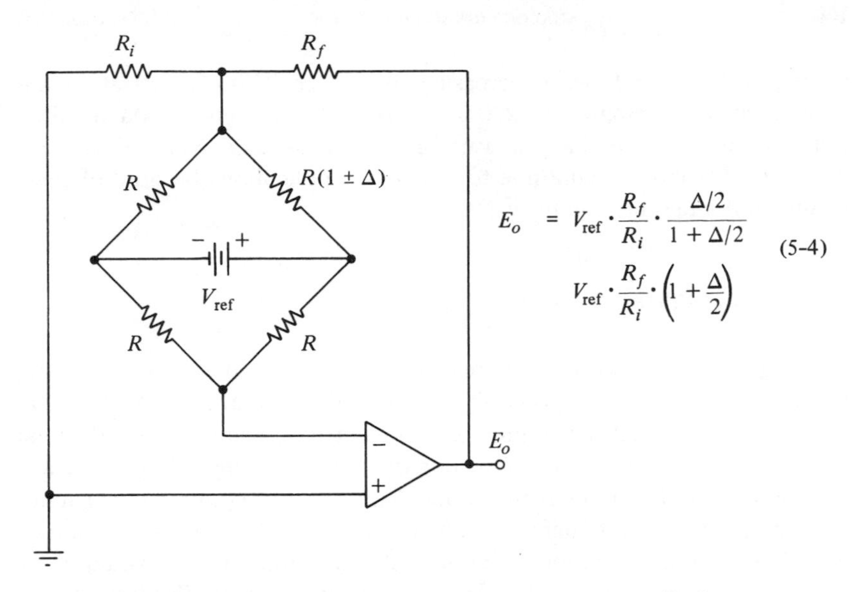

FIGURE 5–7. Nonlinearized Bridge Circuit with Gain

ity. A nonlinearized bridge sensing circuit is shown in Figure 5–7 for the common case of balanced impedances in each arm of the bridge circuit. Fortunately, bridge nonlinearity is described by a simple mathematical relationship which can be compensated for by converting the bridge circuit and the addition of an operational amplifier. Figure 5–8 is useful for sensitive linear bridge measurements, but requires the use of a low input-uncertainty amplifier. Chopper-stabilized operational amplifiers provide good performance in this application when configured in a differential-input arrangement. Bridge nonlinearity reaches significant

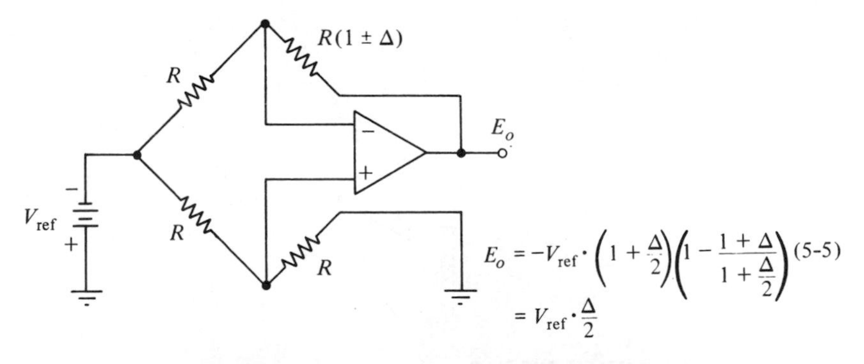

FIGURE 5–8. Linearized Bridge Circuit

values, 50% at $\Delta = 1$, with increasing imbalance. With linearization the variable arm can range over 200%, or up to the reference voltage value. Both circuits assume that the variable arm resistance $R(1 \pm \Delta)$ is itself linear. Bridge circuits continue to find new applications because of their duality and inherent symmetry.

5-2 LOGARITHMIC OPERATIONS

The logarithm is becoming increasingly important in signal processing applications. Its utility primarily is its ability to accommodate wide dynamic range signals encountered with electro-optical sensors and signal compression and expansion. A secondary but increasingly important application of log functions is in the mechanization of computational functions. Logarithmic arguments are always dimensionless, so that in practical circuit implementations, the log of the ratio of two voltages or currents is realized with the denominator normally a fixed reference value.

Present logarithmic circuit realizations employ silicon bipolar devices in matched monolithic pairs for good thermal stability. At the small operating currents involved, however, amplifier offset voltage can develop a bias current error in the feedback path as a function of the input resistance. Bias current errors are usually minimized by using FET-input operational amplifiers. An additional problem is to ensure that the bipolar device in the amplifier feedback path does not result in instability under any operating conditions. Amplifier lag compensation is normally used to ensure unconditional stability. The basic logarithmic circuit relationship is

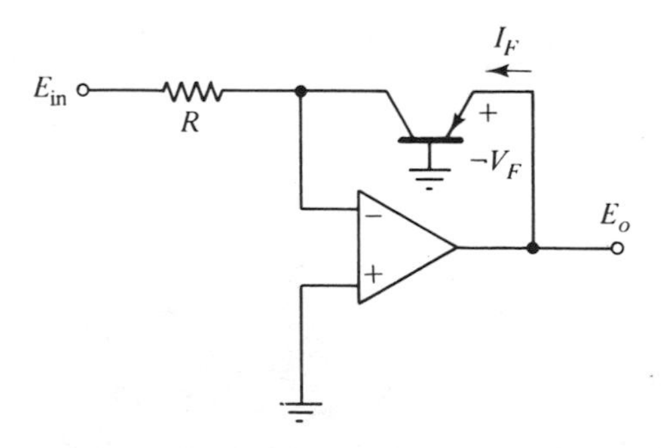

FIGURE 5–9. Basic Log Circuit

TABLE 5–3. Standard Logarithmic Functions

Transfer Function	Description
$E_o = K \log_{10}\left(\frac{E_{in}}{E_{ref}}\right)$	Voltage log
$E_o = K \log_{10}\left(\frac{I_{in}}{I_{ref}}\right)$	Current log
$E_o = E_{ref} \cdot 10^{-E_{in}/K}$	Antilog
$E_o = K \log_{10}\left(\frac{E_1}{E_2}\right)$	Log ratio
$E_o = K \sinh^{-1}\left(\frac{E_{in}}{2E_{ref}}\right)$	Bipolar log
$E_o = K \sinh\left(\frac{E_{in}}{E_{ref}}\right)$	Bipolar antilog

derived as follows (see also Figure 5–9 and Table 5–3):

$$I_F = I_s\left(e^{+V_F/nV_T} - 1\right) \tag{5-6}$$

$$\ln I_F = \ln I_s + \frac{V_F}{nV_T}$$

$$E_o = nV_T\left(\ln I_F - \ln I_s\right)$$

$$= nV_T\left[\underset{\text{(variable)}}{\ln\left(\frac{E_{in}}{R}\right)} - \underset{\text{(constant)}}{\ln I_s}\right]$$

$$= nV_T \ln\left(\frac{E_{in}}{RI_s}\right)$$

$$= K \log_{10}\left(\frac{E_{in}}{E_{ref}}\right)$$

where $V_T = \frac{°K}{11{,}600}$	volt-equivalent of temperature
$I_s = 10^{-15}\ A$	reverse saturation current
$E_o = V_F$	due to the base–emitter junction
$I_F = \frac{E_{in}}{R}$	by Ohm's law
$n = 2$	for silicon
$-\ 1$	dropped for $I_F \gg I_s$

Input voltage or current for the log function is positive, and the output negative for $E_{in} > E_{ref}$ or $I_{in} > I_{ref}$ and reversed for $E_{in} < E_{ref}$ or $I_{in} < I_{ref}$. Output voltage for the antilog or exponential function is always positive. These functions are described by Figures 5–10 and 5–11. The available bandwidth of log devices varies from about 100 Hz to 100 kHz for inputs between allowable minimum and maximum signal levels, respectively. And log conformity accuracy typically is within 1%. With the log-ratio device, both numerator and denominator input variables may take on arbitrary values which will determine the output response range, but unipolar polarity is always maintained. The denominator variable is usually restricted in dynamic range to preserve accuracy. The log-ratio circuit implementation is obtained by subtracting the logs of the two input signals.

Commercially available log devices have performance extending over four decades of voltage, typically from 1 mV to 10 V, and six current decades, from 1nA to 1mA. The log-ratio device is useful over seven decades, with four decades in the numerator and three in the denominator. The bipolar log function is symmetrical about and linear in the vicinity of zero input. Its response is bipolar and typically extends over

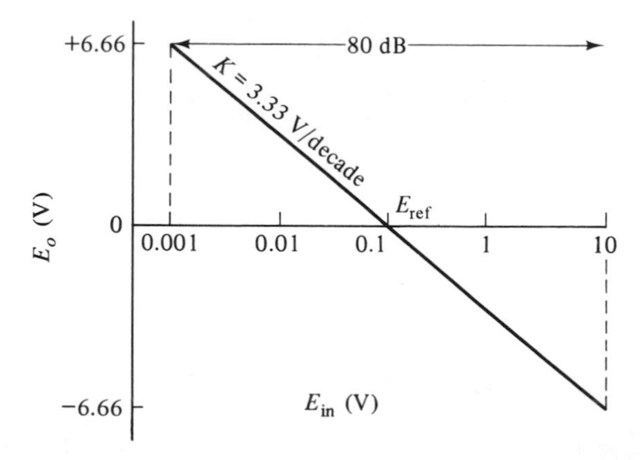

FIGURE 5–10. Logarithmic Voltage Function Adjusted for 3.33 Volts per Decade

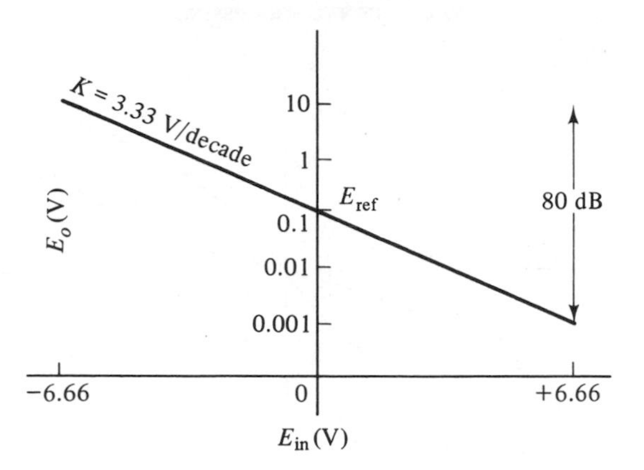

FIGURE 5–11. Antilog Voltage Function Adjusted for 3.33 Volts per Decade

±3 decades. A practical realization of this function is the inverse hyperbolic sine, $\sinh^{-1}$, which can be implicitly mechanized by an Euler's identity and a pair of complementary antilog exponential functions. Equation (5-7) and Figure 5–12 describe this implementation.

$$E_{in} = E_{ref} \cdot 10^{E_o/K} - E_{ref} \cdot 10^{-E_o/K} \tag{5-7}$$

$$\frac{E_{in}}{2E_{ref}} = \frac{\exp(2.3E_o/K) - \exp(-2.3E_o/K)}{2}$$

$$= \sinh\left(\frac{2.3E_o}{K}\right)$$

$$E_o = K \sinh^{-1}\left(\frac{E_{in}}{2E_{ref}}\right)$$

The use of a logarithmic function at the input of a data-conversion system allows a reduction of the resolution of the A/D converter. This technique is primarily of merit for processing high-resolution sensor signals by truncated binary word-length processors. Once converted, the data may be antilogged using software. If the data eventually are to be reconstructed in analog form, an analog antilog operation following output D/A conversion is required to restore signal linearity. For example, a 16-bit-quality signal existing over a 1000 : 1 dynamic range from 10 mV to 10 V can be resolved to about 1% throughout this range by a 10-bit A/D converter following unipolar logarithmic compression. A bipolar log function would be used for signals that are zero-centered.

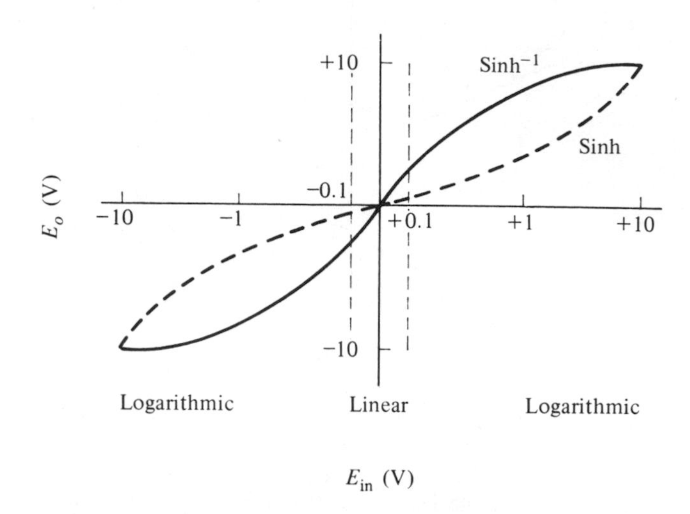

FIGURE 5–12. Bipolar Log and Antilog Functions

The transfer function of a suitable log device is shown by Figure 5–10, and its compression scale factor K value is determined as follows. For an A/D converter that accepts 10 V full scale and an input range spanning three decades of voltage, K is adjusted to equal 10 V/3=3.33 V/decade. With reference to Figure 5–10, the value of input voltage for which zero output is obtained occurs at 100 mV instead of the desired 10 mV. The required shift can be obtained with a dc offset voltage at the log device output shown in Figure 5–13.

Compression is achieved by exponentially distorting the relative value of the A/D converter LSB. For the three-decade compressor of K=3.33 V/decade and a span of 10 V, high-level signals are attenuated by an average factor of 3.33 V/5 V=0.66 and low-level signals amplified by an average factor of 3.33 V/0.05 V=66. Consequently, a constant

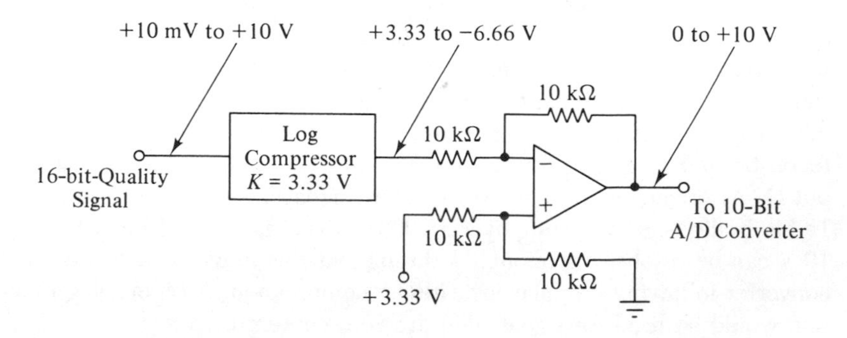

FIGURE 5–13. Preconversion Signal Compression

fractional error is maintained throughout the signal dynamic range at the expense of high resolution at any point within the range. A 16-bit-quality signal (LSB = 153 μV) may therefore be resolved with a 10-bit A/D converter (LSB = 9.7 mV) due to the gain provided at minimum-input-signal levels. The transfer curve of an appropriate antilog device is described by Figure 5–11. An inversion plus positive dc input biasing provides expansion over the appropriate three voltage decades for linear signal reconstruction (Figure 5–14). The combination of compression and expansion is commonly referred to as *companding*.

Besides the obvious A/D converter cost savings, an improvement in the A/D conversion speed is also obtained with signal compression. Another effect of compression is to provide a larger number of A/D quantizing levels at the lower signal amplitudes, which is equivalent to introducing a nonlinear quantization characteristic. The quantization noise is thus effectively smaller at the lower signal levels. Therefore, companding enhances the signal-to-noise ratio,which may be of interest if remote data acquisition is required. The actual improvement depends upon the noise encountered over the transmission path but is greatest for low SNRs, where the improvement with unipolar log devices ranges up to 20 dB (power) and 10 dB for bipolar log devices. This is an appreciable gain and worthwhile when enhancement of signal quality is necessary. Companding does produce a nonlinear operation on the signal, however, which results in harmonics and a greater transmission bandwidth requirement than linear transmission.

Log-ratio devices are useful for rendering photometric and radiometric measurements independent of background interference. With reference to Table 5–3, consider the application of staring (nonscanning) infrared sensors mounted on the tail of a fighter aircraft to provide warning of an approaching missile. A narrow field-of-view rear-looking sensor provides the signal E_1, and its side-looking twin the reference input

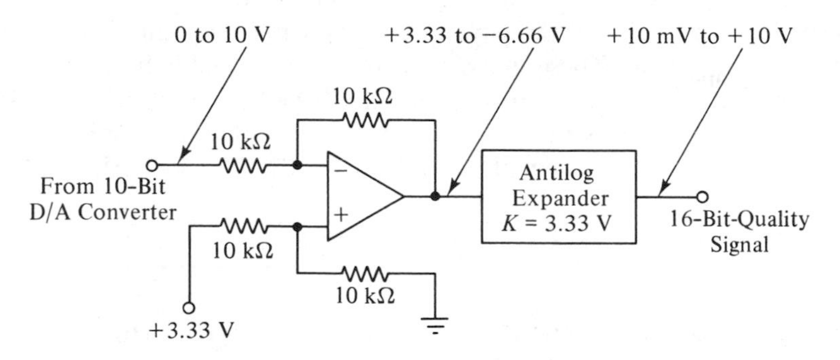

FIGURE 5–14. Postconversion Signal Expansion

E_2. Use of the log-ratio device, therefore, permits increased sensitivity and independence from background radiation, plus a wide dynamic range, resulting in a reduced threat-warning threshold.

5-3 COMPUTATION CIRCUITS

The requirement occasionally arises to perform a precision ac-to-dc conversion for signals down to millivolt levels (Table 5–4 and Figure 5–15). Passive full-wave rectification is inadequate for this task, because silicon diodes will not conduct until the applied voltage reaches about 600 mV. Active full-wave rectification and smoothing permits an accurate realization of this conversion to submillivolt signal levels. A Fourier expansion may be examined to determine the required smoothing filter cutoff frequency to provide the harmonic suppression and hence conversion accuracy of interest. Equation (5-8) presents the first three Fourier terms for a full-wave rectified sinusoidal signal. A 1% conversion accuracy is a practically realizable value and will be determined primarily by the amount of harmonic distortion in the dc output. For the single-pole RC smoothing filter, which has a $-20\,\mathrm{dB/decade}$ attenuation factor, a cutoff frequency of $1/RC$ radians placed 1 decade below the signal frequency ω will provide this accuracy. However, reduced accuracy may be necessary if a faster speed of response is required. This converter will also function as an absolute value circuit.

$$E = \frac{2}{\pi} E_m + \frac{4E_m}{3\pi} \cos 2\omega t + \frac{4E_m}{15\pi} \cos 4\omega t \tag{5-8}$$

An especially useful logarithmic-based device is the multifunction module, which combines multiplication and division with the ability to raise a voltage or voltage ratio to an arbitrary positive or reciprocal power. The magnitude of the power may be greater than unity (power) or less than unity (root). These unipolar modules are available from a variety of manufacturers, such as Analog Devices, Teledyne Philbrick, and Intronics, with accuracies to 0.1% of their full-scale output. These devices typically implement an equation such as (5-9), in which the X, Y, Z

TABLE 5–4. Ac-to-dc Converter Response

Parameter	E	E_o	% of dc
Dc component	$0.636E_m$	$0.636E_m$	100
2nd harmonic	$0.424E_m$	$4.2\times10^{-3}E_m$	0.6
4th harmonic	$0.085E_m$	$8.5\times10^{-6}E_m$	1.3×10^{-3}

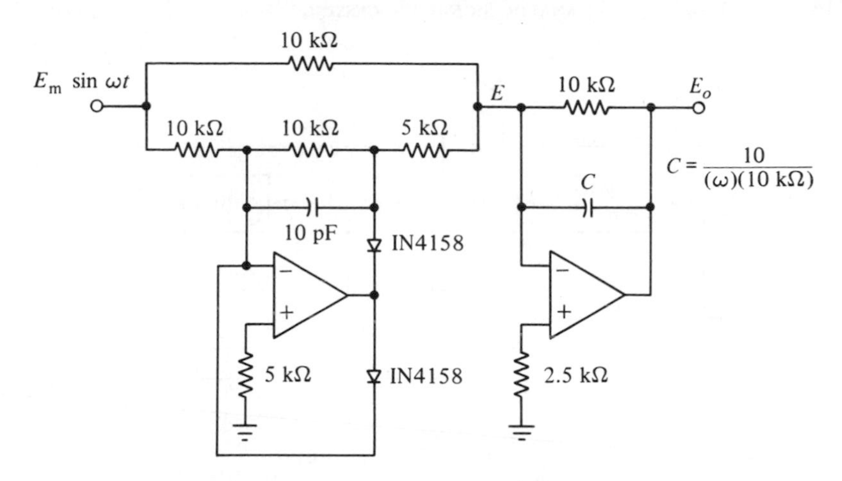

FIGURE 5–15. Precision AC to DC Converter

variables can assume positive values between 0 and 10 V, and M can be any fixed value between 0.2 and 5. The combination of multiplication, division, and exponentiation within a single module yields computation power comparable to a small analog computer.

$$E_o = Y \cdot \left(\frac{Z}{X}\right)^M \tag{5-9}$$

The multifunction device can be connected to perform numerous functions directly plus additional ones with external circuitry. Several are tabulated in Table 5–5. The log–antilog device mechanization is shown in block-diagram form in Figure 5–16. The symmetrical circuit arrangement provides for very low scale-factor and offset errors. Output noise is on the

TABLE 5–5. Multifunction Module Operations

Function	Transfer Equation
Multiplication	$YZ/10$
Division	$10(Z/X)$
Root of ratio	$Y(Z/X)^M \quad M<1$
Power of ratio	$Y(Z/X)^M \quad M>1$
Reciprocal power	$Y(Z/X)^M = Y(X/Z)^{-M}$
True rms	av. E_{in}^2/E_o
Trigonometric	$\sin Z = Z - 0.17(Z)^{2.83}$
	$\cos Z = 1 + 0.235Z - 0.7(Z)^{1.5}$
	$\arctan\frac{Z}{X} = (E_{90^\circ} - E_o)(\frac{Z}{X})^{1.21}$

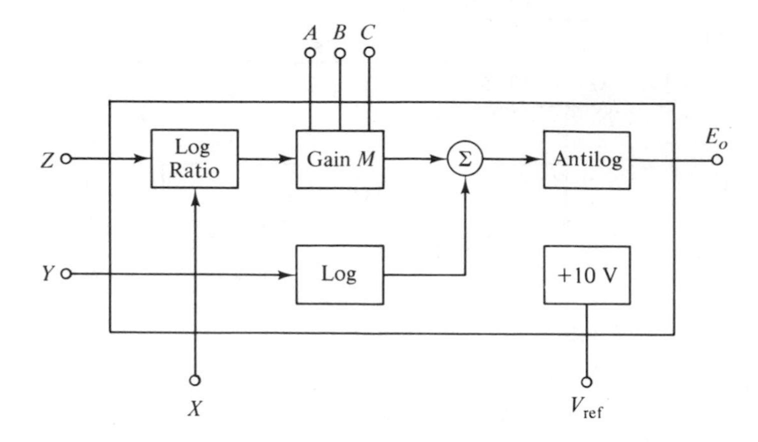

FIGURE 5–16. Log–Antilog Multifunction Module

order of 100 μV, and bandwidth is a function of the input level, varying from about 1 kHz to 100 Hz for 10 mV to 10 V input, respectively. Some example multifunction module operations are shown by Figures 5–17 through 5–19.

An example of the extended capability of the multifunction module is in the analog computation of process data. A single printed-circuit-board analog computer for the real-time calculation of both volumetric flow and mass flow rate of combustion-source stack emissions is shown in Figures 5–20 and 5–21. The rationale for an analog realization is that the transducer inputs are already available in analog form, and the circuit can be constructed to provide an accuracy of 1% at a cost below that for a microprocessor-based system which includes a data-conversion subsystem. These analog-computed flow data may then be transmitted to a remote computer or used locally as required.

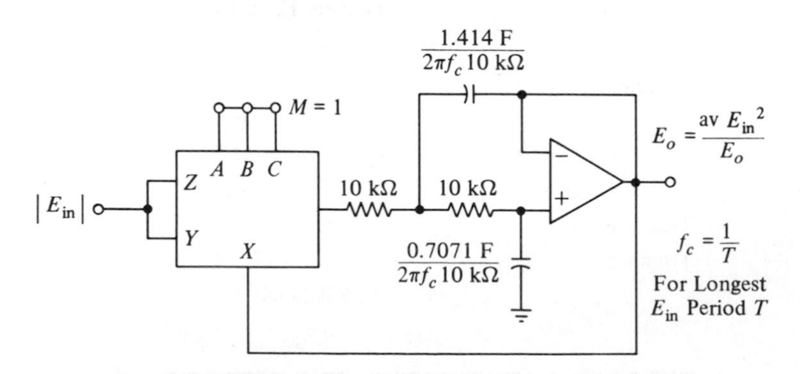

FIGURE 5–17. True RMS Extraction

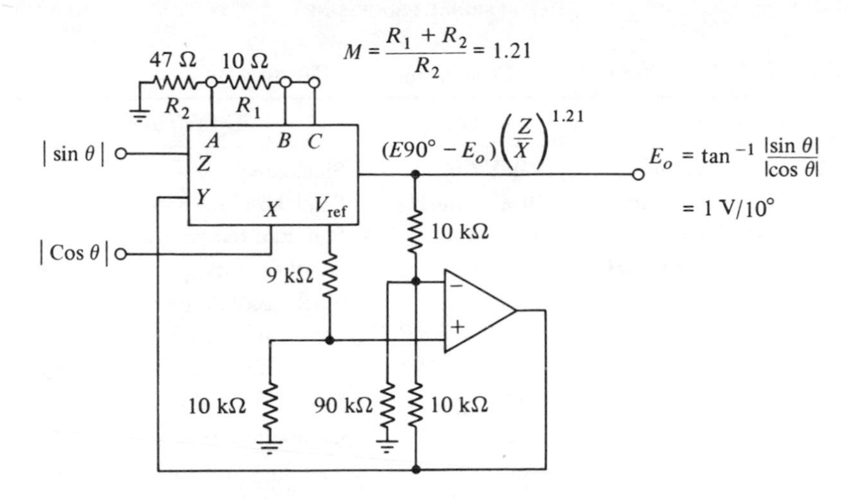

FIGURE 5–18. Arctangent Computation

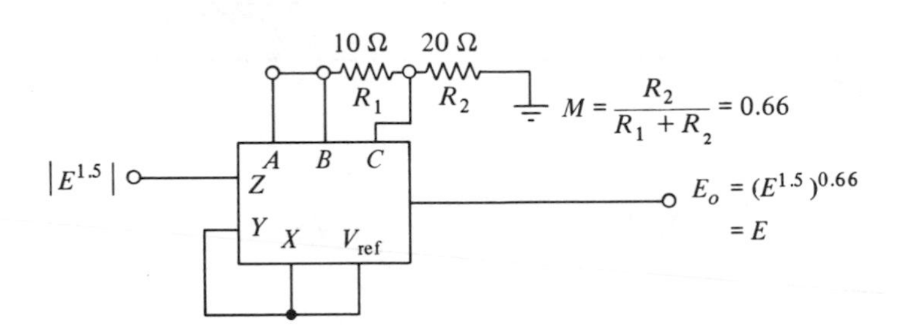

FIGURE 5–19. Transducer Linearization

The computations to be performed are described by equations (5-10) to (5-12) and consist of 15 mathematical operations. The pressure and temperature transducers and their scaling circuitry plus an infrared chemical analyzer and two voltage settable coefficients are external to the board for simplicity of presentation. The signal conditioning operations are treated elsewhere in this volume, but all functions are tabulated in Table 5–6. In the example presented, this analog computation processing unit is applied to a large fossil-fuel stationary source having a stack diameter of 100 m^2 with an on-line SO_2 emission analyzer. The only manual operation is the periodic use of a wet chemistry orsat, perhaps daily, to update the total stack effluent molecular weight M_W. Of interest in the mechanization of these computations by the circuit of Figure 5–20 is the austere component count and the absence of trimpots or other adjustments.

TABLE 5–6. Computation Processing Unit Parameters

Parameter	Value	Scaling	Description
A_n	$100\,m^2$	$10\,mV/m^2$	Stack area
P	900 mm Hg	10 mV/mm Hg	Stack absolute pressure
T_{std}	293°K	0.293 attn	Standard temperature
P_A	720 mm Hg	10 mV/mm Hg	Absolute atmospheric pressure
T	423°K	10 mV/°K	Stack absolute temperature
ΔP	$12\,mm\,H_2O$	$100\,mV/mm\,H_2O$	Stack differential pressure
M_w	28 moles	100 mV/mole	Total effluent molecular weight
ppm	$303\ SO_2$	1 mV/ppm	Stack chemical analyzer output
M_{w_s}	$64\ \text{moles}\ SO_2$	64 gain	Compound molecular weight
C_p	1.0	Unity	Sampling probe coefficient
K_p	$34.97 m^2/s$	3.497 gain	Dimensional constant $\left[\dfrac{(g/g\ \text{mole})(\text{mmHg})}{(°K)(\text{mmH}_2\text{O})}\right]^{1/2}$

$$Q = A_n \cdot C_p \cdot K_p \cdot \sqrt{\frac{\Delta p \cdot T}{P \cdot M_w}} \cdot \frac{P \cdot T_{std}}{P_A \cdot T} \qquad m^3/s \tag{5-10}$$

$$= (1\,V) \cdot (3.5) \cdot \left[\frac{(1.2\,V)(4.23\,V)/10\,V}{(9.0\,V)(2.8\,V)/10\,V}\right]^{1/2} \cdot \frac{(9.0\,V)(0.293)}{(7.2\,V)(4.23\,V)/10\,V}$$

$$= 1.35\,V \qquad \text{corresponding to } 1350\ m^3/s$$

$$Q_f = f(Q) \qquad kHz/V \tag{5-11}$$

$$= 1.35\,kHz \qquad \text{corresponding to } 1350\ m^3$$

$$M = \frac{Q \cdot \text{ppm} \cdot M_{w_s}}{22.4} \qquad kg/s \tag{5-12}$$

$$= \frac{(1.35\,V)(0.303\,V)(2.86)}{10\,V}$$

$$= 0.117\,V \qquad \text{corresponding to } 1.17\ kg/s \text{ of } SO_2$$

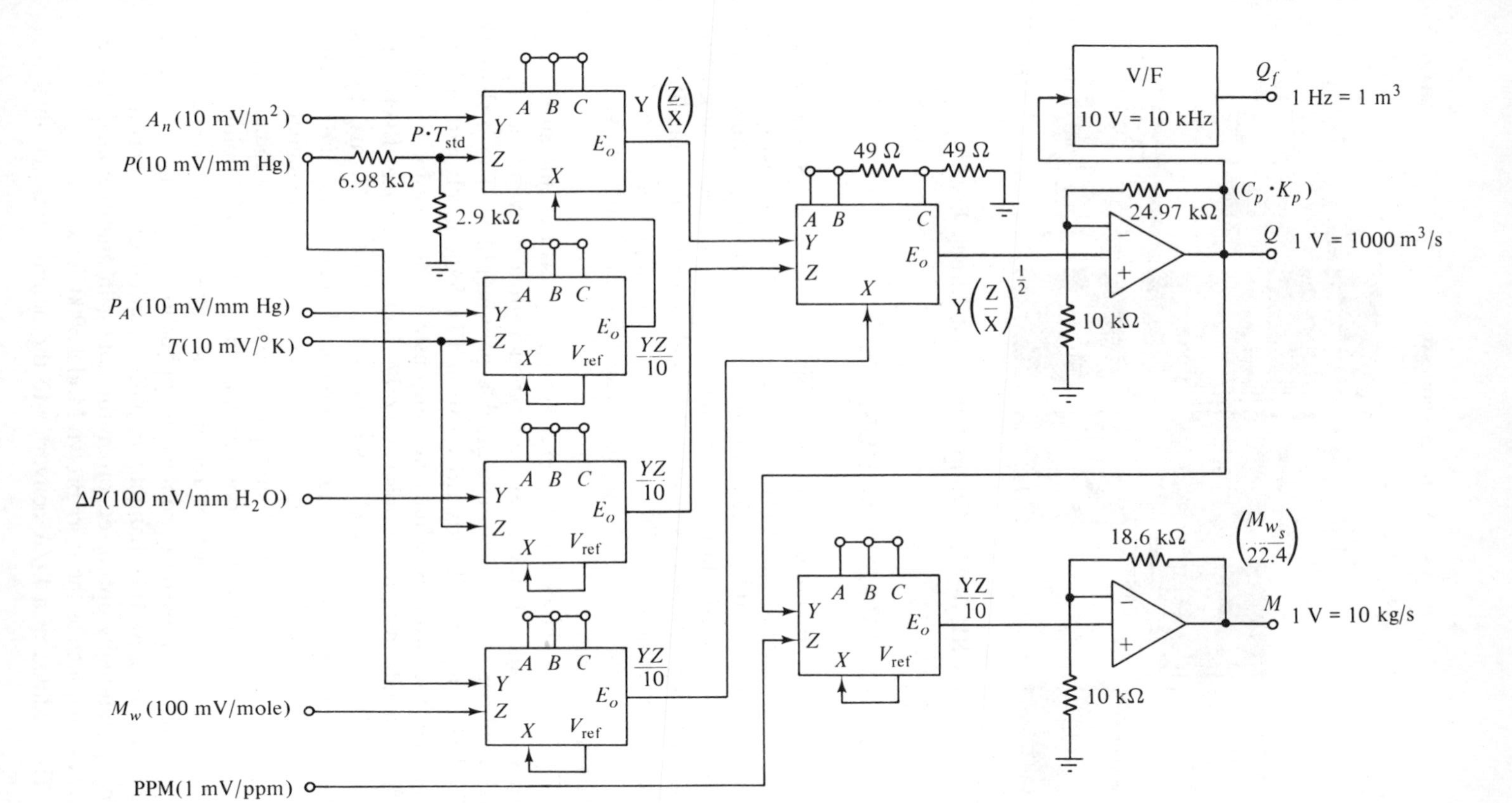

FIGURE 5–20. Computation Processing Unit

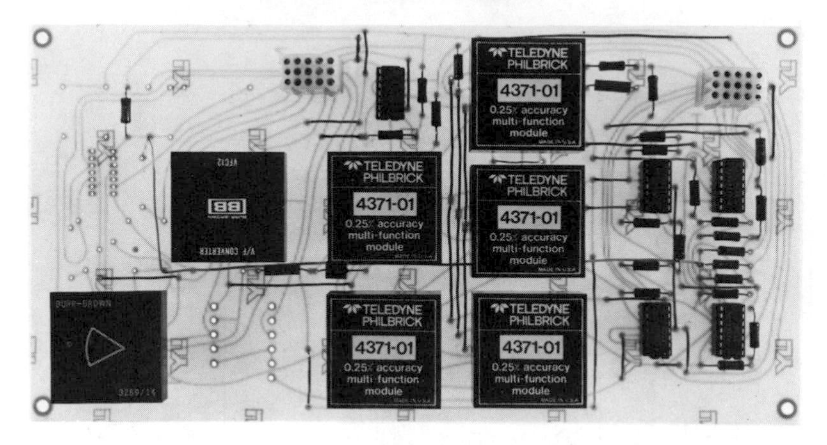

FIGURE 5–21. Computation-Unit Circuit Board

5-4 PROGRAMMABLE FUNCTIONS

It is occasionally required of data-acquisition systems to provide signal conditioning functions under remote program control of a microprocessor or minicomputer. Useful functions include programmable gain operational amplifiers to allow adaptation to changing signal amplitudes; subtractor circuits, which combine a D/A converter and programmable amplifier to remotely enhance the visibility of portions of an input signal; and programmable lowpass filters, to permit adaptation to changing signal and interference conditions.

Figure 5–22 shows a multiplexer switch such as the Intersil IH5011 constant-impedance JFET array, combined with a conventional operational amplifier to form a programmable gain amplifier. The *p*-channel JFET devices may be directly driven from TTL logic levels with a logic "1" opening the switches, while simultaneously forward-biasing the shunting diodes to eliminate input noise and other high-impedance effects. And since the JFET drains are clamped between about ± 50 mV by the operational amplifier summing junction nominal input swing, the switches are prevented from becoming forward-biased by input signals. Gain changing occurs in the feedback path from shunted combinations of feedback resistors. This technique minimizes the effects of amplifier input errors, since the input resistor remains unchanged. Nevertheless, offset voltage error can present a problem in applications requiring a low input uncertainty, because the changing amplifier gain affects this error. Complete and internally optimized programmable gain amplifer modules are also available, such as the Burr Brown Model 3600 device.

The addition of a D/A converter to the noninverting terminal of a

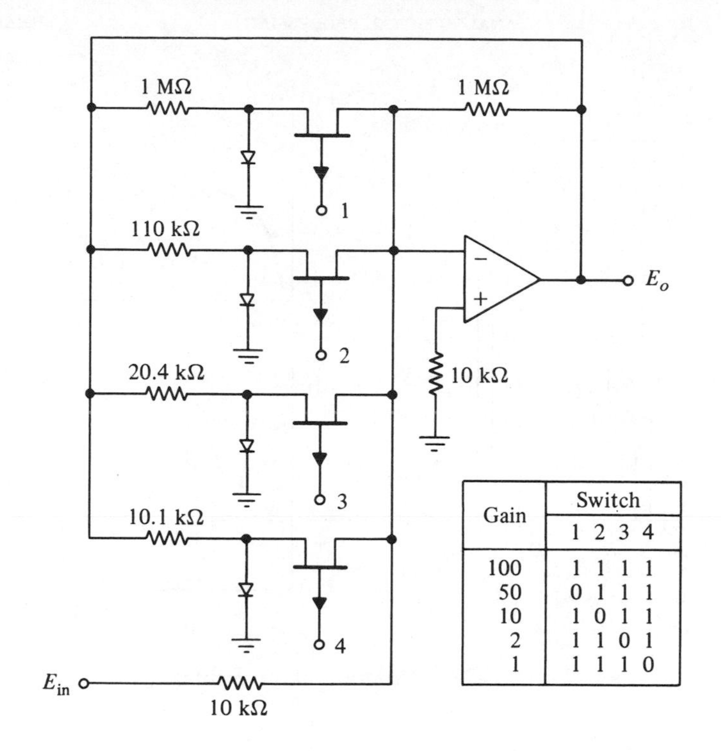

Gain	Switch 1 2 3 4
100	1 1 1 1
50	0 1 1 1
10	1 0 1 1
2	1 1 0 1
1	1 1 1 0

FIGURE 5–22. Programmable Gain Amplifier

programmable gain amplifer provides a subtractor circuit useful for enhancing the resolution of selectable portions of the input signal. This is achieved by first subtracting a segment of the signal to move the remainder down to the baseline, and then increasing amplifier gain to expand the signal portion of interest to the full-scale amplitude limit of the system. This is illustrated in Figure 5–23. The single-pole remotely tunable lowpass filter of Figure 5–24 can be tuned over two decades of frequency with excellent stability by means of the digital input word $D_o - D_N$. Stopband attenuation is -20 dB/decade with a flat amplitude response in the vicinity of dc and a gradual rolloff toward the cutoff frequency, which is useful for many instrumentation applications. For the full-scale equivalent multiplying D/A-converter digital input $D_o - D_N$, the filter cutoff will be at its highest value, $1/2\pi RC$. For a full-scale/100 input value to $D_o - D_N$, the cutoff value will be 2 decades below the highest value. The quantity MDAC $= (D_o - D_N)$/full scale.

$$\frac{E_o}{E_{in}} = \frac{1}{1 + 2\pi fc(\mathrm{R/MDAC})} \tag{5-13}$$

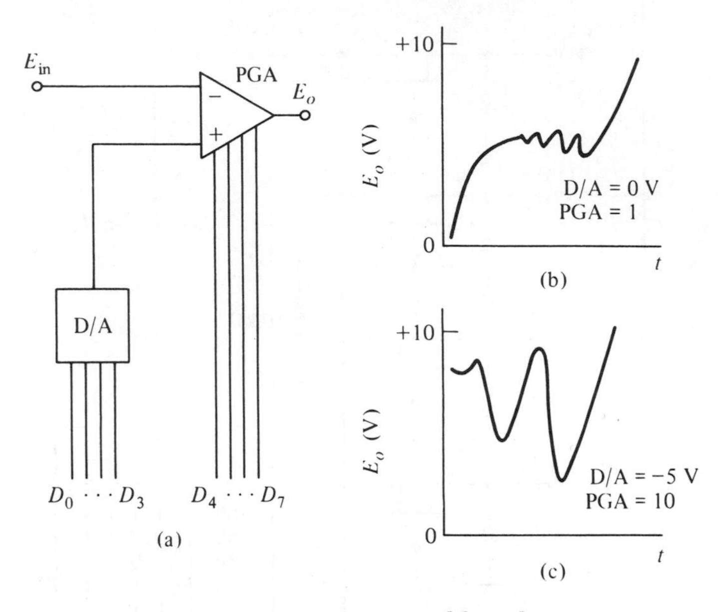

FIGURE 5–23. Programmable Subtractor

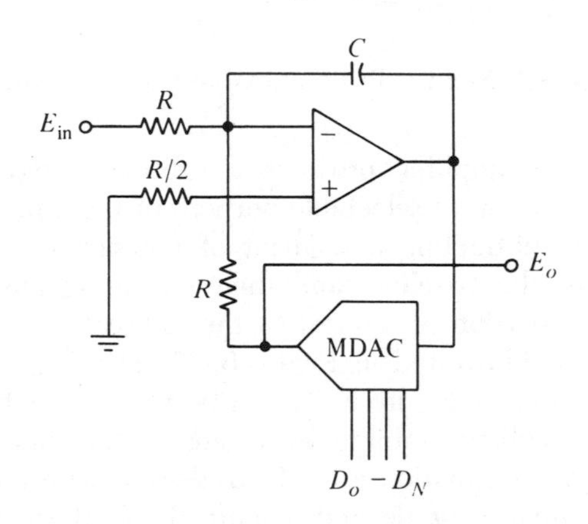

FIGURE 5–24. Programmable Lowpass Filter

PROBLEMS

5-1 Obtain the quadratic linearizing coefficients for the following thermocouple measurements. Then design a linearizing circuit with an output of 1 mV/°C and indicate all component values.

°C	0	200	400	600	800
mV	−.016	1.54	3.27	5.8	11.7

5-2 The nonlinearized Wheatstone bridge of Figure 5–7 may be linearized with an output-feedback multiplier circuit. Rearrange equation 5–4 in terms of $V_{ref} \cdot \frac{\Delta}{2}$ and describe a linearizer block-diagram model.

5-3 The implicit use of an output variable to assist in solving an equation for itself by appearing twice in the equation as a result of feedback generally results in improved accuracy and reduced dynamic range requirements. Implement the implicit solution for the vector sum below with a multifunction module circuit showing all components.

$$E_o = \sqrt{E_x^2 + E_y^2}$$

$$= E_y + \frac{E_x^2}{E_o + E_y}$$

5-4 The inverted multiplier circuit is typically used to form an analog divider which is useful for ratioing and other signal processing operations. With the amplifier summing junction nulled and in steady state, derive the expression shown for E_o. Show how this circuit can be connected to form a square rooter.

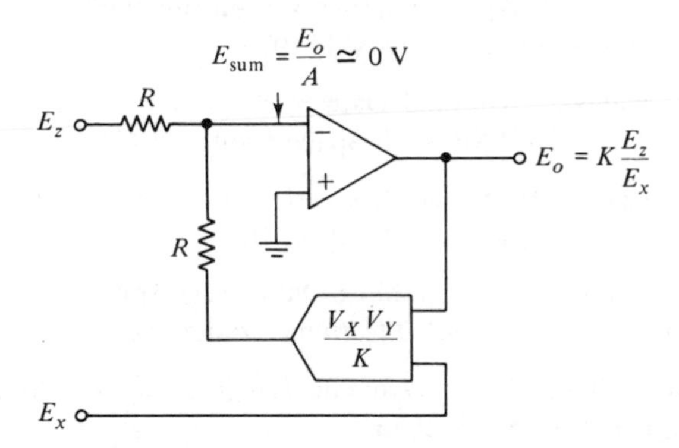

5-5 A magnetically recorded signal is logarithmically compressed over a 4-decade range between 0.1 and 1 V peak to minimize the saturation effects and for SNR enhancement. Implement a bipolar expander to recover this analog signal where the maximum expander output is scaled for 10 V. Use the devices of Table 5–3, Figure 5–12, and tabulate the input and output signal to fit the expander function.

5-6 A prototype cruise missile uses an 8-bit microprocessor to perform terrain-following computations for each of the roll, pitch and yaw axes. Each axis input has an inertial sensor with an analog output between 10 mV and 1 V, and shutter actuators for guidance control whose power amplifiers accept a 10 mV to 1V input signal. Design unipolar logarithmic compressor and expander circuits of 10 V full-scale to provide the equivalent of 12-bit resolution for these analog transducer signals. Use the devices of Table 5–3, Figures 5–10 and 5–11, and show the completed circuits developed from log gain requirements.

REFERENCES

1. A. Annunziato, "Prevent Damage to Loads and Supplies," *Electronic Design*, April 29, 1971.
2. R. S. Burwen, "Linearize Almost Anything with Multipliers," *Electronic Design*, April 15, 1971.
3. T. Cate, "Voltage Tune Your Bandpass Filters with Multipliers," *Electronic Design News*, March 1, 1971.
4. R. C. Dobkin, "Logarithmic Converters," *IEEE Spectrum*, November 1969.
5. R. G. Durnal, "Approximating Waveforms with Exponential Functions," *Electronics*, February 1, 1973.
6. C. A. Halijak, "Sampled Data Systems and Generating Functions," *NASA CR-61349*, Marshall Space Center, 1972.
7. R. Kreager, "AC-to-DC Converters for Low-Level Input Signals," *Electronic Design News*, April 5, 1973.
8. D. R. Morgan, "Get the Most Out of Log Amplifiers by Understanding the Error Sources," *Electronic Design News*, January 20, 1973.
9. G. Niu, "Get Wider Dynamic Range in a Log Amp," *Electronic Design*, February 15, 1973.
10. *Nonlinear Circuits Handbook*, Analog Devices, Norwood, Mass. 02062, 1974.
11. A. Santoni, "True RMS Measurements Reveal the Power Behind the Waveform," *Electronics*, March 18, 1976.
12. D. H. Sheingold, "Approximate Analog Functions with Low-Cost Multiplier/Dividers," *Electronic Design News*, February 5, 1973.
13. *Synchro Conversion Handbook*, Data Devices Corporation, Bohemia (Long Island), N. Y. 11716, 1974.

6

DATA CONVERSION SYSTEMS

6-0 INTRODUCTION

Sensor-based data acquisition systems for industrial and laboratory applications contain assemblies of components for signal conditioning, processing, and conversion purposes. It is common practice to share components in the configuration of data-conversion systems for economy purposes. This is explored in the first section, including variations in the partitioning of these components. Sampled data considerations, including sampling, quantizing, and encoding, are examined next, and then the characteristics and operation of the individual data-conversion components are considered. Finally, computer interfacing and data reconstruction are presented.

Users can choose from among three approaches to implement a data-conversion system: (1) buy modules and ICs and construct a system, (2) buy basic modular/PC board subsystems and configure a system, or (3) purchase a complete system. This chapter develops all three approaches, but the advantage lies with the second approach, because the overall accuracy of the subsystem is specified in advance and includes the necessary timing and control logic. This is also a flexible approach, with the capability of adding signal processing and conditioning as required. Typical modular/PC board subsystems include an eight-channel analog multiplexer, a high-speed sample hold, a 12-bit A/D converter with an overall 50-kHz throughput rate, and a timing and control programmer.

6-1 BASIC SYSTEM CONFIGURATIONS

Figure 6–1 describes the most popular data-acquisition system arrangement, which is efficient and capable of high performance. Efficiency results from the sharing of the sample hold and A/D converter with the analog multiplexer, which seeks the next channel while the sample hold is having its output converted. Performance results from the ability to tailor the signal conditioning in each input channel plus the accommodation of additions to the basic structure, such as signal processing linearizers and programmable gain amplifiers (described in detail in Chapter 5). The digital output is available in various binary or BCD codes at TTL or CMOS logic levels and in parallel or serial formats as needed. This arrangement is recommended for low-level signals, defined as signal levels below 1 V.

Figure 6–2 presents a more austere and correspondingly lower cost and lower performance system. Its utility is in sharing a common instrumentation amplifier with all input channels. However, this imposes the disadvantage of providing identical signal conditioning for each channel. A further disadvantage of high-level multiplexing is the difficulty in maintaining balanced differential inputs for common-mode rejection, plus the varying settling times for switched signal lines with finite impedances. The considerations required to obtain adequate performance with this approach result in it being useful for only the more undemanding applications, such as high-level signals, defined as signal levels of 1 V and above.

Moving the multiplexer away from the analog inputs results in a minimum number of shared elements. Placing the multiplexer at the input of the A/D converter shown in Figure 6–3 is certainly more expensive, owing to the use of multiple sample-hold devices. However, this approach

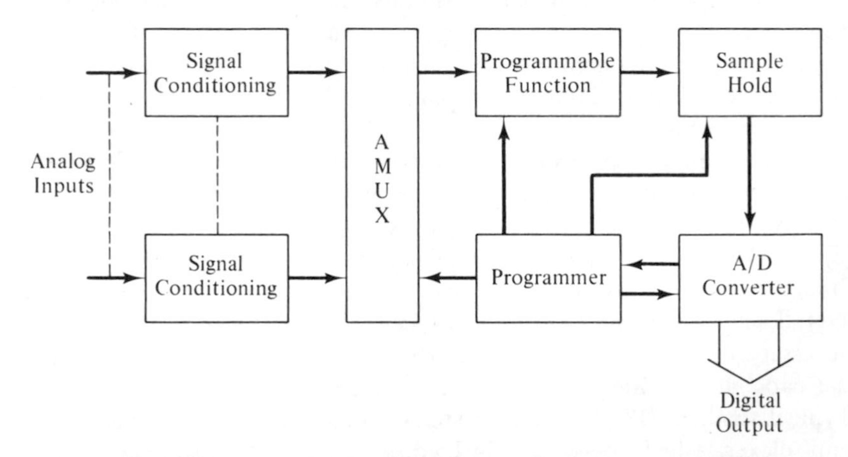

FIGURE 6–1. Multiplexed Signal Conditioning Outputs

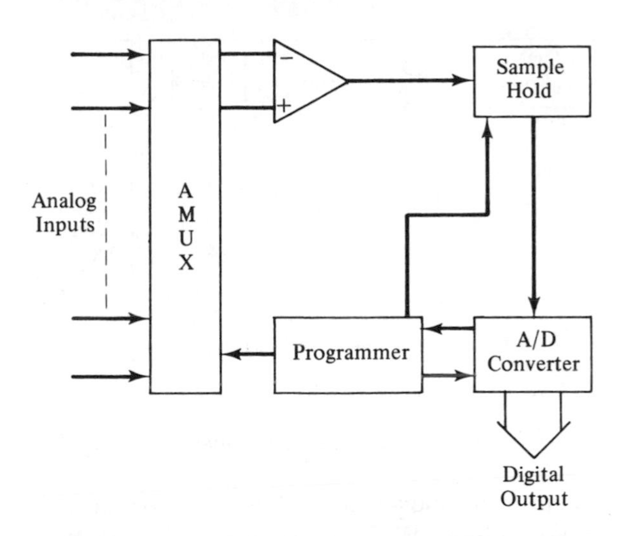

FIGURE 6–2. Multiplexed High-Level Inputs

is useful for capturing multichannel single-event phenomena, such as seismographic measurements and wind tunnel applications.

A fourth approach using parallel conversion transfers the multiplexing task from the analog to the digital domain. This permits use of a slower and lower-cost A/D converter and elimination of the sample hold (Figure 6–4). The benefits of this include elimination of the multiplexer and sample-hold analog errors, which constitute the majority of the

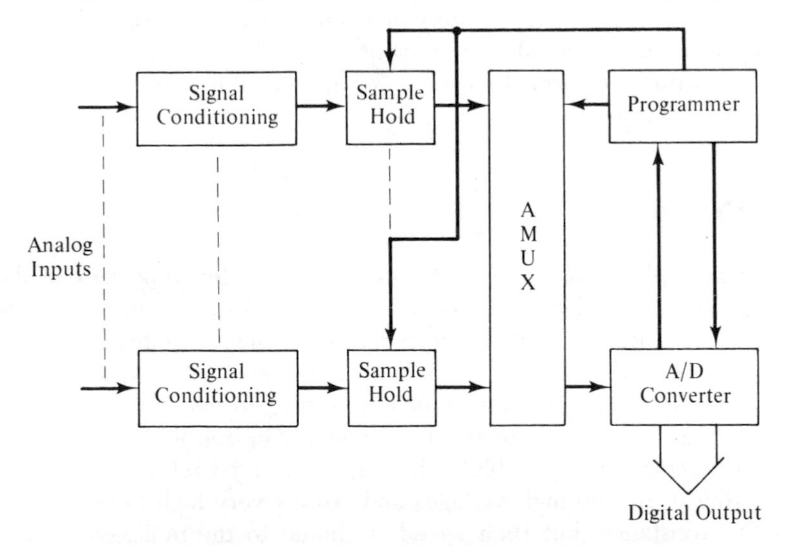

FIGURE 6–3. Multiplexed Sample-Hold Outputs

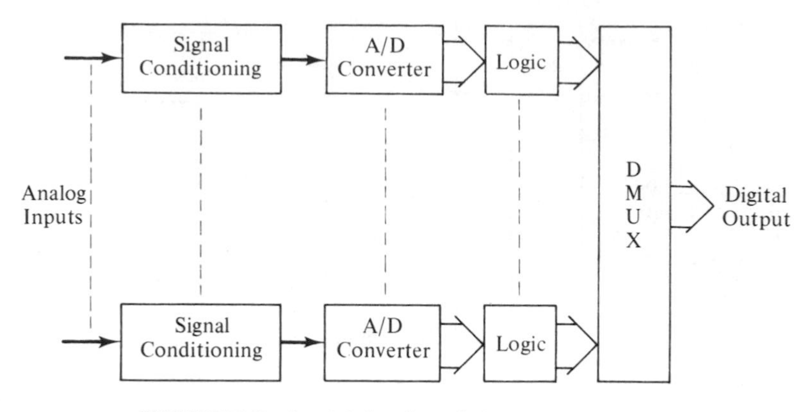

FIGURE 6–4. Multiplexed Converter Outputs

conversion system error budget. More important, perhaps, is that this is the trend of the future. With source conversion at the sensor and improved signal transmission integrity to the computer, the computer involvement can be streamlined by facilitating redundancy reduction of the sampled data. The latter can be achieved by a local logic decision on the dynamic characteristics of the data, which is impossible with analog multiplexed systems, since the data must be sampled before such a decision can be rendered. The declining cost of monolithic A/D converters and the higher performance of source conversion will result in increased application of this arrangement. The trend toward intelligent data-acquisition systems will continue, with the modular/PC board subsystem mounted in minicomputers or microcomputers being only a temporary solution. Eventually, intelligent acquisition circuitry will be integrated with computer hardware for better utilization of computer resources.

6-2 ANALOG MULTIPLEXERS

Analog multiplexers are difficult to precisely characterize because of their internal and external parameters, such as channel source impedance and stray capacitance. Of primary importance in their specification is that they operate at a speed consistent with the sample rate requirements of the data-acquisition system without introducing an unacceptable transfer error. Three switching elements are commonly in use, whose characteristics are summarized by Table 6–1. Mechanical reed relay switches have the ability to handle high voltages and possess very high OFF and very low ON resistance, but their speed is limited to the millisecond range. Field-effect transistors, both JFET and CMOS, are universally used for

TABLE 6–1. Multiplexer Switch Comparison

Type	Speed	ON Resistance	OFF Resistance
Reed	1 ms	0.1 Ω	10^{12} Ω
CMOS	1 μs	1.5kΩ	10^{8} Ω
JFET	100 ns	200 Ω	10^{10} Ω

electronic multiplexer switches and have superseded bipolar transistors because of the voltage offset problems of the latter.

Junction FET devices are capable of higher speeds and lower OFF leakage current, but CMOS is becoming dominant for multiplexer applications. CMOS advantages include the ability to multiplex voltages up to the system supply voltages, a stable ON resistance as the input signal amplitude varies due to the symmetry provided by paralleled *p*- and *n*-channel devices, and an unfailing turn-off when the power is shut off. Figure 6–5 presents a CMOS switch equivalent circuit.

Analog multiplexers exhibit two significant dynamic errors: (1) OFF-channel leakage current, which is temperature-dependent in the JFET, and (2) a settling time constraint resulting from the *RC* time constant formed by the device capacitance and its ON resistance. Consider a 32-channel CMOS analog multiplexer with 1.5kΩ ON resistance and each OFF device contributing 5 nA of leakage current into 50 pF of capacitance per channel. This results in 155 nA of leakage into 1.5kΩ, producing 233 μV of offset voltage, which is substantially less than 1/2LSB of a 12-bit A/D converter that may follow it. Half an LSB for a 12-bit A/D converter corresponds to 1.245 mV. However, the 31 OFF channels summed capacitance of 1650 pF and 1.5kΩ ON resistance form a settling-time constant of 2.5 μs. Settling to 0.01% of full scale for 12-bit accuracy can require up to 9 time constants, or 22.5 μs, in the event of

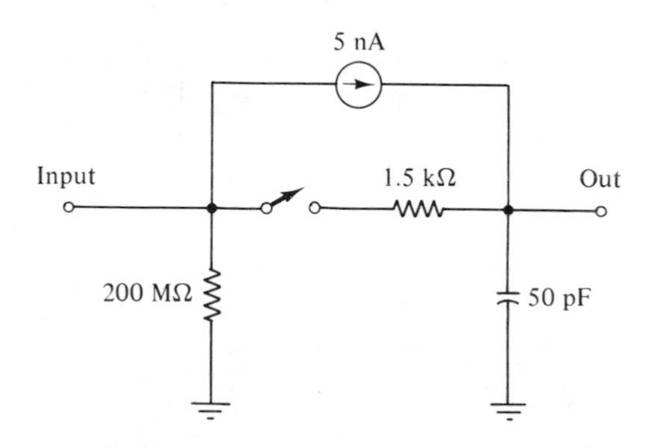

FIGURE 6–5. CMOS Switch Equivalent Circuit

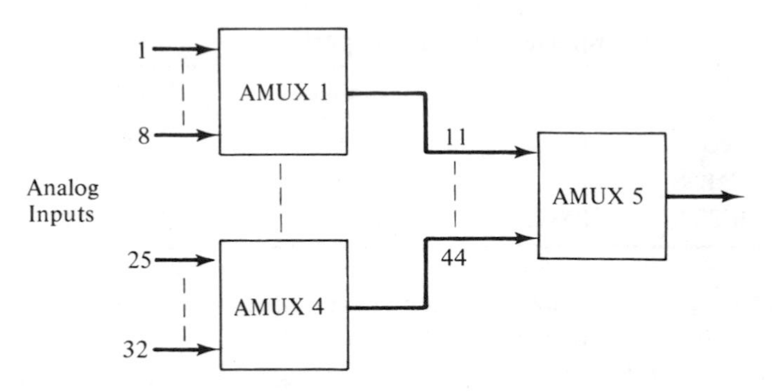

FIGURE 6–6. Eight × Four Tiered Multiplexer Array

signal rollover from full-scale positive to full-scale negative values. This would likely be an unacceptable time penalty in a high-speed data-acquisition system. Two-level tiered multiplexing is a practical solution to these errors and typically reduces them by an order of magnitude where accuracy and speed requirements justify the additional complexity. This scheme is illustrated by Figure 6–6. The voltage divider effect of the multiplexer ON resistance and its terminating impedance can generally be kept below 0.01% error by the use of an output operational amplifier follower.

Below about 10 mV signal level, mechanical switching is recommended over solid-state switching. Mercury-wetted reed devices minimize contact potential and other analog errors for low-level signal multiplexing. The flying capacitor multiplexer is a once popular industrial multiplexer method for low-level switching which offers high isolation at the multiplexer interface and good common-mode rejection (Figure 6–7). In this mechanization a capacitor is differentially transferred between the input and output circuits, thereby eliminating common-mode interference trans-

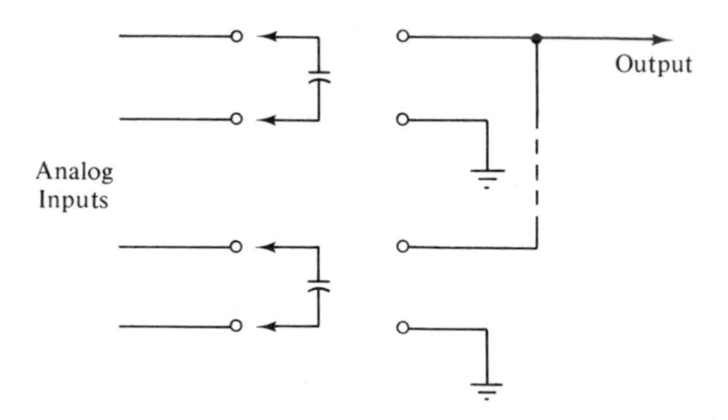

FIGURE 6–7. Flying Capacitor Multiplexer

fer and providing a single-ended output. However, normal-mode interference is transferred with each sample and cannot be reseparated. Accordingly, straight-through multiplexing is now preferred, with conventional signal conditioning operating on both the common-mode and normal-mode interference. An isolation amplifier can provide high voltage or galvanic isolation where required.

6-3 SAMPLE-HOLD DEVICES

Sample holds are used to "freeze" fast-changing signals during conversion in data-acquisition systems and to store multiplexer outputs between updates in data-distribution systems. Sample holds usually have unity gain and are noninverting. The control input is usually TTL-compatible with logic "1" the sample command and logic "0" hold. Figure 6–8 presents a representative circuit in which the feedback loop enforces tracking accuracy by means of the high-gain difference amplifier. Common-mode and offset errrors of the output follower amplifier are compensated for with this arrangement.

Principal errors associated with sample holds occur during the sample-to-hold and hold-to-sample intervals. Aperture time is the elapsed time between the command to hold and the actual opening of the hold switch. The result of this delay is an amplitude uncertainty dependent upon the rate of change of the sampled signal. Figure 6–9 is an aperture–time selection curve presented in terms of required A/D bit quality. For example, interpolation of the curves shows that for a 1 kHz maximum signal frequency, a sample-hold aperture time of 100 ns is adequate for 10-bit A/D conversion, but 50 ns is required if 12-bit accuracy is of interest.

During hold, capacitor droop and sample-hold feedthrough can contribute errors. Droop is caused by the input bias current requirement of

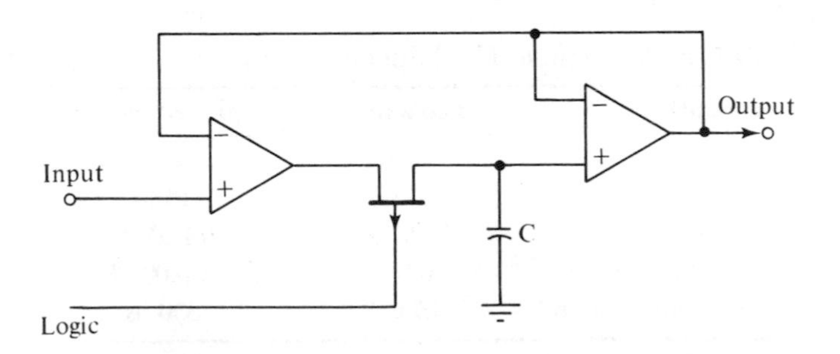

FIGURE 6–8. Sample-Hold Circuit

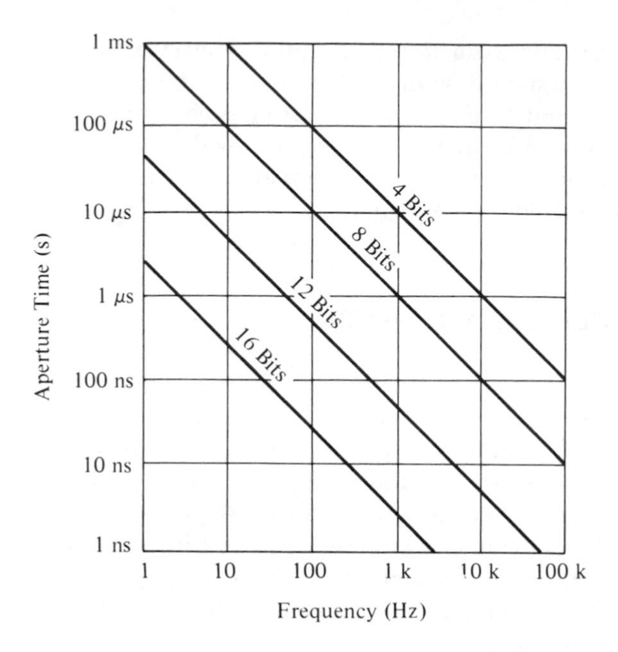

FIGURE 6–9. Aperture Criteria

the output amplifier, which is supplied by the capacitor during the hold interval. Droop is usually of consequence only in long hold intervals such as those found in data-distribution systems. Feedthrough is the fraction of input signal that appears at the output during hold and is primarily due to capacitance across the switch. The principal transient disturbance associated with a sample hold is the hold-jump voltage. This is a constant voltage added to the output by the charge transferred to the capacitor during sample-to-hold switching. The acquisition-time specification is illustrated by Figure 6–10. This is the time duration an output signal must be applied for sampling to the desired accuracy. Table 6–2 summarizes key sample-hold specifications.

TABLE 6–2. Sample-Hold Specifications

Parameter	Economy	High Performance
Gain	+1.0	+1.0
Aperture	100 ns	10 ns
Droop	1 μV/s	0.1 μV/s
Feedthrough	±0.01%	±0.001%
0.01% Acquisition	15 μs	350 ns

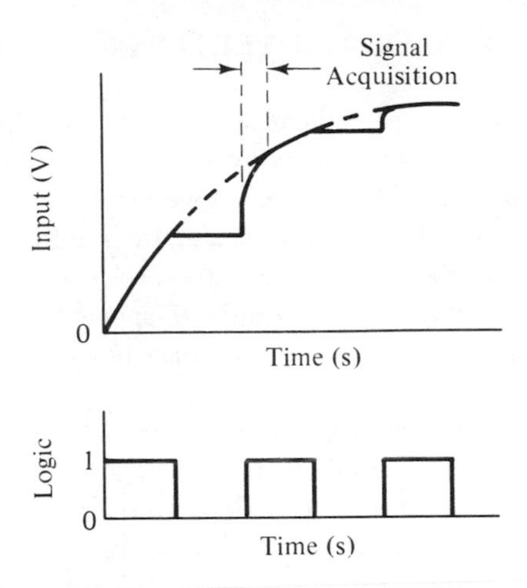

FIGURE 6–10. Acquisition Time

The decision of whether or not to use a sample hold at the input of an A/D converter essentially depends on the maximum rate of change of the input signal. A digital panel meter is an example of direct conversion where a free-running A/D converter will accurately convert the input signal as long as it does not exceed the rate of change specified by equation (6-1). $T = 100$ ms is the assumed time for a conversion, considering $n = 6$ for a 6-bit converter. Introduction of a sample hold at the front of an A/D converter increases the permissible signal rate of change as a function of the sample-hold aperture time t_a. For the same converter and a 100-ns aperture time sample hold, we obtain a six-decade tracking rate improvement.

$$\text{tracking rate} = \frac{2^{-n} \cdot \text{FS}}{T} \tag{6-1}$$

$$= \frac{(1/64)(10\,\text{V})}{0.1\ \text{s}}$$

$$= 1.56\ \text{V/s} \qquad \text{converter only}$$

$$\text{tracking rate} = \frac{2^{-n} \cdot \text{FS}}{t_a}$$

$$= \frac{(1/64)(10\,\text{V})}{0.1\ \mu\text{s}}$$

$$= 1.56\ \text{V}/\mu\text{s} \qquad \text{with sample hold}$$

6-4 DIGITAL-TO-ANALOG CONVERTERS

The most descriptive way of indicating the relationship between analog and digital quantities involved in conversion is to plot a graph. Figure 6–11 graphs an example 3-bit D/A converter of eight discrete coded levels ranging from zero to $\frac{7}{8}$ of full scale. In practical D/A converters (DACs), the zero bar may not be exactly zero, due to offset error; the range from zero to $\frac{7}{8}$ may not be exactly as specified, due to gain error; and differences in the heights of the bars may not change uniformly, as a result of nonlinearity.

Offset error is the output voltage of a DAC with a zero input code. It is caused by the analog amplifier or comparator devices and can be trimmed to zero. Gain error is the departure from the design output voltage for a given input code. In this case variance in the reference voltage, ladder resistance values, or output amplifier gain is usually at fault. Linearity error describes the departure from a linear transfer curve and does not include the $\pm\frac{1}{2}$-LSB quantizing error. Differential nonlinearity indicates the difference between actual analog voltage change and the ideal 1-LSB voltage change for any code increment. For example, a DAC with a $1\frac{1}{2}$-LSB step at a code change exhibits $\frac{1}{2}$-LSB differential nonlinearity. Differential nonlinearity may be twice the LSB increment,

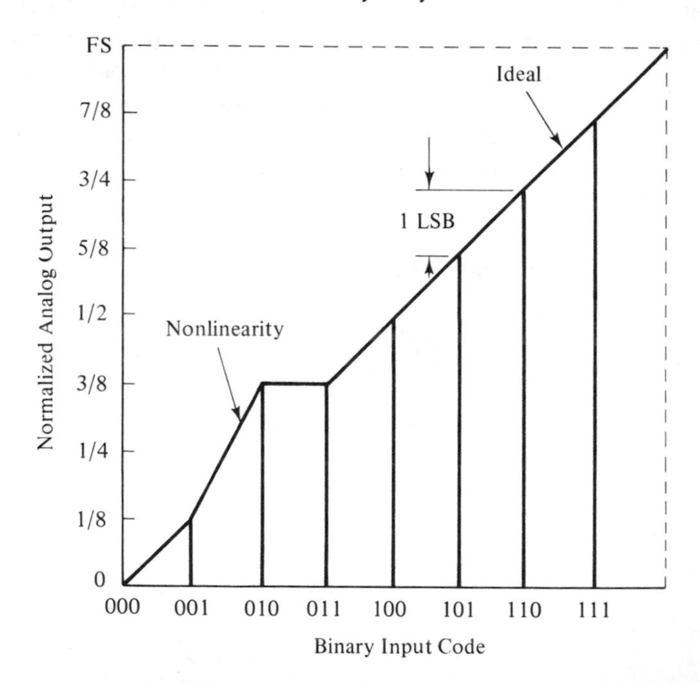

FIGURE 6–11. Three-Bit D/A Converter

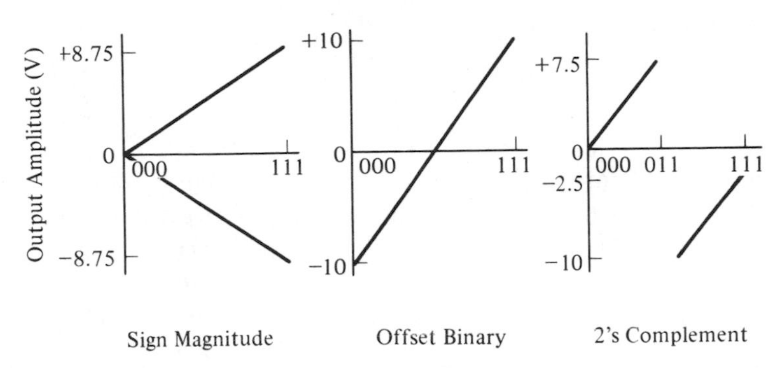

FIGURE 6–12. Three-Bit DAC Relationships

but if the error exceeds 1 LSB, the converter transfer curve is said to be nonmonotonic and is no longer single-valued.

Frequently used input codes for D/A converters are the sign magnitude, offset binary, and 2's-complement bipolar codes illustrated by Figure 6–12 for a 3-bit DAC. Sign magnitude is a straightforward method of expressing analog quantities digitally and is especially useful for outputs which are frequently in the vicinity of zero. The binary input code does not undergo a major bit change at zero permitting linear transitions from small positive to negative voltages, or vice versa. Offset binary is the easiest code to implement with converter circuitry and has a single unambiguous code for zero, unlike sign magnitude. However, a major bit transition occurs for the zero output code, making it susceptible to glitches and offset errors in this region. Offset binary is easily converted to the computer-compatible 2's-complement code by simply complementing the MSB.

The 2's-complement code consists of a binary number for the positive magnitudes and the 2's complement of each positive number to represent its negative values. The 2's complement is implemented by complementing the binary number and adding one LSB. Table 6–3 compares these three codes for a 3-bit binary word. Note that the sign magnitude code exhibits twice the resolution of the other two codes, but requires a fourth sign bit in its implementation. By omitting the sign bit a unipolar binary code can be obtained for either positive or negative output voltages, depending upon the reference polarity chosen.

The D/A converter can be thought of as a digitally controlled potentiometer that produces an analog output current or voltage that is a normalized fraction of its full-scale value. If the reference for the full-scale value can assume varying positive and negative values and the DAC provides a bipolar output, then four-quadrant analog multiplication is possible. If the reference is restricted to a single polarity, then two-

TABLE 6–3. Binary Code Values

+	−	N	E_o(V)	N	E_o(V)	N	E_o(V)
0	1	111	8.75	111	10.00	011	7.5
0	1	110	7.50	110	7.14	010	5.0
0	1	101	6.25	101	4.29	001	2.5
0	1	100	5.00	100	1.43	000	0.0
0	1	011	3.75	011	−1.43	111	−2.5
0	1	010	2.50	010	−4.29	110	−5.0
0	1	001	1.25	001	−7.14	101	−7.5
0	1	000	0.00	000	−10.00	100	−10.00
Sign Magnitude				Offset Binary		2's Complement	

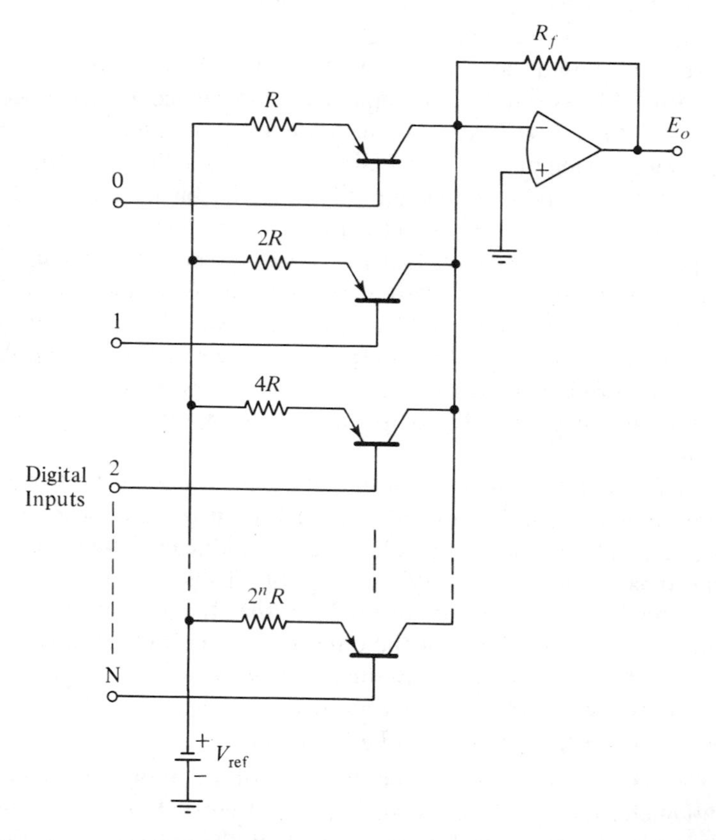

FIGURE 6–13. Weighted Resistor DAC

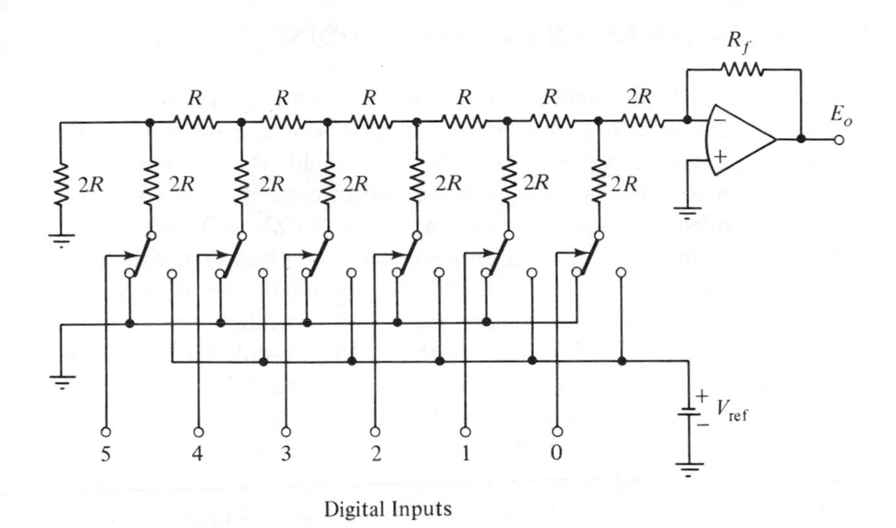

FIGURE 6–14. R–2R Network DAC

quadrant multiplication is possible. The polarity of the output product is then a function of the analog reference polarity, the digital code, and the conversion relationship. The use of DACs in this manner is occasionally of value in applications requiring a digitally controlled variable attenuator or programmable function as described in Section 5-4.

A complete description of D/A converter implementation methods and circuits is beyond the scope of this chapter. However, the basic D/A converter consists of a voltage source, which is usually a temperature-compensated zener, a set of binary-weighted precision resistors, and a gang of electronic switches. Each switch closure adds a binary-weighted current increment to an output summing bus. A current-output DAC is therefore provided by omitting the output current-to-voltage conversion operational amplifer. Current output DACs offer higher speed in the amount of settling time saved by omitting this amplifier. A 12-bit D/A converter requires a range of resistance values of 4096:1 in the weighted-resistor network method and a typical LSB value of 40 MΩ. The use of a limited number of repeated resistance values in the R–2R ladder arrangement is an efficient method of reducing this resistance range and is now almost universally employed. These two converter methods are shown in Figures 6–13 and 6–14 configured for voltage outputs. DAC output accuracy is typically 0.01%, with conversion speeds of 0.1 μs for current output and 20 μs for voltage output.

6-5 SAMPLING, QUANTIZING, AND ENCODING

The process of analog-to-digital conversion involves three distinct phases: (1) sampling, (2) quantizing, and (3) encoding. It is of interest to examine these three phases in some detail for the insight they provide into data-conversion systems. Sampling can be performed either by a sample-hold circuit which imposes nonreturn to zero (NRZ) sampling on the input signal, or by an analog multiplexer in time-division multiplexed systems which imposes return to zero (RTZ) sampling on the input signal. Examination of Figure 6–15 illustrates the significant difference between these methods. The sampled data for both cases is presented in both time and the complementary frequency domains. For the RTZ system, the bandwidth to the first null is described by the $\sin X/X$ gating function as the inverse sampling pulse width $1/\tau$ Hz. The envelope of sampling components is described by the sampling frequency f_s and its multiples nf_s, which is defined by $1/\mathrm{T}$ Hz and n/T Hz. Of special interest are the sideband frequency components about the sampling frequency f_s which are produced by the inverse input signal period $1/T$ Hz. Multiple signal frequencies simply result in a spread spectrum about each f_s bounded by the highest signal frequency present. Note that this is analogous to the production of sidebands in amplitude modulation.

TABLE 6–4. Decimal Equivalents of 2^n and 2^{-n} (FS = 1 V)

Bits, n	Levels, 2^n	LSB Resolution, 2^{-n}	Dynamic Range (dB)
0	1	1.0	0
1	2	0.5	−6
2	4	0.25	−12
3	8	0.125	−18
4	16	0.0625	−24
5	32	0.03125	−30
6	64	0.015625	−36
7	128	0.0078125	−42
8	256	0.00390625	−48
9	512	0.001953125	−54
10	1,024	0.0009765625	−60
11	2,048	0.00048828125	−66
12	4,096	0.000244140625	−72
13	8,192	0.0001220703125	−78
14	16,384	0.00006103515625	−84
15	32,768	0.000030517578125	−90
16	65,536	0.0000152587890625	−96

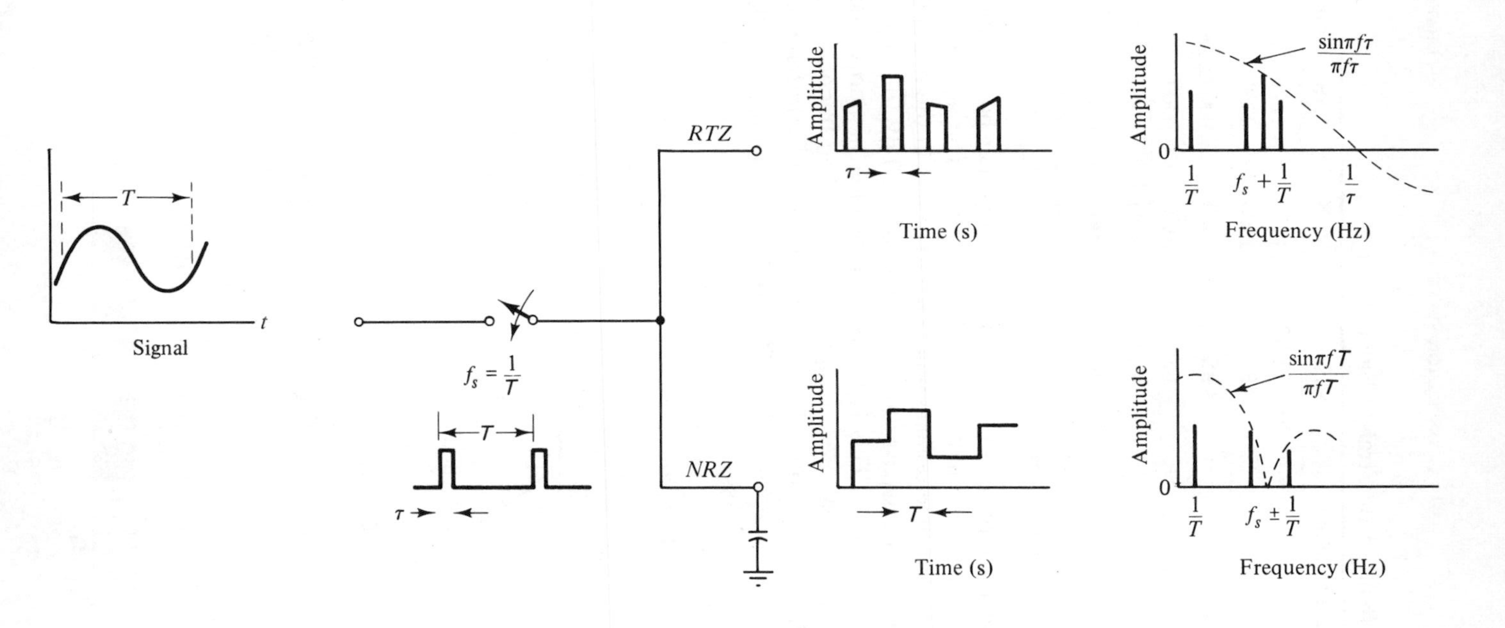

FIGURE 6–15. Sampled Data Time and Frequency-Domain Relationships

TABLE 6–5. 8-Bit Straight Binary Code

Decimal Fraction	Scale	MSB	LSB
0.996	FS − 1 LSB	1111	1111
0.750	$\frac{3}{4}$ FS	1100	0000
0.500	$\frac{1}{2}$ FS	1000	0000
0.250	$\frac{1}{4}$ FS	0100	0000
0.125	$\frac{1}{8}$ FS	0010	0000
0.004	1 LSB	0000	0001
0.000	0	0000	0000

The NRZ characteristic is imposed by the zero-order hold action of sample-hold devices at the input of an A/D converter. This action serves to stretch the sampled time-domain function and results in the imposition of essentially a $\sin X/X$ lowpass filter asymptote of -20 dB/decade plus up to -60-dB nulls at f_s. This is a useful realization of normal-mode filtering on the input signal. For example, if the sampling frequency f_s is chosen as 60 Hz, a sharp null will occur for rejection of interference at this frequency. Note that in both RTZ and NRZ sampling, the signal frequency(s) of interest reside in the spectrum adjacent to 0 Hz. This coincides with the choice of the presampling filter cutoff frequency discussed in Chapter 4, which is usually superimposed on the sampling frequency spectrum.

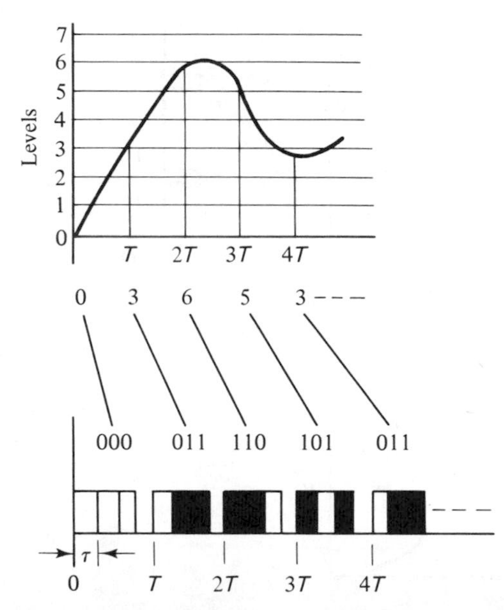

FIGURE 6–16. BCD Encoded A/D Conversion

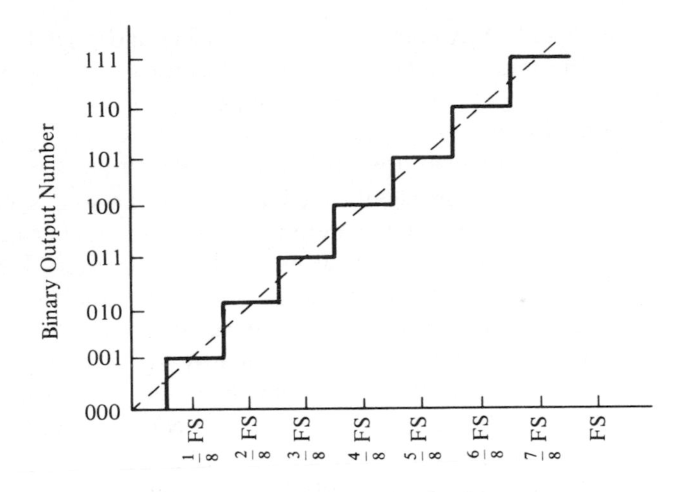

(a)

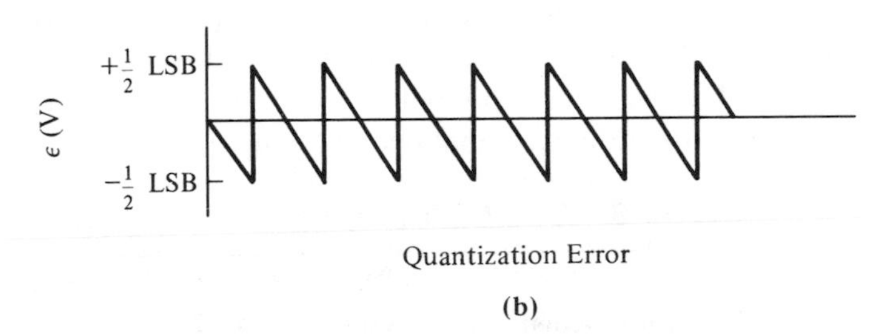

Quantization Error

(b)

FIGURE 6–17. Three-Bit A/D Converter Relationships

Quantization of the sampled analog waveform involves the assignment of a finite number of amplitude levels, corresponding to discrete values of voltage increasing from zero to some full-scale (FS) value, frequently 10 V. The quantizing level 2^{-n} represents the least significant bit (LSB) resolution limit for A/D converters of FS volts and 2^n levels, as tabulated in Table 6–4. The uniform quantizing algorithm is dominant, whereby if the analog signal exceeds a quantizing level 2^{-n} by $\frac{1}{2}$, the next higher level is taken as the value to be encoded. The resulting quantization error may range up to $\pm a/2$ V, which is an irreducible noise added to the converted signal equivalent to a 6-dB SNR loss. This was discussed in Section 4-1.

$$a = 2^{-n} \cdot FS \quad \text{volts, level spacing} \tag{6-2}$$

$$\epsilon = \pm \frac{a}{2} \quad \text{volts, maximum error} \tag{6-3}$$

Both A/D and D/A converters relate analog and digital values by means of an appropriate digital code. The codes used are various binary-related codes, the most common of which is perhaps natural binary (Table 6–5). The first bit in A/D and D/A converters is called the most significant bit (MSB) and has a weight of $\frac{1}{2}$, the second has a weight of $\frac{1}{4}$, and so on down to the least significant bit, which has a weight of $\frac{1}{2}^{n} \cdot$FS. The resolution of the converter is determined by the number of bits, of course, where the size of the LSB is FS/2^n. Converters have both unipolar and bipolar analog scaling. Note that all 1's in the digital output code does not correspond to the full-scale value, but to $(1-2^{-n}) \cdot$FS. For the eight-level 3-bit A/D converter suggested by Figure 6–16, a conversion is performed once each sample period T and a numerical value assigned to each quantizing level, which is then converted to the output code.

Figure 6-17 presents the graph for a simple 3-bit A/D converter. The analog input is quantized into eight discrete ranges according to the previously discussed quantization algorithm. Therefore, the A/D converter suffers an inherent $\pm\frac{1}{2}$ LSB quantization uncertainty in addition to the errors previously described for D/A converters. These errors are principally due to the analog circuit components, which are implied by the following equation. And where a D/A converter with excessive differential nonlinearity exhibits a nonmonotonic output, the A/D converter

TABLE 6–6. Two-Digit BCD Code

Decimal Fraction	MSQ 8 4 2 1	LSQ 8 4 2 1
0.00=0.00+0.00	0 0 0 0	0 0 0 0
0.01=0.00+0.01	0 0 0 0	0 0 0 1
0.02=0.00+0.02	0 0 0 0	0 0 1 0
0.03=0.00+0.03	0 0 0 0	0 0 1 1
0.04=0.00+0.04	0 0 0 0	0 1 0 0
0.05=0.00+0.05	0 0 0 0	0 1 0 1
0.06=0.00+0.06	0 0 0 0	0 1 1 0
0.07=0.00+0.07	0 0 0 0	0 1 1 1
0.08=0.00+0.08	0 0 0 0	1 0 0 0
0.09=0.00+0.09	0 0 0 0	1 0 0 1
0.10=0.10+0.00	0 0 0 1	0 0 0 0
|	|	|
|	|	|
|	|	|
0.99=0.90+0.09	1 0 0 1	1 0 0 1

manifestation of this error is missed output codes. Table 6–6 is an example of a two-digit BCD code.

$$\text{analog error} = \underset{\text{(offset)}}{E_{os}} + \underset{\text{(gain)}}{K(1 \pm \Delta)E_{\text{in}}} + \underset{\text{(nonlinearity)}}{f(E_{\text{in}}/^{\circ}\text{C})} \quad \text{volts} \qquad (6\text{-}4)$$

6-6 ANALOG-TO-DIGITAL CONVERTERS

A larger number of methods are in common usage for A/D conversion than for D/A conversion. This is so because A/D conversion lends itself to several indirect counter and feedback mechanizations. Table 6–7 lists the prevalent conversion methods and their features. The first five listed are the most frequently applied converter types and are widely available commercially. The less frequently applied methods are generally either not cost-competitive or lack comparable features available with other converters.

A/D converter methods can be categorized into those which require a DAC in their mechanization and those which do not. Methods that require DACs generally have more expensive circuit realizations but are not necessarily superior. For example, successive approximation converters utilize a DAC and dual-slope converters do not, yet both have features that are advantageous for specific applications. A second general classification is methods which are of the integrating type and those

TABLE 6–7. A/D Conversion Methods

Type	Conversion Rate	Resolution (bits)	Features
Successive approximation	1 MHz	10	Iterative, constant rate
	1 kHz	16	
Dual slope	100 Hz	12	Integrating, self-calibrating
Voltage to frequency	40 Hz	8	Integrating, eliminates S/H
Counter ramp	40 kHz	8	Tracking, eliminates S/H
Parallel	50 MHz	4	Very high speed
Hybridized	20 MHz	8	Speed-resolution compromise
Single slope	1 kHz	8	Integrating, low cost
Charge balancing	100 Hz	12	Integrating, complicated
Logarithmic	20 kHz	15 log	0.1% resolution over 120 dB dynamic range

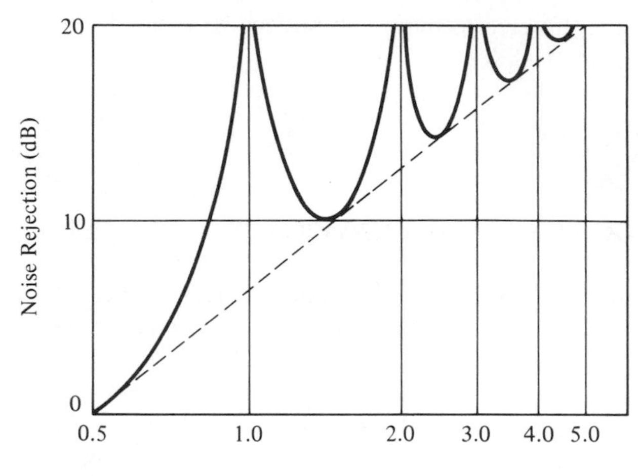

FIGURE 6–18. Integrating Converter Noise Rejection

which are not. Integrating converters provide noise rejection to the input signal at an attenuation rate of 20 dB/decade of frequency, with up to 60-dB nulls at multiples of the integration period as shown by Figure 6–18. This results in additional improvement in the signal-to-noise ratio, with notch filtering at multiples of the integration period. Inexpensive digital panel meters usually employ single-slope A/D conversion with an integration period of $16\frac{2}{3}$ ms. This provides a useful null to 60-Hz interference.

The successive approximation method is the most widely applied converter, because of its combination of high resolution and speed. It operates by comparing the output of an internal D/A converter against the analog input signal, one bit at a time. Therefore, n-fixed time periods are needed to deliver an n-bit output with the conversion time a constant as illustrated by Figure 6–19. Conversion accuracy depends upon the stability of the DAC reference, the ladder network, and the comparator. The successive approximation converter is typically used in multiplexed, multiple-input computer data-conversion systems, where its fixed conversion rate and relatively high speed are advantageous.

Integrating A/D converters operate by the indirect method of converting a voltage to a time period that is then measured by a counter. Single-slope, dual-slope, and triphasic converters are all variations of this basic principle. The most popular type is the dual-slope converter, which frequently includes the triphasic third integration for improved accuracy about the zero endpoint, as shown in Figure 6–20. Dual-slope operation is self-calibrating, which makes it immune to long-term component drift.

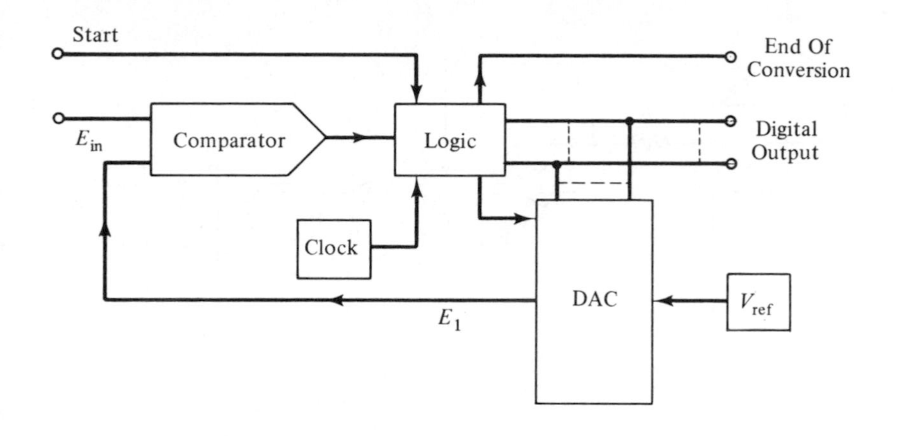

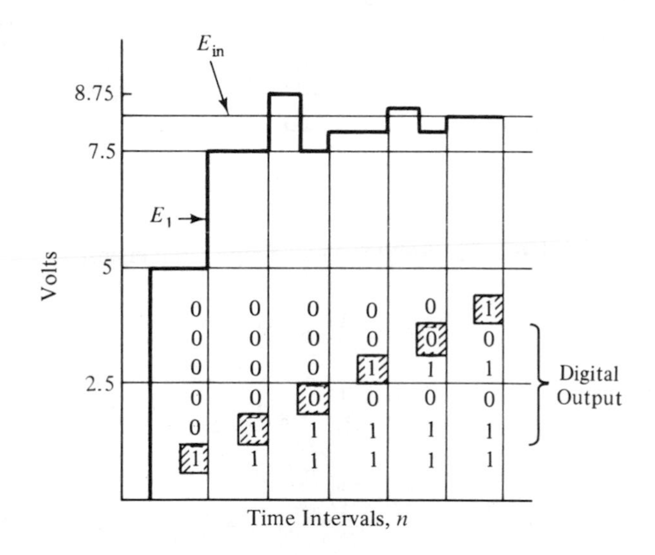

FIGURE 6–19. Successive Approximation Conversion

Operation occurs in three steps. The first is the auto-zero step, whereby analog errors are stored by the integrator with the input grounded. During the second portion, the input signal is integrated for a fixed time, providing an integrator output proportional to the input voltage. In the final portion of the conversion cycle, the input is connected to a reference voltage of opposite polarity, and integration proceeds to zero. The clock pulses counted during the third portion provides a digital measure of the

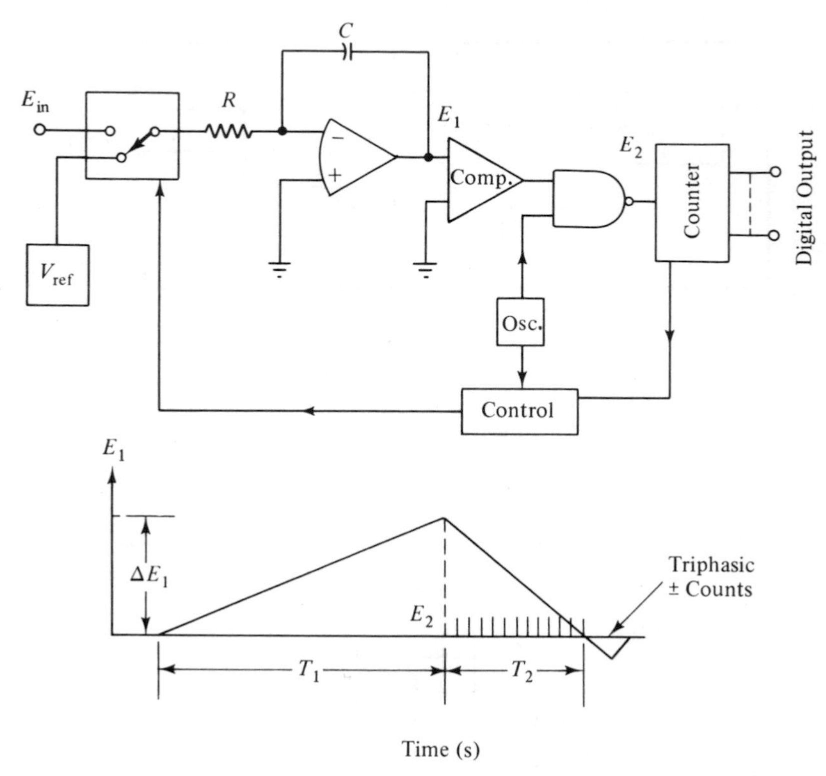

FIGURE 6–20. Dual Slope Conversion

$$\Delta E_1 = \frac{1}{RC} \cdot E_{in} \cdot T_{1_{constant}} \tag{6-5}$$

$$= \frac{1}{RC} \cdot V_{ref} \cdot T_{2_{variable}}$$

$$T_2 = \frac{E_{in} \cdot T_1}{V_{ref}} \tag{6-6}$$

input voltage. For triphasic conversion, integration proceeds below zero in the previous third portion and is then integrated back to zero in a final iteration. Dual-slope conversion is typically used for precision instrumentation applications such as digital voltmeters. However, since its conversion time is in the millisecond range utilization is restricted to low data rates.

Voltage-to-frequency A/D conversion has achieved some popularity as a low data rate method. Features include noise rejection comparable to other integrating-type converters and a simple mechanization (Figure 6–21). Economical source conversion with excellent SNR is possible with

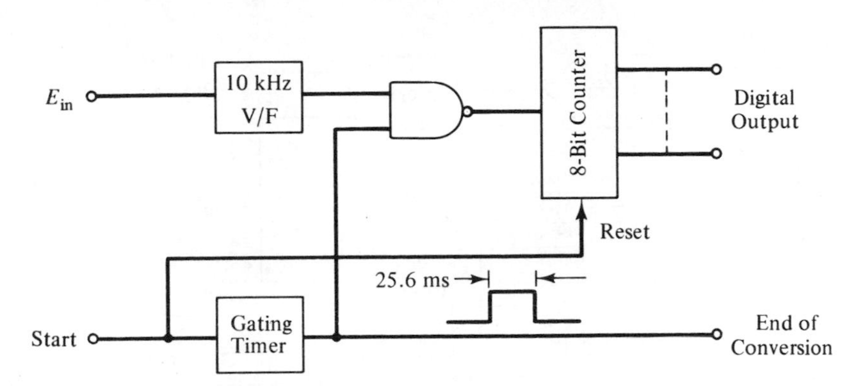

FIGURE 6–21. Voltage-to-Frequency A/D Conversion

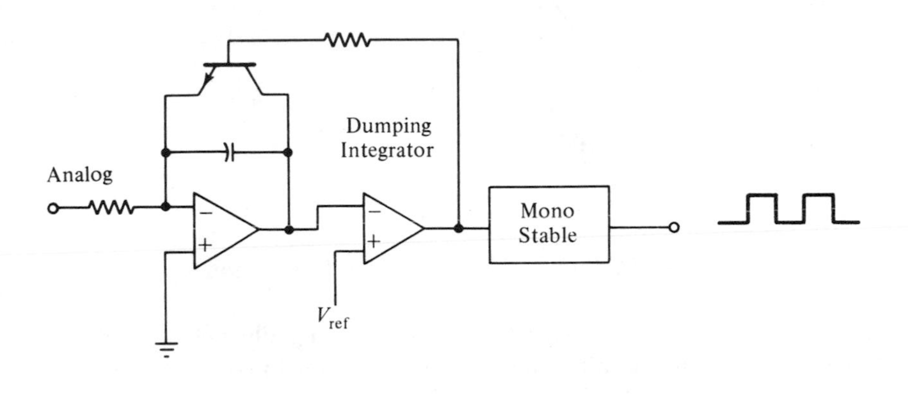

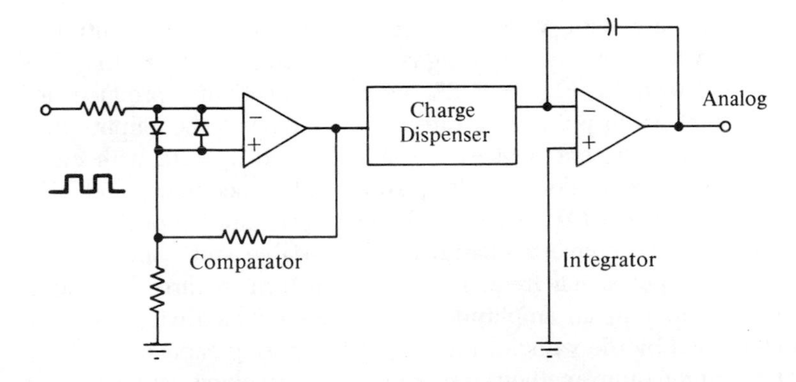

FIGURE 6–22. V/F and F/V Converters

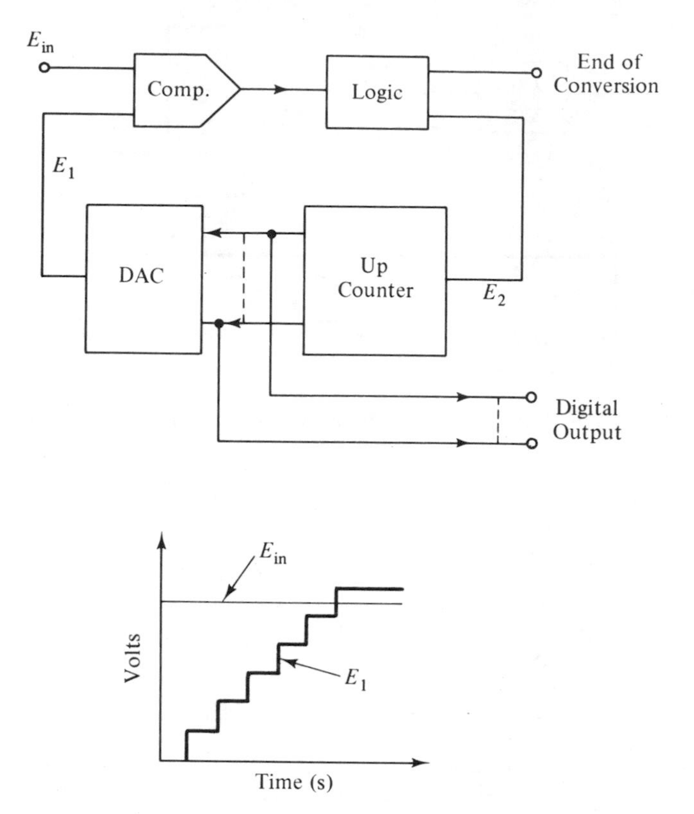

FIGURE 6–23. Counter Ramp Conversion

a V/F device located at each transducer and digitally multiplexed to a counter and gating circuit located at the computer to complete the A/D conversion. For the popular 10-kHz V/F converter, a 0.0256-s gating period is required for an 8-bit A/D conversion. No input sample-hold circuit is necessary with V/F A/D conversion, because the output is always the average of the input signal. Representative V/F and F/V circuits are shown by Figure 6–22, which, respectively, produce and accept constant-width pulses at a rate corresponding to the amplitude of the analog signal. Present devices are unipolar and operate with either positive or negative analog signals, provide 0.01% accuracy, and offer frequency outputs to 1 MHz with a 6-decade representation of the analog signal voltage. V/F converter bandwidth is variable and approximately equal to the output signal frequency which, in turn, is directly proportional to the input signal amplitude. F/V converter bandwidth is primarily determined by the value of the output integrating capacitor.

The counter ramp method, also known as a tracking converter, can form the basis of a low-cost A/D conversion system because it will track

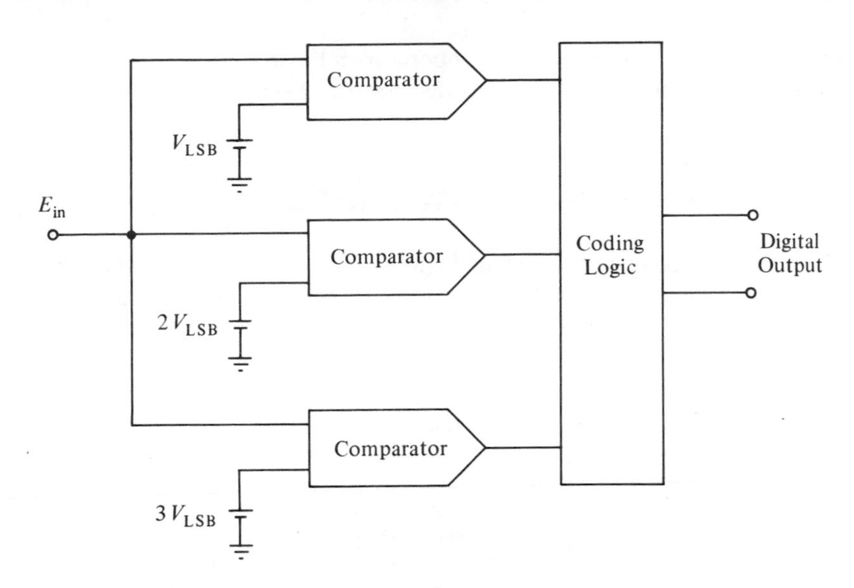

FIGURE 6–24. Two-Bit Parallel Conversion

varying input signals without the requirement for a sample-hold device (Figure 6–23). In operation its conversion time is variable and tracks the input signal at a rate up to 2^{-n} per count of the counter for an n-bit converter. For example, an 8-bit converter with an internal 10-MHz clock can track an input signal up to a $2^{-8}\cdot 10$ MHz or 40-kHz rate, with 256 counts per conversion. And since it is free-running a simple conversion system can be configured without a logic programmer. A variation of this converter is the servo type, in which an up-down counter replaces the up counter. This converter has the advantage of being able to follow small changes in the signal more rapidly than the up-counter version.

The parallel converter method, also known as the simultaneous or flash technique, is capable of 50-MHz conversion rates at 4 bits (Figure 6–24). This method employs an input quantizer composed of 2^n-1 comparators biased 1 LSB apart by a reference supply. The quantization process is accomplished in the switching time of the comparators; however, an output decoder is required to realize the binary output code of interest. The hybridized converter efficiently combines the parallel and successive approximation methods, trading off speed for additional resolution, and overcomes the parallel converter geometrical comparator increase with increasing bit length. The single slope converter is an austere mechanization requiring periodic calibration and is primarily employed in inexpensive digital panel meters. The charge balancing converter is similar in form to the dual-slope converter, but is not widely used. The Analogic AN8020L logarithmic A/D converter provides an efficient mechanization of a logarithmic operator followed by a 15-bit linear converter. The mechanization was discussed in Section 5-2.

6-7 CONTROL LOGIC AND INTERFACING

Modular data conversion system logic programmers provide the timing and control signals to coordinate the analog multiplexer with the sample-hold and A/D converter (Figure 6–25). Programmer inputs and outputs are typically TTL compatible and provide ready/busy control functions

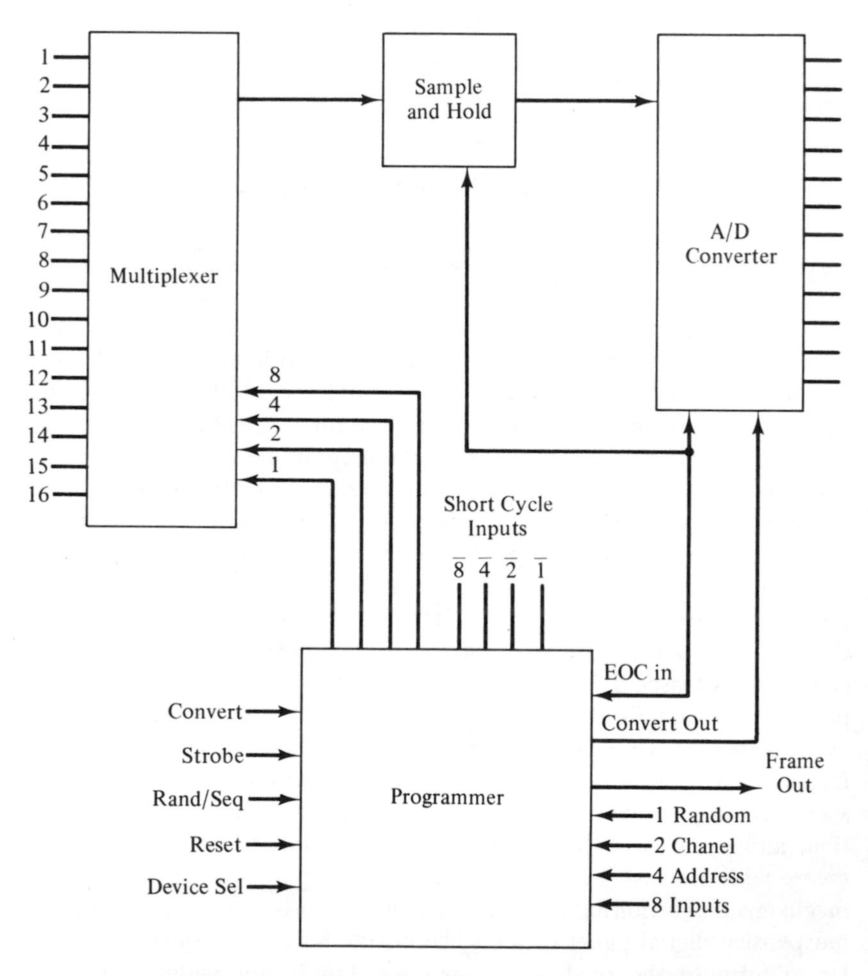

FIGURE 6–25. Subsystem Logic Programmer

with selectable random or sequential operation. Most programmers provide for up to 16 multiplexer channels, an A/D short cycle capability when less than the total available output bit length is required, plus a frame synchronization output for system expansion. A cycle is initiated with the device select input plus a strobe pulse, which allows either party line or computer bus operation. In sequential operation an internal counter increments automatically to select the next multiplexer input channel. Under random operation, specific channels can be accessed by an external discrete address.

Figure 6–26 describes a typical conversion cycle. First, the multiplexer switches channels and settles before the sample hold is commanded to acquire a new input signal. After receiving this command the sample hold is allowed to settle prior to initiating the A/D conversion. The programmer also accounts for the requirement of successive approximation converters to clear all registers before beginning a new conversion. Table 6–8 shows a representative data-conversion system timing budget with a maximum throughput speed of 21 μs, corresponding to a 48-kHz rate per channel. Equation (6-7) defines the maximum available sampling rate for a data-conversion system channel considering uniform sampling of each channel.

$$\text{channel sampling rate} = \frac{\text{conversion system throughput rate}}{\text{number of multiplexer channels}} \qquad (6\text{-}7)$$

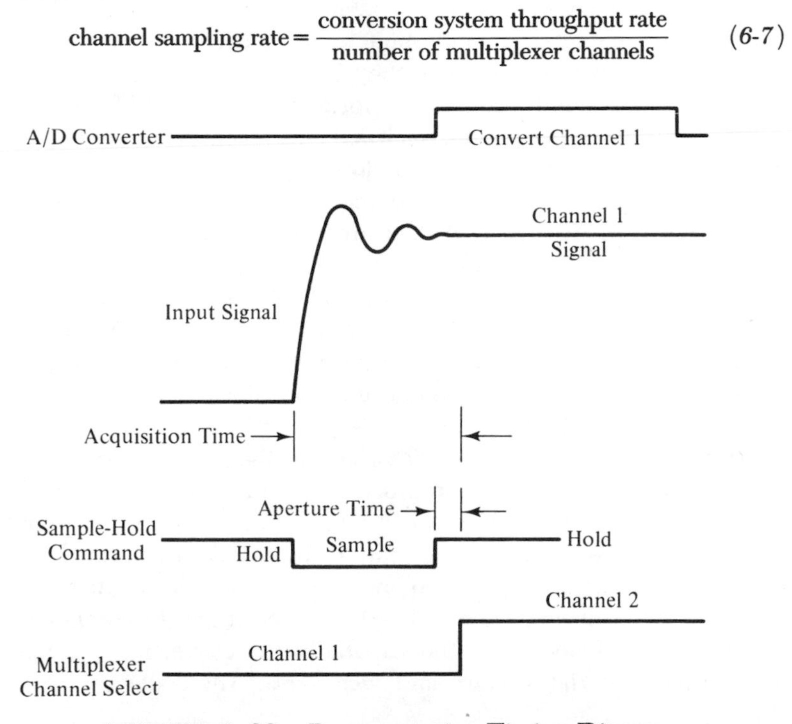

FIGURE 6–26. Representative Timing Diagram

TABLE 6–8. Representative Timing Budget

Parameter	Multiplexer (μs)	Sample-Hold (μs)	A/D (μs)
Settling	2	1	
Acquisition		8	
Conversion			10

Conversion system interfaces utilize one of three possible interrupt schemes for data transfer to the computer. Nonvectored interrupts halt the processor and institute a polling routine to identify which peripheral is to be serviced. However, if there are many interrupting devices, polling can be slow and inflexible. Vectored interrupts furnish an address to the interrupt handler to identify the interrupting peripheral. Both of these arrangements are under program control of software instructions. Direct memory access (DMA) is a third technique which transfers data directly to a memory location. Additional hardware is required, but speed is typically increased by one third. DMA controllers, such as the Intersil 6102 or Motorola 6840 devices, facilitate the implementation of this method for microcomputers.

Interface circuits are important components in minicomputer and microcomputer systems, because they handle functions the computer is not equipped to handle alone. Two formats are available for data transmission between a peripheral, such as a data-conversion system, and a computer input—remote serial and close-in parallel. For high data rates a data-conversion system should be located near the computer with a parallel interface. However, if data are gathered some distance away, a serial interface is indicated. Remote data-conversion systems can be interconnected by means of a universal asynchronous receiver/transmitter (UART). This device can communicate directly with most computers or another UART. Parallel microcomputer interfacing, on the other hand, is handled by programmable interface devices which provide for addressing, interrupts, and data transfer.

Programmable interface devices, such as the Motorola 6820 and Intel 8255, communicate with a microprocessor over an 8-bit bidirectional data bus and provide two bidirectional 8-bit inputs/outputs for peripheral equipment. These devices are intentionally flexible and provide various handshaking functions, plus two interrupt request lines. Asynchronous communications devices such as the Intersil 6402 and Motorola 6850 are also bidirectional and have the capability for converting parallel data formats into a serial stream, and vice versa. These devices also have

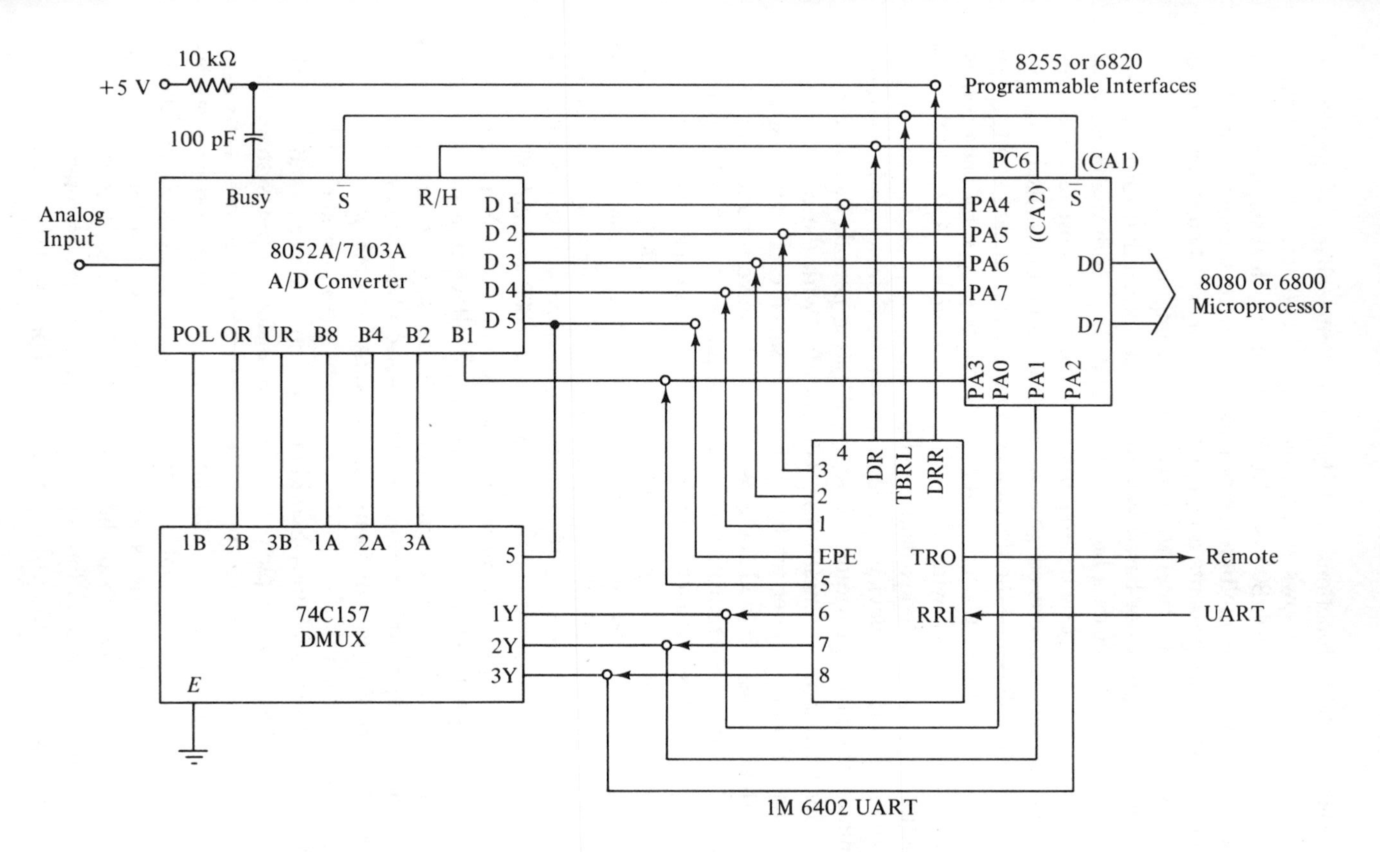

FIGURE 6–27. Microprocessor Parallel and Serial Interface

various selectable functions, including baud rate, character length, and parity. Figure 6–27 shows an example parallel and serial microcomputer interface. The Intersil 8052A/7103A monolithic dual-slope A/D converter and a digital multiplexer provide the correct control signals for both. Figure 6–28 presents a complete modular/PC board data conversion subsystem for the Intel 8080-based microcomputer.

For microprocessor-based systems, direct connection to the bidirectional microprocessor data bus with three-state byte-addressable logic will minimize interface circuitry requirements. Since the cost of a data-conversion system can exceed that of the microcomputer itself, there is considerable interest in the development of low-cost analog input/output methods. And if the microcomputer is to serve as part of the data-conversion system, such as with the voltage-to-frequency A/D method of Section 6-6, asynchronous data handling must be provided for. A programmable interface device can interface the V/F device and an external counter, the latter providing the required gating period. Two interrupts, one for each signal, complete the data transfer, with the resetting of an internal software counter totalizing the V/F signal each gating period.

An additional method is the use of a D/A converter and comparator to form a software-controlled successive approximation A/D converter. The D/A converter is accessed like a read-only memory which minimizes the conversion time, interface circuitry, and program length. In addition, the D/A converter can also serve as an analog output channel. The Burr Brown MP10/11 8-bit device is an example of such a nonmultiplexed, one-word data conversion system which can provide a single input and output analog channel for either the Motorola 6800 or Intel 8080 microprocessors (Figure 6–29). An external comparator controls a register that turns the required D/A converter bits on or off via the programmable interface device. The microprocessor software support requirement is accordingly simplified to essentially a sequence of decision points and is available from Burr Brown. Conversion time is about 900 μs.

A more versatile but costly approach is to use the MP 20/21 16-channel 8-bit thick-film hybrid analog input systems and the MP 10/11 devices as a complete two-channel analog output system. Since these devices are memory-mapped, microprocessors treat them as memory locations instead of accumulator input/output devices, and programmable interface devices are not required. Both of these devices are directly interfaced with the address and data busses and can be adapted to microprocessors other than the 8080 and 6800. The MP 20/21 also accepts eight differential low-level analog signals, has an internal instrumentation amplifier, and utilizes successive approximation conversion.

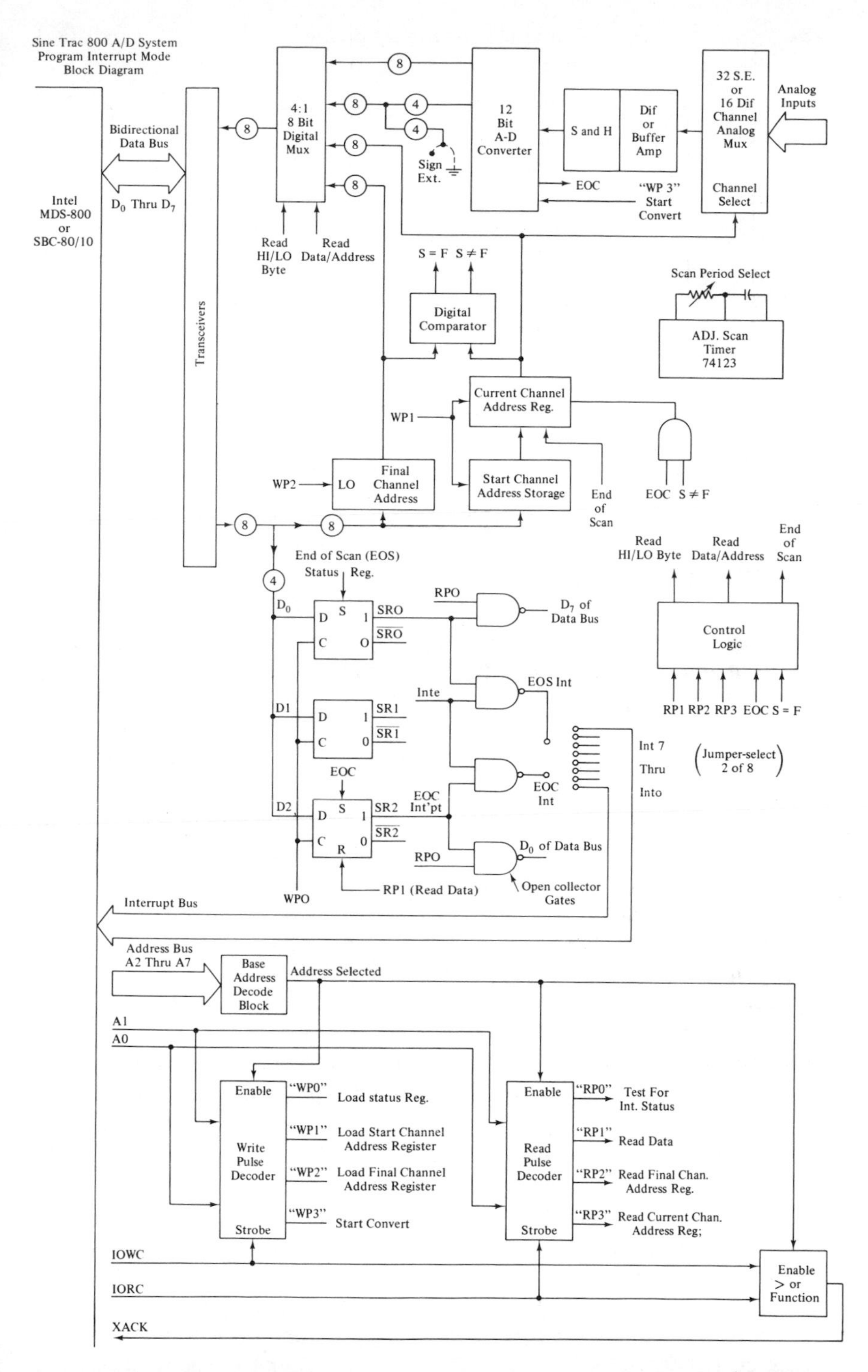

FIGURE 6–28. Modular PC/Board Data Conversion Subsystem (*Courtesy* Datel Systems)

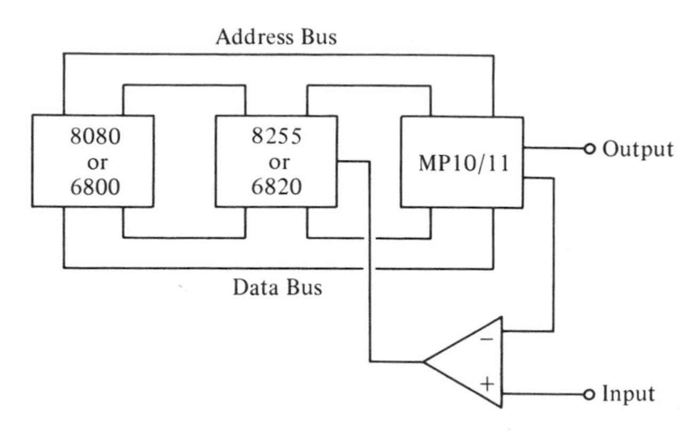

FIGURE 6–29. Single Channel Microprocessor Analog I/O

6-8 OUTPUT SIGNAL RECONSTRUCTION

Data distribution generally poses fewer problems than data acquisition, but the problems are of a different nature. Two output methods are available: digital distribution employing a D/A converter per channel, and analog distribution with a sample-hold per channel (Figure 6–30). Digital distribution using monolithic DACs provides higher performance at about the same cost as sample holds and is preferred to analog distribution for the following three reasons: (1) an indefinite hold without the need for input refreshing, (2) rapid updating with minimum settling time, and (3) minimization of analog offset and drift. Similarly, a serial data exchange receiver available from Analog Devices may be used as a self-multiplexed serial output distributor with up to six D/A converters (Figure 6–31). Its features include a standard 20-mA current loop, parity, handshaking functions, and transmission up to 2 miles at a 600-baud rate.

In signal recovery a sampling spectrum is created as a result of the computer update rate of the D/A converter. How closely the recovered signal approximates the original signal is determined by many factors: the A/D and D/A converter linearity and resolution, the sample rate, sample-hold aperture and feedthrough errors, the signal-to-noise ratio, and the characteristics of both the presampling and signal recovery filters. In the case of applications sensitive to envelope delay, a linear-phase recovery filter may be necessary to prevent phase distortion of the recovered signal. Further, the step transitions of the D/A converter output introduce harmonics which are not a part of the original analog signal.

Smoothing the discrete output steps to eliminate the harmonics requires a sharp-cutoff lowpass filter with a cutoff frequency above the signal spectrum but below the lowest repetitive harmonic component of

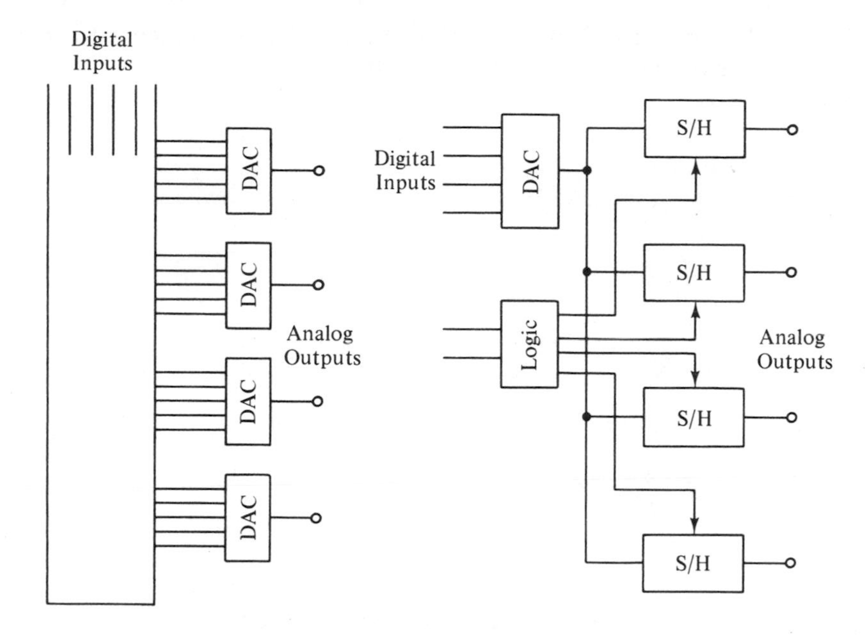

FIGURE 6–30. Data Distribution Options

the output sampling spectrum. Consequently, the specifications for the signal recovery filter may be approached in the same way as the presampling filter criteria developed in Chapter 4. The application of computer output digitized values to a D/A converter at an update rate of f_s results in the product of a frequency-dependent $\sin X/X$ function times the signal spectrum where $X = \pi \cdot f/f_s$. Therefore, passband signal attenuation

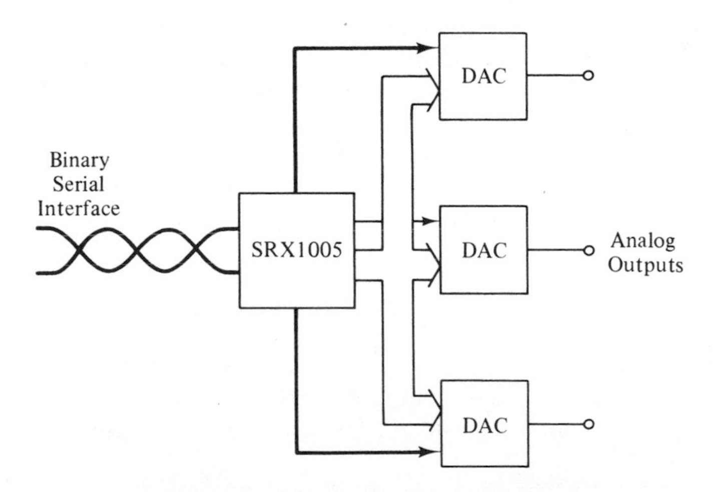

FIGURE 6–31. Serial Data Distribution

imposed by this $\sin X/X$ function should be evaluated. Insight into the origin of this response can be obtained with reference to Figure 6–15 for NRZ sampling.

By way of example, consider reconstruction of the signal used in the examples of Chapter 4 having a maximum signal frequency of 40 Hz and an update rate f_s of 160 Hz (Figure 6–32). This provides a $\sin X/X$

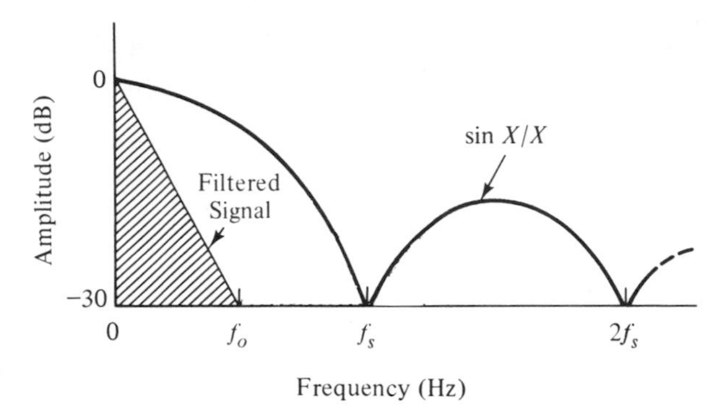

FIGURE 6–32. Signal Reconstruction Spectrum

amplitude attenuation at the maximum signal frequency of 0.9 dB from equation (6-8). At the output sampling spectrum folding frequency $f_o = f_s/2$, or $X = \pi/2$, the $\sin X/X$ attenuation is -4 dB. In order to prevent aliasing of the reconstructed signal, adequate overlap suppression of the output sampling spectrum must be provided at f_o. Even though the NRZ signal reconstruction method of updating the D/A converter has output nulls at f_s, the sidebands remain under the $\sin X/X$ envelope and can produce aliasing at f_o if not suppressed. Therefore, a six-pole Butterworth recovery filter with a 50-Hz cutoff frequency will result in a -30-dB output attenuation at f_o when the $\sin X/X$ attenuation is also considered (Figure 6–33). This choice of cutoff frequency also provides -0.1 dB at

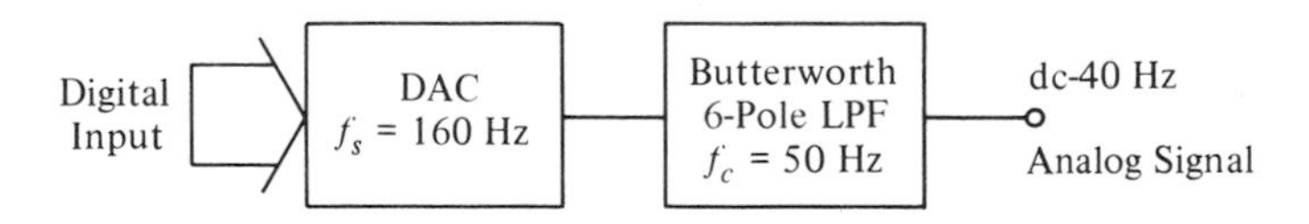

FIGURE 6–33. Signal Recovery Subsystem

40 Hz, which when summed with the $\sin X/X$ contribution provides a total of -1 dB at the maximum signal frequency. The filter design data and curves of Chapter 3 are useful for determining the specific mechani-

zation of the signal recovery filter.

$$\text{attenuation} = 20\log\left[\sin\left(\frac{\pi f}{f_s}\right)/\frac{\pi f}{f_s}\right] \qquad (6\text{-}8)$$

$$= 20\log\left[\sin\left(\frac{\pi}{4}\right)/\frac{\pi}{4}\right]$$

$$= 0.9 \text{ dB} \qquad \text{at } f = 40 \text{ Hz}$$

PROBLEMS

6-1 Characterize and block diagram two remote 8-bit source conversion data acquisition systems using the different approaches of V/F and direct A/D conversion. Identify the components required up to the computer interface if each method uses serial transmission and multiplexed digital channels, and justify your choice of the method which offers the highest performance/cost ratio.

6-2 A popular method for D/A conversion is the R-2R ladder technique shown in Figure 6-14. Operation of this network is based upon the binary division of current as it flows down the ladder. For a 4-bit version of this network consider the LSB ON and the other bits at common ground potential. Determine: (a) the fraction of V_{ref} across each resistor of the network, and (b) the left-right resistance at a point *X* immediately to the left of the center resistor *R*.

6-3 Design an 8-bit digital sample-hold circuit using an output holding register which requires 100 ns to change state. Determine: (a) the A/D converter best suited for this circuit, and (b) the highest signal frequency which can be sampled. Show a block diagram of this circuit.

6-4 A 1-bit A/D converter is required for a temperature controller which is implemented by a TTL-compatible 1-bit microprocessor in an appliance controller. The input is a DC 0-10 mV thermocouple signal, and the output a logic ONE for heater ON and a ZERO for heater OFF. Design an austere signal conditioning and conversion circuit showing scaling and component values, and include an adjustable temperature setpoint which determines the ONE-ZERO switching point. Show calculations for a 1 Hz signal, a preamp output SNR requirement of 100, an $f_s = 25$ Hz, and determine the minimum allowable input SNR.

6-5 Develop a building-block model of a circuit which provides an output frequency equal to the absolute difference between two input frequencies over a 10 kHz range, or $f_3 = |f_2 - f_1|$. Use V/F and F/V converters and show all required circuit elements including the voltage and frequency scaling at each point in the circuit.

6-6 A 3.3 MHz video signal has been digitized at a 10 MHz rate and is to be reconstructed using an 8-bit D/A converter operating at the same rate. Specify, but do not implement, a Butterworth reconstruction filter which results in not greater than a total of -3 dB attenuation over the output signal passband, and at least -30 dB at the output frequency spectrum folding frequency $f_o = f_s/2$. Sketch the output frequency spectrum.

REFERENCES

1. R. Allen, "A/D And D/A Converters: Bridging the Analog World to the Computer," *Electronic Design News*, February 5, 1973.
2. *Analog-Digital Conversion Handbook*, Analog Devices, Norwood, Mass. 02062, 1972.
3. B. M. Gordon, "The ABC's of A/D and D/A Converter Specifications," *Electronic Design News*, August 1972.
4. B. M. Gordon, "Digital Sampling and Recovery of Analog Signals," *Electronic Equipment Engineering*, May 1970.
5. D. F. Hoeschele, Jr., *Analog-to-Digital, Digital-to-Analog Conversion Techniques*, John Wiley, New York, 1968.
6. M. Lindheimer, "Guidelines for Digital-to-Analog Converter Applications," *Electronic Equipment Engineering*, September 1970.
7. L. Solomon and E. Ross, "Educating Dumb Data Acquisition Subsystems," *Digital Design*, November 1976.
8. D. Stantucci, "Data Acquisition Can Falter Unless Components Are Well Understood," *Electronics*, November 13, 1975.
9. D. Stantucci, "Maneuvering for Top Speed and High Accuracy in Data Acquisition," *Electronics*, November 27, 1975.
10. G. E. Tobey, "Ease Multiplexing and A/D Conversion," *Electronic Design*, April 12, 1973.
11. E. Zuch, "Consider V/F Converters," *Electronic Design*, November 22, 1976.

7

SIGNAL TRANSMISSION METHODS

7-0 INTRODUCTION

The transmission of data between instrumentation, control and remote data-acquisition or distribution systems and computers is a frequent requirement. Both analog and digital signals are encountered, and it is of interest to preserve their accuracy over the transmission link to at least the quality possessed at the sending end. Industrial locations where data acquisition and process control systems are commonplace usually present a difficult interference environment. Therefore, some design effort is required to ensure data-transmission integrity. This leads to the application of specific transmission methods depending upon the signal type, transmission link, and distance involved.

A primary concern is maintaining the signal-to-noise ratio over the transmission link at a level to preserve the required accuracy of the signal. Another factor essential to digital transmission is minimizing intersymbol interference which results in signal derogation and reduction of the useful transmission distance. And there are many competing trade-offs. For example, SNR can be improved with wideband FM or PCM (pulse-code modulation) methods. However, for the frequently used voice-grade telephone channel, such methods are precluded, because of the 3.2-kHz bandwidth restriction. This chapter presents seven signal-transmission methods for analog and digital signals which are tabulated in Table 7–1, and provides a development of their implementation and an analysis of their performance.

TABLE 7–1. Signal Transmission Methods

Method	Format	Distance	Speed	Qualification
Direct wire	Analog voltage	100 ft	1 MHz	Limited utility
Voltage–Current converters	Analog current	1000 ft	10 kHz	Process control standard
V/F–F/V converters	Encoded analog	5000 ft	Variable	Assumes line drivers
Balanced line drivers	Baseband digital	5000 ft	600 bps	Inexpensive digital method
Frequency shift keying	Audio tones	50,000 ft	1200 bps	Limited-distance MODEM
Phase shift keying	Phase modulation	Telephone system	2400 bps	Line conditioning required
Radio	FSK	10 miles	300 bps	11-meter band

7-1 ANALOG TRANSMISSION

When it is required to send an analog signal for some distance, transmitting a current replica of the signal is advantageous for two reasons. First, resistive line-drop problems are eliminated as a source of error since current is identical at all points in a series circuit. Second, the receiving-end termination is normally a low impedance, which minimizes the development of noise at the output due to induced interference on the line. A Norton equivalent network is described by Figure 7–1, whereby

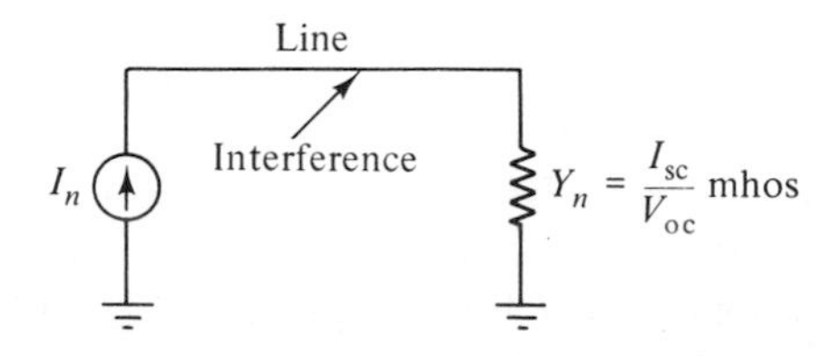

FIGURE 7–1. Norton Equivalent Network

the terminating admittance Y_N is determined by the short-circuit current to open-circuit voltage ratio.

Practical voltage and current converter circuits are shown by Figure 7–2. They satisfy the Norton equivalent network requirements, including the ability to short-circuit the current-source output without altering its linearity or tracking. The current-source output may be terminated in any resistance between 0 and 250 Ω without degradation of accuracy. And the use of operational amplifiers provides stable and accurate conversion, owing to their high open-loop gain. The voltage-converter output amplifier must be capable of delivering 20 mA, which can be met, for example, by the Burr Brown 3268/14 device. Note that the transmission speed for this method is not restricted by the bandwidth of the line. Instead, the closed-loop gain of the operational amplifiers result in a bandwidth typically on the order of 10 kHz, which is usually adequate for instrumentation applications. Practical transmission distances in an industrial environment are limited to a thousand feet or so, depending upon the severity of the interference. For direct-wire transmission of analog volt-

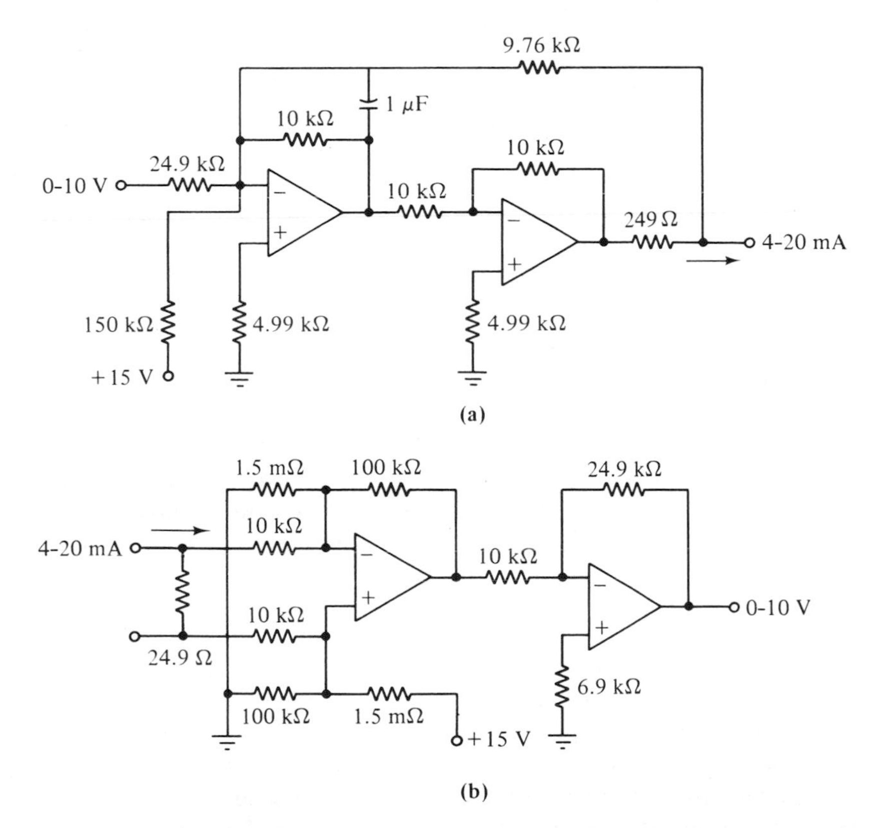

FIGURE 7–2. Voltage and Current Converters

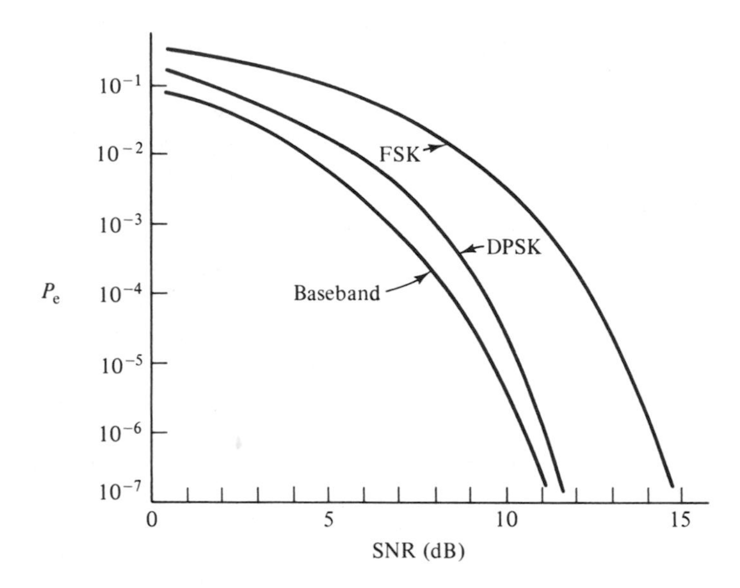

FIGURE 7–3. Error Probabilities for Digital Detection (*Courtesy* McGraw Hill Book Co.)

ages, however, the range is limited to about 100 ft. Shielded cable is beneficial for both methods. The advantage of digital encoding and transmission is the substantially reduced SNR requirement for binary detection in comparison with analog signal estimation. Figure 7–3 presents a comparison of frequently applied digital transmission methods in terms of the probability of detection error versus SNR.

7-2 DIGITAL TRANSMISSION

Although highly efficient and virtually errorless data transmission is possible, the majority of applications simply do not warrant the cost and complexity demanded by a near-ideal communication system. Consequently, the design of a practical signal transmission system is usually simpler and based on two requirements: (1) the required bandwidth or data rate, and (2) the necessary transmission quality or allowable error. Just as analog signals have a wide range of bandwidths, digital signals have a wide range of bit rates. Baud rate refers to the maximum allowable bit rate over a transmission link for a specified error rate. Unlike signaling speed, the specification of an acceptable error rate is often arbitrary. Nevertheless, error rates on the order of 10^{-4} are suitable for many applications and typical for MODEMs (modulators/demodulators) operating over voice-grade telephone lines. Savings can be realized by not employing a more complex signal transmission method than is actually required (Table 7–1). This section develops the characteristics of the frequently used baseband digital transmission method.

Except for the 20-mA Teletype current loop and the Electronic Industries Association RS232C and RS422 electrical standards, no standard computer interfacing method exists other than the specialized Hewlett-Packard bus, which is gaining wider acceptance. RS232C and the newer RS422 are for serial binary-data interfaces. They do not define the coding to be transmitted across the interface, although seven-level ASCII is commonly used. An ASCII transmission pattern for the letter U is shown in Figure 7–4. These standards are primarily intended for TTL levels and are summarized in Table 7–2. Table 7–3 presents the full ASCII character set.

Differential line drivers and receivers, such as the Fairchild 55109 and 55107A devices, will accommodate common-mode noise up to ±3 V when used with balanced and properly terminated transmission lines. A 62-Ω resistor in each leg of Figure 7–5, for example, will terminate a 125-Ω impedance twisted pair. This allows a high data rate because line reflections are virtually eliminated. Data are impressed on a balanced line by unbalancing the line voltage with driver current. Line-sharing systems conserve wiring costs by using the party-line technique. The strobe feature of the line receiver and inhibit of the driver permit either data-bus or party-line operation over a single twisted-pair line.

Transmission lines do not have to be perfectly terminated at both ends. However, the signal impressed on the line will reflect back and forth between line terminations in an imperfectly terminated system until it reaches the final dc value. Signal rise time also increases with distance, as suggested by Figure 7–6, because high-frequency components are

TABLE 7–2.

	RS232C		RS422	
Parameter	**Driver**	**Receiver**	**Driver**	**Receiver**
ONE signal	− 5 V min − 15 V max	−3 V max threshold	A negative	A<B
ZERO signal	+ 5 V min + 15 V max	+3 V max threshold	B positive	A>B
Impedances	Unspecified	3 kΩ min input 7 kΩ max input	<100Ω balanced	>4 kΩ
Maximum levels	±500 mA	±25 V max	150 mA	6 V max
Data rate	0–20 k bits	Unspecified	10 M baud	Unspecified

TABLE 7–3. ASCII Character Set

Binary Code				b_7	0	0	0	0	1	1	1	1
				b_6	0	0	1	1	0	0	1	1
				b_5	0	1	0	1	0	1	0	1
b_4	b_3	b_2	b_1		Nonprintable		Printable Characters					
0	0	0	0		NUL	DLE	SPACE	0	@	P	\	p
0	0	0	1		SOH	DC1	!	1	A	Q	a	q
0	0	1	0		STX	DC2	//	2	B	R	b	r
0	0	1	1		ETX	DC3	#	3	C	S	c	s
0	1	0	0		EOT	DC4	$	4	D	T	d	t
0	1	0	1		ENQ	NAK	%	5	E	U	e	u
0	1	1	0		ACK	SYN	&	6	F	V	f	v
0	1	1	1		BEL	ETB	/	7	G	W	g	w
1	0	0	0		BS	CAN	(	8	H	X	h	x
1	0	0	1		HT	EM	)	9	I	Y	i	y
1	0	1	0		LF	SUB	*	:	J	Z	j	z
1	0	1	1		VT	ESC	+	;	K	[	k	{
1	1	0	0		FF	FS	,	<	L	\	l	:
1	1	0	1		CR	GS	—	=	M	]	m	}
1	1	1	0		SO	RS	.	>	N	∧	n	~
1	1	1	1		SI	US	/	?	O	—	o	DEL

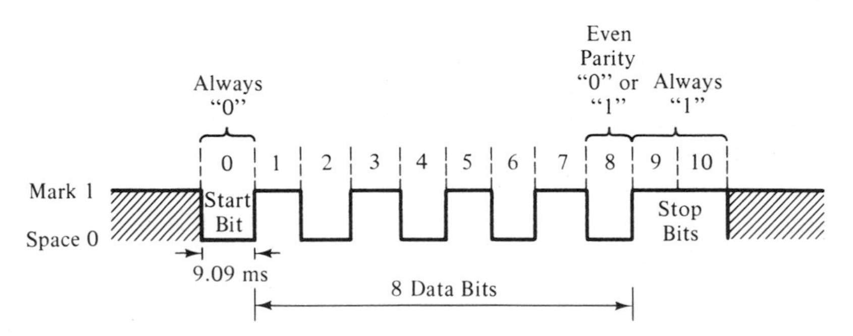

FIGURE 7–4. ASCII Transmission Pattern for Letter U

attenuated and delayed more than low-frequency components. This distortion results in a timing uncertainty in the recovered signal which ultimately limits the transmission distance for a given data rate. Conversely, the data rate must decline for increasing distance. Figure 7–7 describes this uncertainty for a line receiver threshold halfway between the ZERO and ONE logic levels.

The utility of this characterization is that it permits the transmission distance, line bandwidth, signaling rate, and error considerations to be

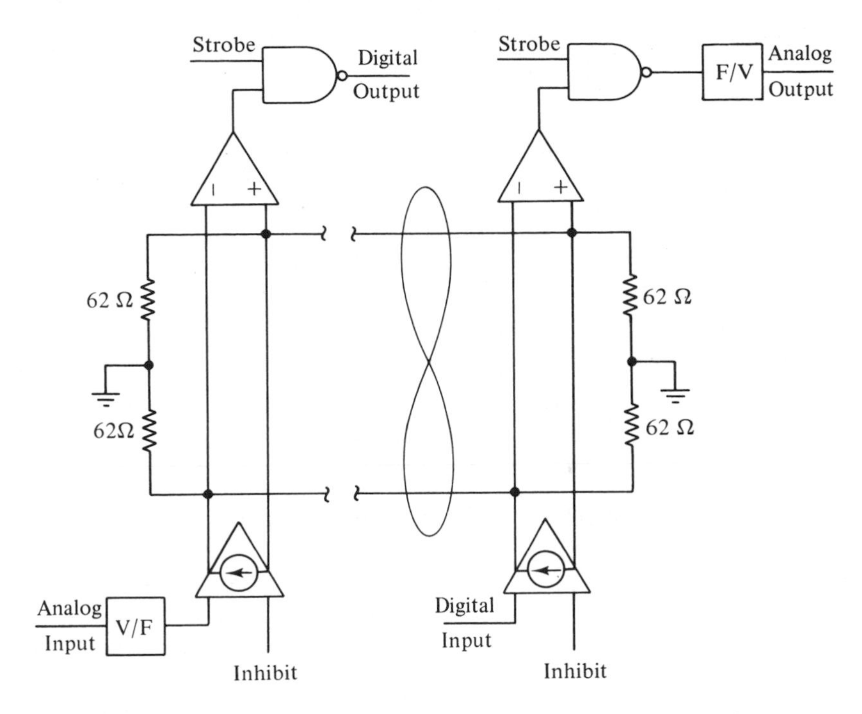

FIGURE 7–5. Balanced Line Transmission

formally characterized for baseband digital networks. It should be evident from Figure 7–3 that the baseband detection SNR requirement is sufficiently modest that it is not the primary distance limitation. Instead, bit-position timing uncertainty will ultimately result in pulse overlapping, or intersymbol interference, at the receiver and worsening of the error rate.

As the bit rise time t_r, defined as the interval required for the pulse amplitude to increase from 10 to 90%, increases with transmission dis-

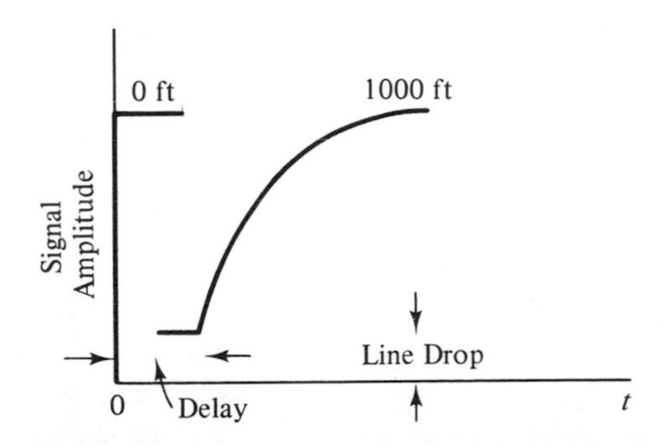

FIGURE 7–6. Line Receiver Input

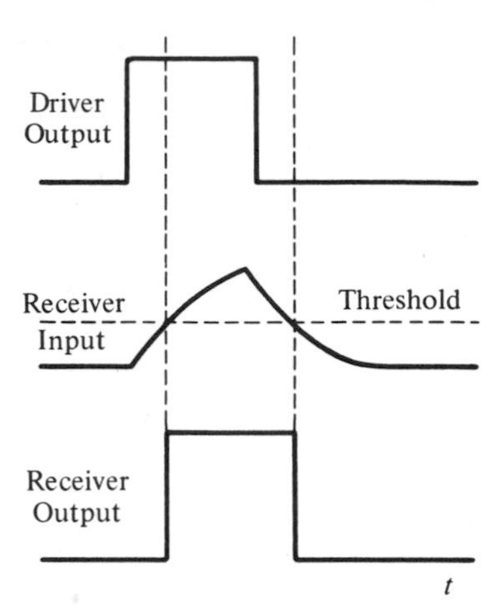

FIGURE 7–7. Bit Timing Uncertainty

tance, intersymbol interference also increases. Bit rise time is an inverse function of the 3-dB bandwidth of the lowpass-modeled transmission line expressed by equation (7-1). This bandwidth (BW) decreases with increasing distance as a result of cumulative shunt capacitance and series line inductance. In addition, the Nyquist rate R defines the maximum allowable signaling rate for minimum intersymbol interference in terms of the same line bandwidth. Consequently, the bandwidth associated with a given line length defines the allowable bit rate for minimum error by equation (7-2). For example, a 1-kHz bandwidth line determined from a receiving-end rise-time measurement of 500 μs will support a maximum signaling rate of 2 kbits/s. This analysis assumes a standard 50% bit duty cycle.

$$t_r \geqslant \frac{1}{2\text{BW}} \quad \text{seconds} \tag{7-1}$$

$$R \leqslant 2\text{BW} \quad \text{bits per second} \tag{7-2}$$

$$t_r \leqslant \frac{1}{R} \quad \text{seconds} \tag{7-3}$$

With the use of line drivers and twisted-pair lines, low data-rate baseband binary signals can be transmitted over several miles of wire. For instance, speeds up to 600 bits/s can normally be transmitted over 5000 ft of No. 22 AWG twisted pair without excessive intersymbol interference. However, higher data rates suffer reduced range with 2400 kbits/s limited to a few hundred feet typically. If line drivers and receivers cannot meet a distance requirement, the next consideration is the limited-distance MODEM. These are usually frequency-shift-keyed devices and are less costly than conventional telephone-line MODEMs. Limited-distance MODEMs can meet the needs of all but the more demanding high-data-rate, long-haul transmission tasks.

7-3 MODEMS

The transmission of digital data over distances greater than about 1 mile using a dedicated line or telephone trunk requires additional system complexity to overcome the previous distance-limiting factors. The MODEM provides a solution to these limitations by encoding the digital data and modulating it by a method suitable for efficient transmission over the available bandwidth of the specific transmission link. Since most wire links are essentially narrowband, the MODEM cannot achieve an SNR improvement by taking advantage of wideband FM or PCM modulation methods which exchange bandwidth for SNR enhancement. For transmission over private lines or voice-grade telephone trunks, however, SNR is normally not the limiting factor as with radio or satellite communication links. Consequently, narrowband modulation methods are used such as FSK and PSK, but with their signal set and detector designed to take advantage of detection rather than estimation SNR requirements.

MODEMs handle data in two ways: in spurts and in continuous streams referred to as asynchronous and synchronous operation, respectively. Asynchronous transmission is advantageous for handling irregular data rates. However, transmission efficiency is low. Synchronous transmission offers higher line efficiency, but equipment costs are correspondingly higher because of the more complex circuitry required. We will be concerned in this section with both limited-distance and conventional telephone MODEMs, which are available for handling data in both of the ways described above.

Most MODEMs transmit in serial fashion and operate in one of three transmission modes—simplex, half duplex, and full duplex. The simplex mode provides unidirectional transmission only or reception only. In the half-duplex mode, transmission can occur in either direction but not simultaneously. This is the most commonly used mode and requires a single wire pair. Full duplex operation permits simultaneous transmission and reception and generally requires two wire pairs. Almost all commercial MODEMs are interfaced in accordance with the EAI RS232C standard. Diagnostic capabilities vary from device to device, but usually include at least a local loop-back test, which returns the transmitter output back to the receiver to check for errors.

The transmission quality of a data link is usually expressed as the bit error rate, which is the probability of a received bit being in error.

Designing for a specific bit error rate may be inadequate, however, because transmission errors are primarily caused by noise bursts lasting from 1 to 50 ms rather than occurring at random. Work performed by the Bell System has shown that the burst error rate is about one tenth of the bit error rate over voice-grade lines, and that both errors can be reduced with the use of error control systems.

Most error control systems use a single method of correction. The commonest is automatic request for repetition (ARQ), in which the detection of an error in a received message causes retransmission. A typical MODEM data block, including check bits and termination characters to facilitate error detection, is shown by Figure 7–8. Less common

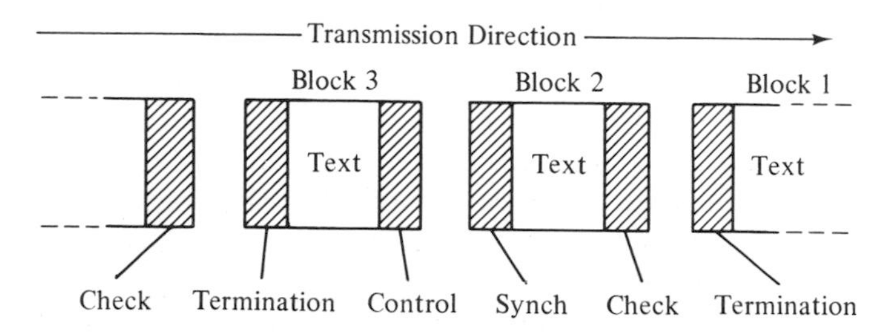

FIGURE 7–8. Encoded Data Block

and requiring more check bits is forward error control (FEC). Sufficient redundancy is built into this code structure to allow accurate message reconstruction at the receiver without retransmission. More complex algebraic codes differ from block codes by interleaving check digits in the coded bit stream. A well-designed Fire code (named for its developer) can correct an error burst 50 bits wide by adding 100 check bits. A factor of 10 improvement in error rate is common from inclusion of an error control system, thereby reducing a typical 10^{-4} bit error rate to 10^{-5} on the average.

A basic MODEM is shown by the block diagram of Figure 7–9. Higher-speed telephone MODEMs generally include voice-grade line conditioning filters, sometimes termed "mop-up" filters, to compensate for attenuation and envelope delay distortion encountered in the telephone network (Figure 7–10). Attenuation distortion results from the signal being attenuated by different amounts as the frequency of the signal changes. Envelope delay occurs because the amount of signal time delay varies with its frequency. This results because the leading or trailing edge of a bit contains high-frequency information, which is subjected to a different delay than the low-frequency content of the top of the bit. And regardless of the modulation scheme used by the MODEM, digital signals

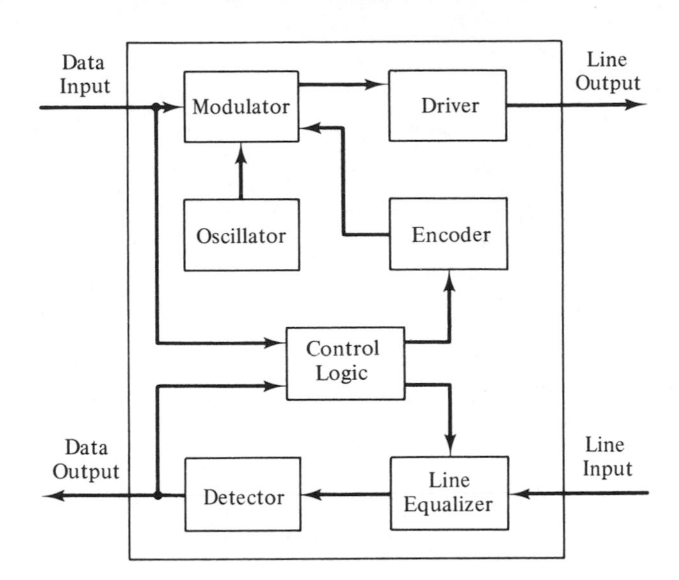

FIGURE 7–9. MODEM Diagram

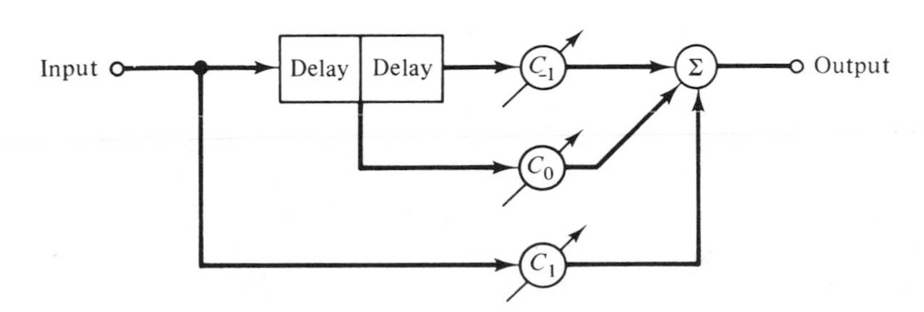

FIGURE 7–10. Transversal Equalizing Filter

result in being transmitted as pulses of one form or another. Attenuation and envelope delay distortion increase intersymbol interference and interfere with accurate detection.

MODEM line-conditioning filters compensate for these distortions frequently by means of a simple transversal digital filter. In operation, a loop-back test is initiated and the filter coefficient tap gains automatically servoed by searching for the point of minimum intersymbol interference (Figure 7–10). These filters may contain as few as three taps and are all-pass networks which vary the phase shift across the filter passband.

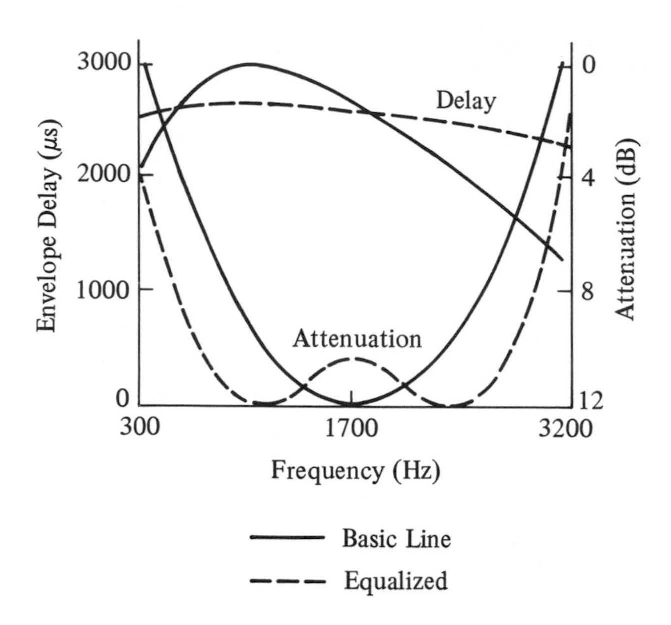

FIGURE 7–11. Line Equalization

Subscribers can also order conditioned voice-grade lines from the telephone company under two tariff specifications: C-conditioning, which minimizes attenuation and envelope-delay distortion and ensures a minimum SNR of 24dB, and D-conditioning, which increases the SNR to 28dB and reduces network harmonic distortion, which is essential for 9600-bit/s transmission. The generally accepted limit for dial-up unconditioned lines is 1200 bits/s.

Limited-distance MODEMs normally employ FSK modulation and operate asynchronously in either the half-duplex or full-duplex modes. They are also usable on voice-grade telephone lines if no induction coils are encountered in the link. The FSK MODEM converts binary signals into two discrete audio tones, one corresponding to a logical ONE and the other to a logical ZERO. These frequencies are typically placed between 1 kHz and 3 kHz symmetrically disposed about a carrier frequency, which is frequently at 1700 Hz. The Motorola MC6860 device shown in Figure 7–12, for example, provides about half of the functions necessary to construct a noncoherent FSK MODEM in a single integrated circuit. It includes a modulator, which transmits eight-step synthesized sine waves, a detector, and supervisory functions. Bandpass filters are used on Transmit to eliminate harmonics, and on Receive to enhance the signal-to-noise

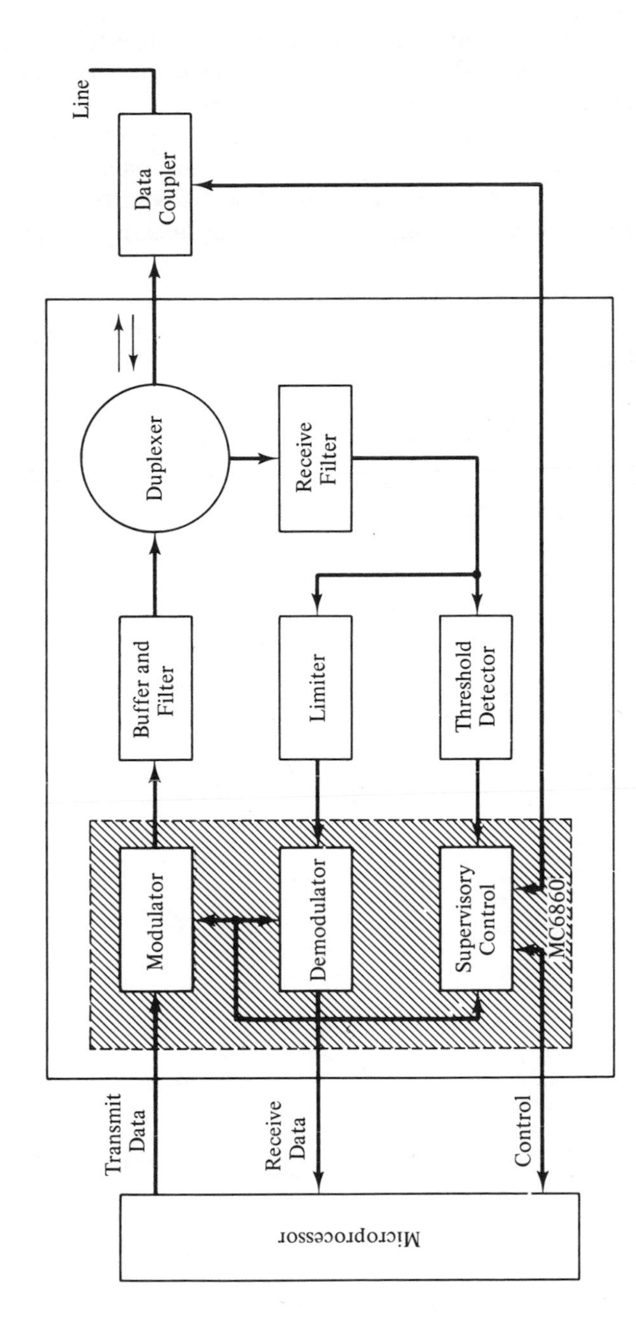

FIGURE 7–12. FSK MODEM Block Diagram (*Courtesy* Motorola Incorporated)

ratio. Linear phase or group delay in the filter passbands is essential, however, because unequal delay of the data frequencies is equivalent to signal distortion and can result in detection errors. Filter group delay is defined by equation (7-4) with an acceptable value typically being 1 ms across the signal spectrum. This will minimize intersymbol interference insofar as the filter contribution. A combination six-pole Bessel lowpass plus six-pole Bessel highpass design can satisfy this linearity requirement. With some design ingenuity a single filter can be switched between the transmit and receive modes. The required filter passband is determined from the spectral occupancy requirements of the specific signal set indicated by Figure 7–13.

$$t_d = \frac{\Delta\phi}{\Delta F} \cdot \frac{1}{360°/\text{cycle}} \text{ seconds} \qquad (7\text{-}4)$$

where $\Delta\phi$ = change in phase degrees
ΔF = change in frequency Hertz

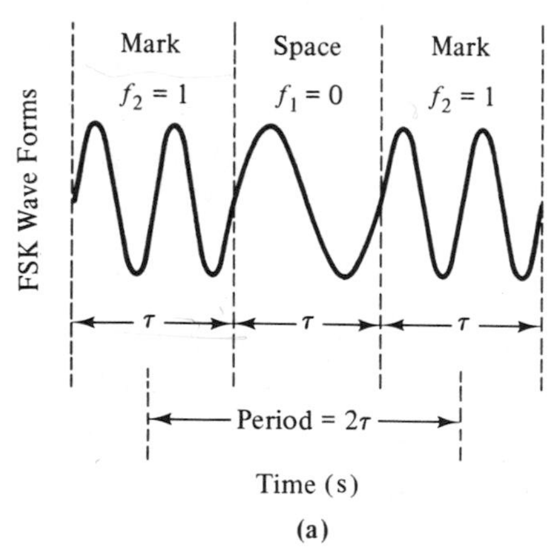

(a)

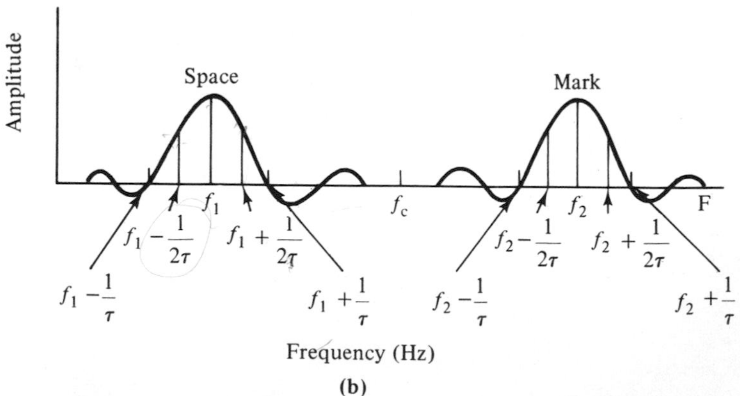

(b)

FIGURE 7–13. FSK Time and Frequency Domain Signal Set

Advantages of FSK modulation include an error rate that is essentially independent of signal amplitude, equal per-digit error probabilities for a ONE and ZERO, and simple noncoherent detection without need to process the carrier signal. Intersymbol interference of the $\sin \pi f\tau / \pi f\tau$ signal envelopes shown by Figure 7–13 primarily limits the ultimate transmission distance over wire links. This occurs because of two mechanisms. First, the contracting bandwidth of extended lines forces a widening of the recovered pulse rise time and ultimately results in overlap and detection errors. Second, over long-line telephone links, frequency-domain multiplexing can produce cumulative frequency offset errors. For example, a 1100-Hz FSK ONE signal may be shifted to 1.1.2 kHz and back to 1090 Hz due to heterodyne frequency drift. An accumulation of these errors, of course, will result in the signal being substantially offset from its recovery bandpass filter. The bandwidth required for transmission of FSK signals is that spectrum above and below the carrier of $2\Delta f + 2/\tau$ Hz.

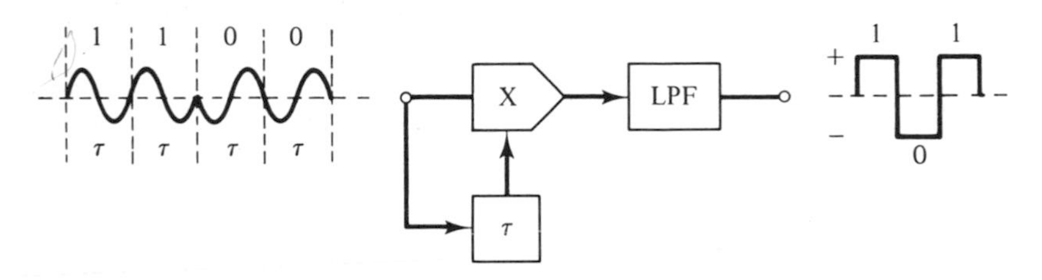

FIGURE 7–14. DPSK Autocorrelator Detector

Phase-shift-keyed modulation involves the transmission of a sinusoidal signal with a phase of 0 degrees for binary ONE and 180 degrees for binary ZERO. A clever technique known as differentially coherent PSK (DPSK) has been devised to get around the synchronization problems required for coherent detection. This is described by the autocorrelation detector of Figure 7–14 in which the fixed delay-line interval τ is chosen to exactly equal the PSK bit spacing. Consequently, if adjacent

TABLE 7–4. DPSK Format

Binary input		1		0		1	
Encoded message	1		1		0		0
Transmitted phase	0		0		π		π
Detector output		+		−		+	
Binary output		1		0		1	

received bits are of like phase, their product results in a positive output or binary ONE, and if of unlike phase a binary ZERO. Since it is the shift between transmitted bits which represents the message information, differential coding is required at the transmitter with an arbitrary first digit. Table 7–4 summarizes this format. DPSK offers a 3-dB SNR advantage over FSK at an error rate of 10^{-4} (Figure 7–3). A disadvantage is that due to the fixed-delay τ associated with the detector, DPSK is committed to synchronous signaling speeds.

7-4 RADIO DATA LINK

An occasional application arises for transmitting digital data over an analog radio link. The principal difference between a radio link and the previously considered wire links is the generally poorer SNR conditions for radio transmission. This is due to both signal power limitations and the manifold noise and interference sources. Therefore, transmission performance over a radio link is found to be primarily dependent upon the received SNR and some additional uncertainties associated with the message error rate which are attributable to propagation anomalies. Nevertheless, a radio system can be adequately characterized and designed to provide a required data rate with reasonable confidence in its error rate. Such an example is developed in this section.

Higher SNR is required to maintain a given error probability with an increasing signaling rate. This is a major trade-off which exists for digital communications systems. Noncoherent FSK is frequently used for digital transmission over narrowband radio links. Its error probability is described in terms of receiver output SNR_o by equation (7-5). This equation assumes optimum detection involving matched filtering of the signal and the output SNR_o is related to the receiver input SNR_i by equation (7-6). However, the matched filter can be closely approximated in practice, for example, with a phase-locked loop device. Table 7–5 presents a tabulation of baud rate versus SNR requirements for error probabilities ranging between minimum and maximum useful values. Note that higher signaling

TABLE 7–5. Signaling Rate Versus SNR

Baud Rate	P_ϵ	SNR_o		B_n/B_s	SNR_i	
300 (bps)	10^{-2}	7.8	8.9dB	33.3	0.23	−6.3 dB
	10^{-4}	17.0	12.3	33.3	0.51	−2.9
600	10^{-2}	7.8	8.9	16.6	0.47	−3.3
	10^{-4}	17.0	12.3	16.6	1.02	+0.1

rates require correspondingly wider postdetection signal bandwidths and result in higher SNR_i requirements because of the reduced receiver processing gain.

In determining the minimum postdetection signal bandwidth B_s, FSK can be recovered from the first sidebands on either side of the center frequency of the $\sin \pi f \tau / \pi f \tau$ functions representing the mark and space data in the frequency domain. Therefore, for a 300-bps data rate, the first sidebands occur at ± 150 Hz on either side of the $\sin \pi f \tau / \pi f \tau$ center, frequencies, yielding a minimum postdetection signal bandwidth of 300 Hz. Figure 6–15 provides a description of the location of the sidebands for a $\sin \pi f \tau / \pi f \tau$ function. And with the typical receiver front-end bandwidth B_n in narrowband service about 10 kHz, the available receiver processing gain can be readily determined from these parameters by equation (7-6).

$$P_\epsilon = \frac{1}{2} \exp\left(-\frac{SNR_o}{2} \right)$$

$$= \frac{1}{2} \exp\left(-\frac{SNR_i \cdot B_n}{2B_s} \right)$$

$$= \frac{1}{2} \exp\left(-\frac{V_s^2 \cdot B_n}{2V_n^2 B_s} \right) \qquad (7\text{-}5)$$

$$\text{receiver processing gain} = \frac{SNR_o}{SNR_i} = \frac{B_n}{B_s} \qquad (7\text{-}6)$$

where V_s = receiver input RMS signal level
V_n = receiver input RMS noise level
B_n = receiver front-end bandwidth
B_s = postdetection signal bandwidth

A noncoherent FSK signal set can be generated with a voltage-controlled oscillator (VCO) and optimally detected by a phase-locked loop tone decoder such as the Exar 2207 and 567 devices. These devices can be connected to the audio input and output of a radio transceiver for half-duplex operation. An example system is designed around these components, a qualitative analysis of phase-locked loop operation presented, and an evaluation of the performance of the radio link developed. The mark and space frequencies are chosen as 3 kHz and 1 kHz, respectively, and FSK generator circuit values accordingly calculated. Figure 7–15 presents an overall diagram of this system, including a phase-locked loop demodulator circuit designed to capture the mark signal.

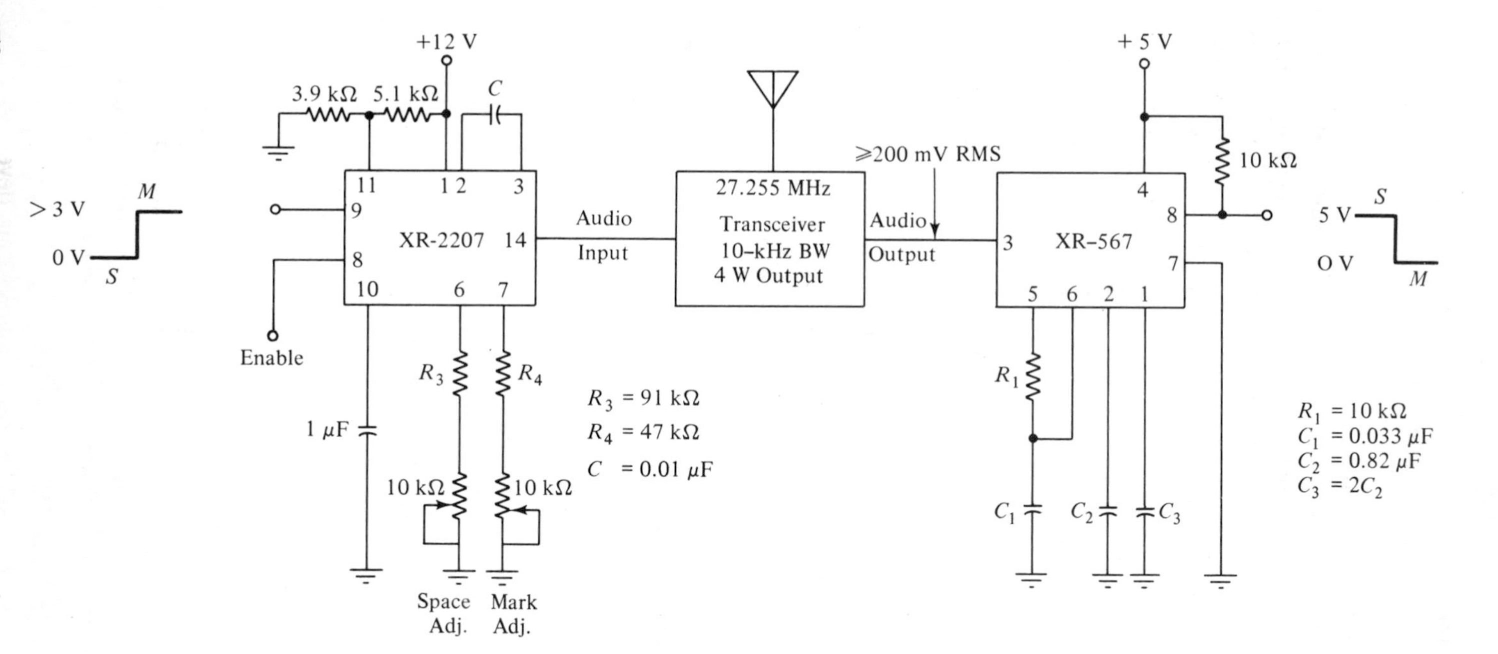

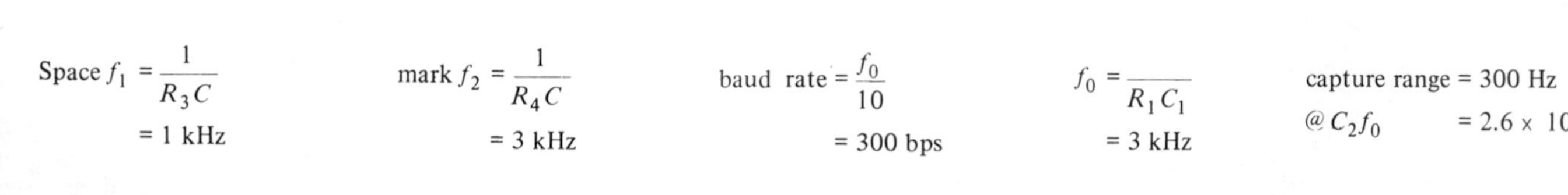

FIGURE 7–15. FSK Radio MODEM

The phase-locked loop (PLL) is basically an electronic servoloop consisting of a phase comparator, lowpass filter, amplifier, and a voltage-controlled oscillator. Its controlled oscillator phase makes possible synchronization with an incoming signal. A rigorous mathematical analysis of this system is cumbersome and beyond the scope of this development. However, the basic principles are presented in conjunction with Figure 7–16. The VCO operates at the free-running frequency f_o with no input signal f_i present. If an input signal is applied, the phase detector provides an output related to the frequency and phase difference between its two input signals. A closer examination of the multiplier phase comparator output discloses both sum and difference frequency or phase terms, denoted by $f_i \pm f_o$, in accordance with a half-angle trigonometric expansion. The lowpass loop filter removes the sum term and applies the difference term to the VCO control terminal as an error signal. Thus, f_o will be driven into synchronism with f_i due to the feedback nature of the loop, providing a clean replica of f_i at the VCO output.

The range of frequencies over which the PLL can acquire lock with an input signal and then maintain lock are, respectively, the capture range and lock range. The capture range is centered about the VCO free-running frequency f_o but is primarily determined by the lowpass loop-filter bandwidth. This is so because the difference frequency term $f_i - f_o$ must be within the filter passband to influence the VCO. It is this capture effect that provides the frequency selective property of the PLL. The lock range, on the other hand, is essentially determined by the VCO tuning range and is not affected by the lowpass filter.

PLL dynamic performance is complex and does not lend itself to simple analysis, especially for noisy input signals, but has been well

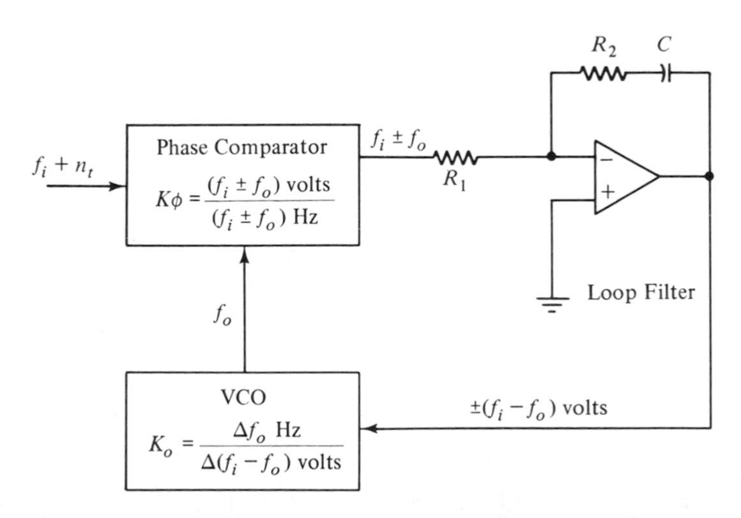

FIGURE 7–16. Phase-Locked Loop

treated in the literature.[12,14] The loop gain is the product of the individual voltage gains provided by the phase comparator, lowpass filter, and voltage-controlled oscillator at the frequency of interest. And the multiplier phase comparator and lowpass filter combination constitute a matched filter for the normally encountered Gaussian noise added to the input signal described by $f_i + n_t$. The lowpass filter increases the capture or pull-in time for a decreasing bandwidth but improves interference rejection and serves as a short-term memory when the PLL is thrown out of lock by a noise transient. However, if the bandwidth is too narrow or the loop gain too high, the PLL can become unstable in response to changes in the input. Generally, an amplifier/filter of the integrator-lead type is used over the capture range to improve the capture effect and transient performance. This circuit is described in Figures 7–16 and 7–17.

Frequency allocations for remote-control purposes are covered under Part 95 of the FCC Rules. Nine frequencies are available under the provisions of this Class C service for fixed-station use involving nonvoice communications which are listed by Table 7–6. Utilization of these frequencies requires only type acceptance of the transmitter by the manufacturer, antenna attachment directly to the transmitter with a gain not exceeding that available from a half-wave dipole, and vertically polarized radiation. Amplitude modulation of 100% tone is permissible with a double-sideband bandwidth up to 8 kHz. This translates into a 4-kHz baseband bandwidth which is adequate for FSK transmission.

The 27.255-MHz frequency coincides with Channel 23 of the citizen's band service. Consequently, a commercial unit can be used directly

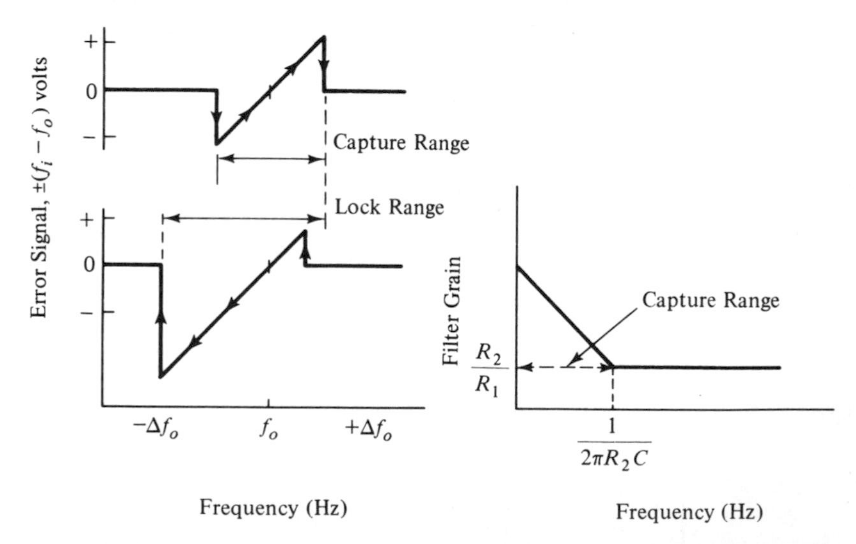

FIGURE 7–17. VCO Tuning Range and Lowpass Filter Response

TABLE 7–6. Remote-Control Frequency Allocations

Frequency (MHz)	Power (W)
26.995	4
27.045	4
27.095	4
27.145	4
27.195	4
27.255	25
72.16	0.75
72.32	0.75
72.96	0.75

with external attachment of the FSK modulator and demodulator to the audio input and output. The standard 4-W output will be effectively quadrupled by the $2\times$gain of both the transmitting and receiving whip antennas. This results in a total effective power of 16 W or 12 dB. With reference to Table 7-5, a 300-bps baud rate having a 10^{-4} bit-error probability requires a receiver SNR_i of -2.9 dB.

Atmospheric, man-made, and receiver front-end noise in this frequency range averages about 2 μV/m of antenna length in a 10-kHz bandwidth.[9] The required signal power at the receiver input for a 1-m-length antenna is therefore determined to be 2 pW by equation (7-7). Considering the 16 W effective transmitter power, this is about a 10^{13} or 130-dB power range. Emissions in this frequency range are propagated essentially by line-of-sight space waves. However, practical considerations usually result in a non-line-of-sight transmission path, or shadow-zone operation. Experience for space-wave propagation shows about a 4-dB/mile power attenuation under shadow-zone conditions. Therefore, the transmission-range estimate for this system is about 32 miles. In practice, unpredictable man-made interference, propagation anomalies, and interfering modulation can reduce the useful range to a fraction of the theoretical estimate. Reliable transmission has been obtained with this FSK radio system in experiments conducted over a 10-mile distance in an urban environment, however.

$$SNR_i = \frac{1}{2} \qquad \text{for } -3\,\text{dB}$$

$$= \frac{S_i}{(2\times 10^{-6}\,\text{V})^2} \tag{7-7}$$

$$S_i = 2\times 10^{-12}\ \text{W}$$

PROBLEMS

7-1 A thermocouple inside the windings of a 4160 V induction motor is to have its signal conditioned and safely transmitted to a remote data logger. Design and block diagram an isolated signal transmission system of the highest integrity conceivable, show the components and power supplies in block diagram fashion, and indicate all interconnections using a Faraday box to house the electronics.

7-2 A 10 kHz output V/F converter and digital line driver is used to drive a twisted-pair line having a bandwidth of 6.7 kHz, due to distributed line constants, over a one mile length. Determine the allowable line length for minimum intersymbol interference.

7-3 A 600 bps data rate is used to generate an FSK signal set with mark and space frequencies of 2.4 kHz and 1 kHz, respectively. Determine: (a) the bandwidth required to accommodate this signal set for transmission purposes, (b) characterize a Bessel lowpass plus highpass type bandpass filter with corner frequencies at the bandwidth extremums of the signal set which also provides $-25\,\text{dB}$ attenuation an octave away, (c) find the attenuation at the mark and space frequencies, and (d) calculate the filter group delay from the combined filter phase shifts between the bandwidth extremums.

7-4 Implement the MODEM filter of Problem 7–3 and provide for an amplitude response within $\pm 1\,\text{dB}$ at the mark and space frequencies. Show the final circuit with component values. Use 10 kΩ resistors where possible.

7-5 An operational amplifier duplexer is used to couple an FSK MODEM to a telephone line as shown. Select resistor values to maximize gains A_1 and A_2 while simultaneously minimizing A_3. Determine the values of these gains.

7-6 A burglar alarm system transmits an intrusion as a binary sequence at 110 baud to a central station via citizen's band radio at 27.255 MHz. For the FSK system of Figure 7–15, determine: (a) the

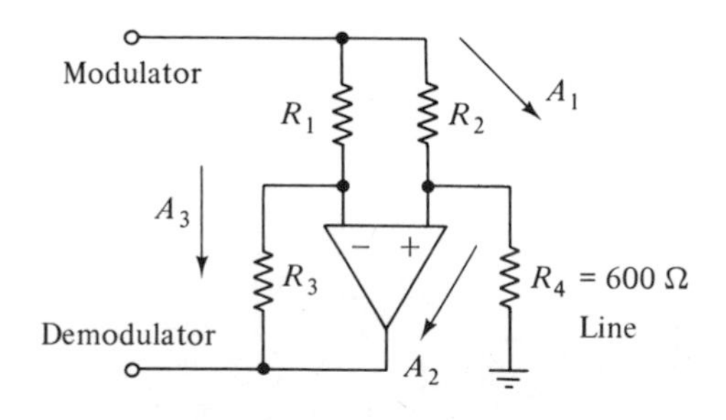

required receiver input SNR for a 10^{-2} error rate, and (b) the predicted transmission range with a 25 W transmitter linear final amplifier.

REFERENCES

1. D. H. Axner, "Compatibility and Transmission Modes Steer MODEM Selection," *Data Comm User*, May 1976.
2. A. B. Carlson, *Communications Systems*, McGraw-Hill, New York, 1975.
3. *The Communications Handbook*, Microdata Corporation, 17481 Red Hill Avenue, Irvine, Calif. 92705, 1973.
4. J. C. Hancock and P. A. Wintz, *Signal Detection Theory*, McGraw-Hill, New York, 1966.
5. N. Kumar, "Forward and Reverse Error Control in Tandem Yields High Throughput," *Data Communications*, November/December 1975.
6. G. Lapidus, "Transmitting Data Pulses Over Short Distances," *Data Communications*, July/August 1974.
7. *Low-Speed MODEM Fundamentals*, Application Note AN-731, Motorola Incorporated, Box 2953, Phoenix, Ariz. 85062, 1974.
8. K. I. Nordling, "Taking a Fresh Look at Voice Grade Line Conditioning," *Data Communications*, May/June 1975.
9. *Reference Data for Radio Engineers*, 29-2, ITT, Howard W. Sams, Indianapolis, Ind., 1975.
10. D. J. Sakrison, *Notes On Analog Communication*, Van Nostrand Reinhold, New York, 1970.
11. *Special Function Data Book*, National Semiconductor, 2900 Semiconductor Drive, Santa Clara, Calif. 95051, April 1976.
12. R. C. Tausworthe, "Theory and Practical Design of Phase Locked Receivers," *NASA Report 32-819*, Vol. 1, 1966.
13. "Transmission Line Characteristics," *National Semiconductor Application Note AN-108*, 2900 Semiconductor Drive, Santa Clara, Calif. 95051.
14. A. J. Viterbi, *Principles of Coherent Communication*, McGraw-Hill, 1966.

8

PROCESS CONTROLLERS

8-0 INTRODUCTION

The use of digital computers for process automation gained widespread application in the mid-1960's with the availability of the minicomputer. Two methods have subsequently emerged in the application of computers to process control: (1) direct digital control (DDC) whereby the functions of the control loops at the process interface are simulated by the computer software, and (2) the more common supervisory computer control whereby the computer interfaces with discrete analog controllers at the process interface. In both methods, the computer implements an operating strategy by control algorithms which utilize measured process variables. The advent of the microprocessor promises to provide a cost effective DDC replacement for the analog controller, but the external connections and adjustments are likely to remain unchanged because they are determined by the requirements of the process.

The purpose of this chapter is to focus on the essential aspects of process control at the analog controller and process interface including the characteristics and proper adjustment of commercially available controllers. Since the controller is primarily responsible for the realization of good control action with minimum error, the selection and tuning of these devices is one of the more important tasks of engineers and technologists in the process industries, especially since most processes are potentially unstable. A theoretical analysis of control systems is not pursued in favor of a practical development of basic control loops, analog controller characteristics and tuning, and applications considerations.

8-1 CONTROL-LOOP ANALYSIS

In order to control a process, the controlled variable $c(t)$ must be identified. How this variable is affected by actuator positions and process variables such as $x(t)$ must be fairly well, although not precisely known. The input setpoint command $m(t)$ is translated into an actuator forcing function $u(t)$ which is tailored to control the value of $x(t)$. Analysis then enables the designer to determine how the process actuators should be adjusted so that the controlled variable can be held at the desired setpoint.

An example process control strategy could be to maintain the controlled variable $c(t)$ above a specified lower limit X_L 95% of the time. If $c(t)$ in Figure 8–2 has a normal probability distribution with a standard deviation of σ and the uncontrolled operation provides a mean X_0 shown by curve A, application of a control system could reduce the mean of $c(t)$ to X_0' as shown by curve B. The benefit of shifting the mean value down while still exceeding the minimum value X_L 95% of the time is tighter control, resulting in reduced variance of the controlled variable $c(t)$. This not only improves the quality control of the product, but also minimizes the use of feedstocks and conserves utilities used in the operation of the process.

The response of specific process variables to an actuator change can usually be modeled by a first-order lag plus some preceding dead time as suggested by Figure 8–3. A step actuation $u(t)$ at the process input, therefore, will result in a response $x(t)$ which can be expressed as a first-order linear differential equation given by equation (8-1). The parameters L and τ are considered to be constant and the solution of equation (8-1) using Laplace transforms is given in (8-2). The inverse transform of (8-2) conveniently yields the time response $x(t)$, which describes the output in terms of the process time constant τ and dead time L. The process gain K is determined as the ratio of the process change Δx to the actuator change Δu.

$$\tau \frac{dx(t)}{dt} + x(t) = Ku(t-L) \tag{8-1}$$

$$x(s) = \frac{K}{s(1+s\tau)} \cdot e^{-sL} \tag{8-2}$$

$$x(t) = K(1-e^{-(t-L)/\tau}) \cdot u(t-L) \tag{8-3}$$

The basic analog controller has unity feedback and a forward proportional gain K_C shown in Figure 8–4. The transfer function of this controller is defined by equation (8-4) and is a zero-order system because it

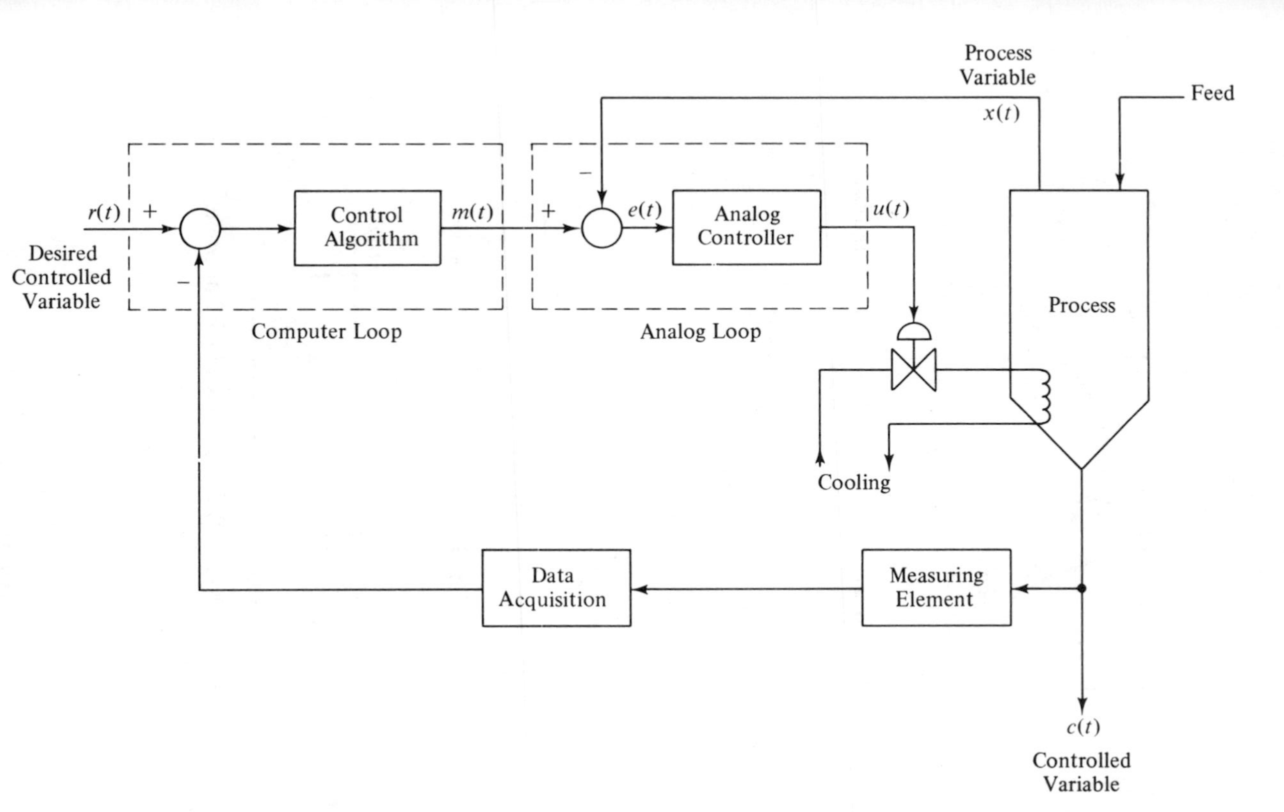

FIGURE 8–1. Computer Process Control with Local Analog Loop

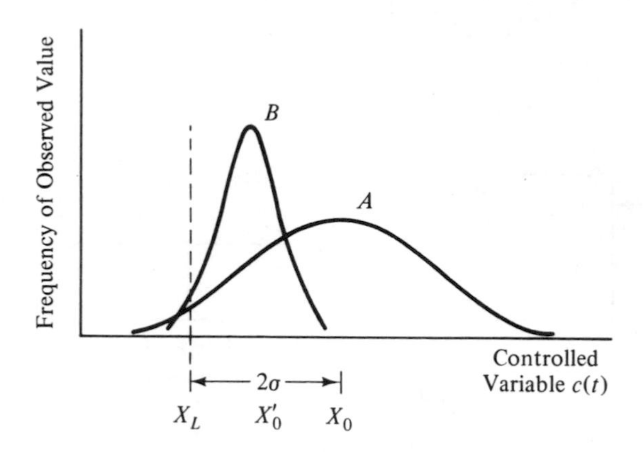

FIGURE 8–2. Controlled Variable Distribution

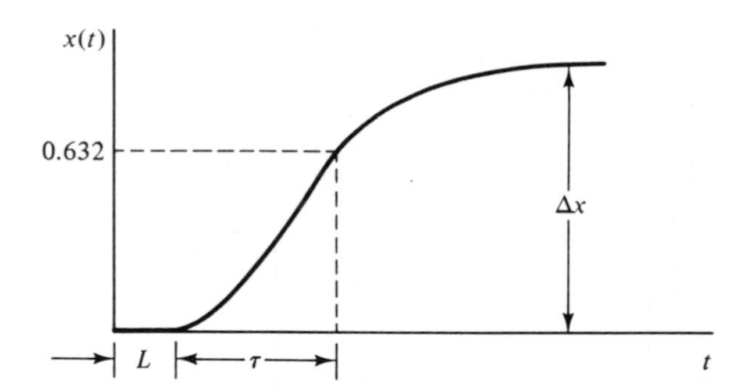

FIGURE 8–3. Process Variable Response

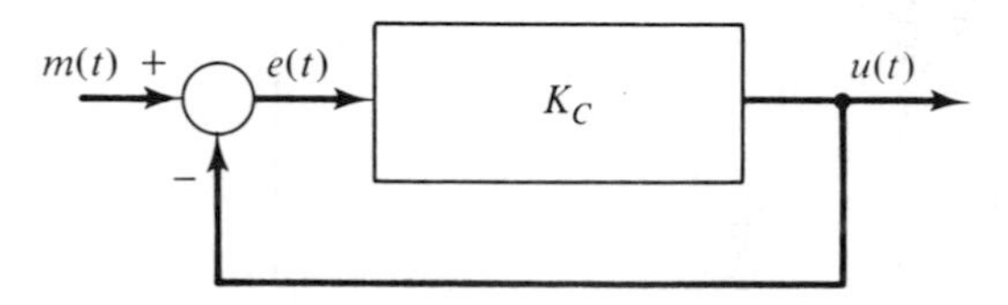

FIGURE 8–4. Basic Proportional Controller

contains no frequency-determining elements.

$$\frac{u(t)}{m(t)} = \frac{K_C}{1 + K_C} \tag{8-4}$$

However, when coupled to a conventional first-order process, the combined response is that of the first-order system described by equation

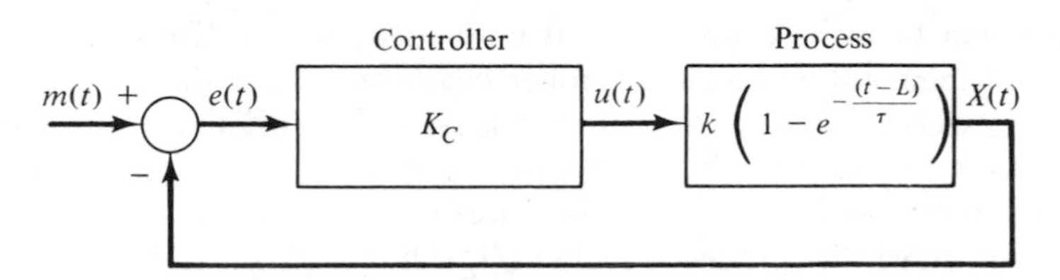

FIGURE 8–5. Proportional Control Loop

(8-5)(Figure 8–5).

$$x(t) = m(t) \cdot \frac{K_C K\left(1 - e^{-(t-L)/\tau}\right)}{1 + K_C K\left(1 - e^{-(t-L)/\tau}\right)} \tag{8-5}$$

Of interest is the steady-state error exhibited by this system, illustrated in Figure 8–6, for displacement, velocity, and acceleration setpoint inputs $m(t)$. For the proportional controller steady-state error settles to zero for a displacement change, is equal to the inverse proportional gain for a constant-rate signal, and approximates this rate error multiplied by time for acceleration setpoint inputs (Figure 8–6). Compensation for these steady-state errors is achieved by modifying the controller forward trans-

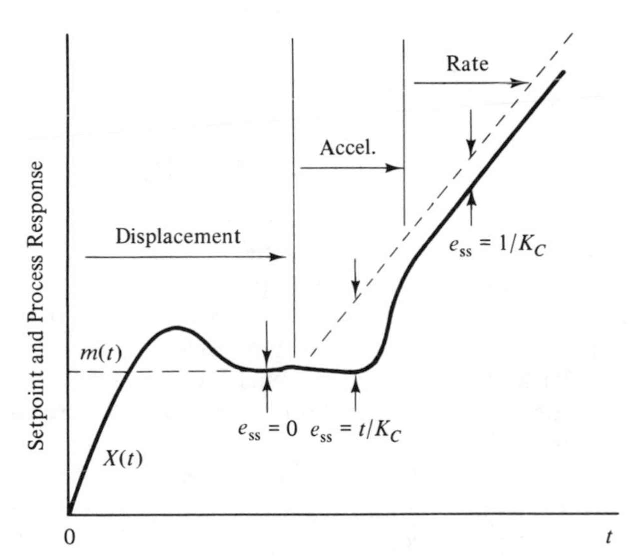

FIGURE 8-6. Proportional Control Loop Process. Variable Response to Step, Acceleration, and Ramp Setpoint Changes (*Courtesy* International Textbook Co.)

fer function to include integral and derivative control. These modifications and their influence on controller characteristics is discussed in the following section. Finally, the actuator is normally sufficiently faster than the process response so that its frequency response appears transparent and does not contribute terms to the transfer function defining the control loop. In contrast, the process variable $x(t)$ exhibits a typical response from a fraction of 1 Hz to about 1 Hz.

8-2 CONTROLLER CHARACTERISTICS

For most commercial analog controllers the terms "proportional gain" and "integral time" are not used. Instead, the terms "proportional band" and "reset rate" are standard. The proportional band is defined as the percentage of full-scale change of the controller input signal required to move the controller output through its full range. For example, if the proportional band is set at 10%, then a 10% change in the input will produce a full-scale output change. The proportional gain K_C in this case is 10, since the controller output change is 10 times the input change. Equation (8-6) expresses this standard definition of proportional band. When the full-scale input and output signals are not equal, the definition of proportional band is defined by equation (8-7).

$$\text{proportional band} = \frac{100\%}{K_C} \tag{8-6}$$

$$= \frac{\mathrm{FS_{out}}}{\mathrm{FS_{in}}} \cdot \frac{100\%}{K_C} \tag{8-7}$$

As an example, consider an electronic controller with a 1- to 5-V input or 4-V range, and a 4- to 20-mA output or 16-mA range. For a 100% proportional band, proportional gain K_C equals 4 mA/V from equation (8-7). Thus, a full-scale 5-V input signal produces a full-scale output of 20 mA. Similarly, for 3- to 15-psi signals, a pneumatic controller with a 200% proportional band will produce a 6-psi output for a 12-psi input signal since the proportional gain is $\frac{1}{2}$.

A disadvantage of the proportional controller is that it will not return a variable to its setpoint following a process load change. The difference between the $m(t)$ input setpoint signal and the new equilibrium value of the process variable $x(t)$ is an offset. This offset is directly proportional to the proportional band setting, (i.e., the smaller the proportional gain K_C, the larger the offset error). Consequently, applications for this type of controller are limited to simple level and pressure controls. Figure 8–7 describes this response.

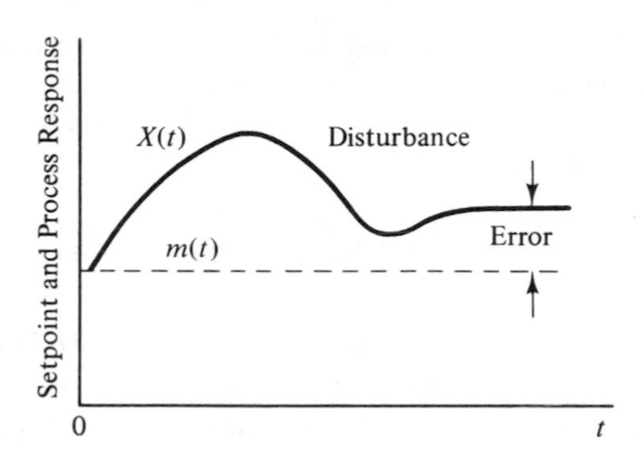

FIGURE 8–7. Proportional Control Loop Error Following a Process Change

Integral control converts the first-order proportional controller plus process into a second-order system which is capable of tracking process disturbances. In many applications backlash and hysterisis associated with the actuator may exceed the controller steady-state errors. Integral control is effective in overcoming these actuator anomalies. The proportional plus integral controller is therefore the most widely applied of the controller types. The minority of control loops in which it is not applicable are primarily those with large time delays L, such as analytical and temperature-related process variables.

The term reset rate is derived from the output response of a PI controller to a step input as shown in Figure 8–8. The response consists of an initial jump from zero to the proportional gain setting K_C followed by a ramp which repeats the initial proportional response each integral time T_i. Therefore, the reset rate is defined as the repeats per minute of the initial proportional response. The reset rate and integral time are related by

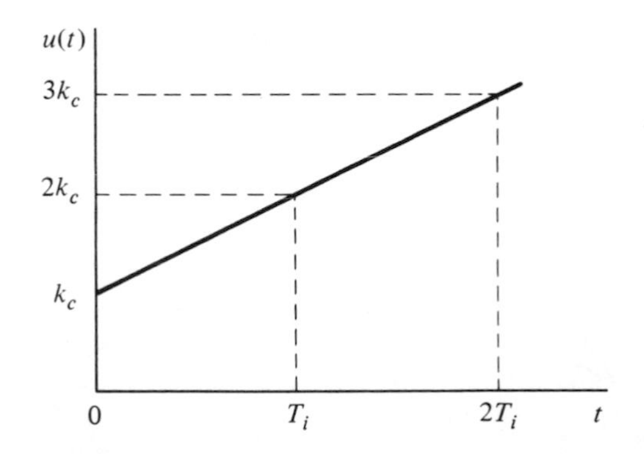

FIGURE 8–8. PI Controller Response to Step Input

equation (8-8). If the reset setting is 1, then for every minute during which the error signal is nonzero, the amount of corrective action added to the controller output signal by the reset will equal that of the proportional band alone.

$$\text{reset rate} = \frac{1}{T_i} \text{ per minute} \tag{8-8}$$

The addition of derivative control to a PI controller results in a three-mode controller. With this feature, corrective action is added to the controller output equivalent to the derivative of the slope of the error curve. The unit of derivative action is called the rate time. If this rate setting is 1, the corrective signal that is generated immediately following an error occurrence is equal to the amount that a proportional controller would output in 1 minute acting alone. Derivative control decreases the effect of time lag, such as exists in temperature-control loops, by anticipating the extent of a process variable change before it is completed. Derivative time is ordinarily in the range from a fraction of a minute to a few minutes, with a representative three-mode controller response described by Figure 8–9. In practice, the derivative action is usually placed in the controller feedback path rather than the forward path to minimize disturbances from changes in the setpoint. The frequency range over which derivative action is effective can be restricted by a lowpass filter when process noise is a problem.

The mathematical relationship between the controller output $u(t)$ and the error signal $e(t)$ is described by the following equations. These expressions are ideal, however, because in practical controllers there is usually some interaction between the modes. Figure 8–10 presents a block diagram of a typical three-mode controller showing the usual

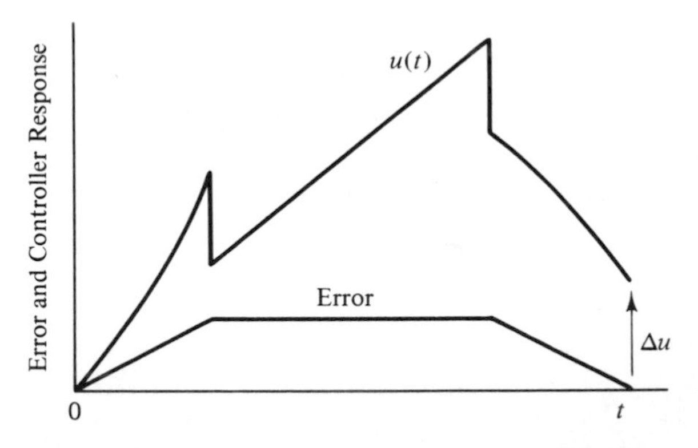

FIGURE 8–9. Three-Mode Controller Response

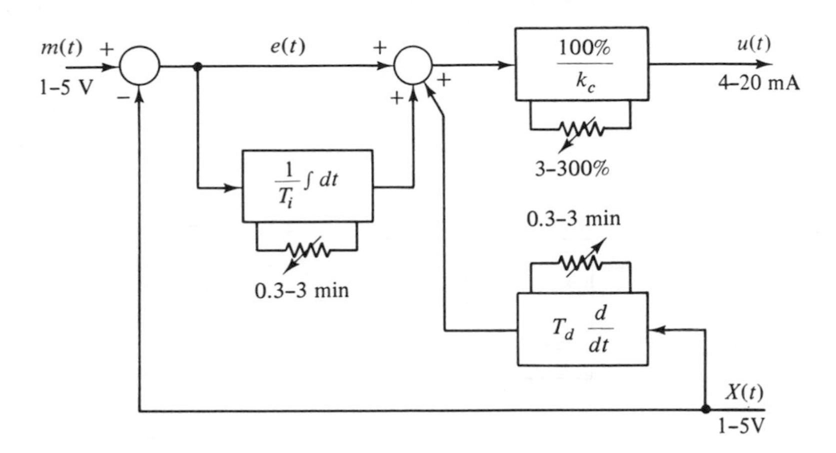

FIGURE 8–10. PID Process Controller Diagram

adjustment ranges for the three modes.

$$\text{P:} \quad u(t) = K_C \cdot e(t) \tag{8-9}$$

$$\text{PI:} \quad u(t) = K_C \cdot \left[e(t) + \frac{1}{T_i} \int_0^t e(t) \cdot dt \right] \tag{8-10}$$

$$\text{PID:} \quad u(t) = K_C \cdot \left[e(t) + \frac{1}{T_i} \int_0^t e(t) \cdot dt + T_d \frac{dx(t)}{dt} \right] \tag{8-11}$$

When the process variable consists of two lags in series as described by Figure 8–11, system performance can usually be improved by cascade control if the dynamics of one lag is faster than the other. An additional benefit is the reduced effect of process disturbances. With this arrangement the master controller output is the setpoint input to the slaved inner-loop controller. Normally, a proportional inner-loop controller is used with a PI outer-loop controller. The response of the inner loop must be equal or faster than that of the outer loop, however. Controller tuning is identical to that of conventional loops, but with the inner loop tuned first. The local control loop of Figure 8–1 could benefit from cascade control, since the cooling flow is faster than the process temperature change. Implementation requires a flow transducer and additional controller. Essentially, the long-term transfer function of the inner loop in a cascade arrangement is unity. Usually, the outer loop is tuned so that the inner loop has time to drive the actuator to the setpoint provided by the outer loop controller faster (by about four times) than that setpoint is able to change to a different value.

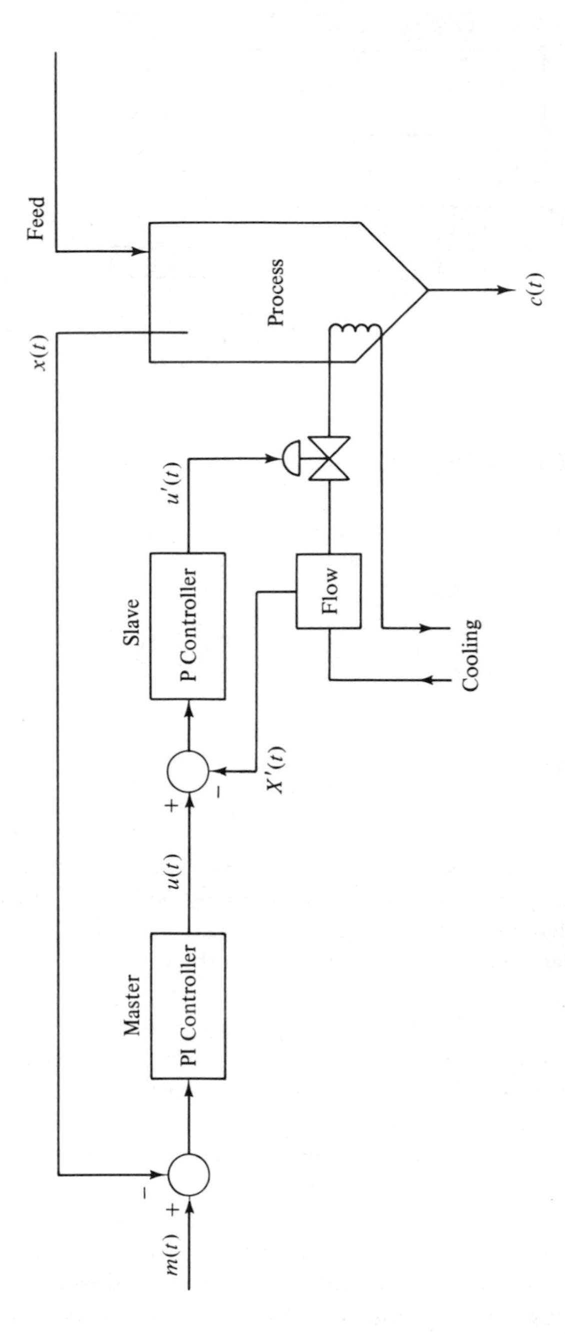

FIGURE 8–11. Cascade Control Implementation

8-3 ANALOG CONTROLLER TUNING

In order to match a controller to a process and obtain the best possible control response requires some knowledge of the frequency response of both the controller and the process. If the process response were known exactly, the ideal controller proportional band and reset-rate mode settings for best stability and steady-state error could be determined mathematically. In practice, however, the effort required to obtain the process frequency response is seldom justified. Instead, the stability of the process is determined by introducing a disturbance and then analyzing the recorded response of this process disturbance to determine the control-loop dynamics. This section is concerned with methods for determining these dynamics and relating them to initial controller tuning adjustments.

Initial analog controller settings are determined from these dynamics by the application of well-known empirical relationships such as those of Ziegler and Nichols.[13] Both the closed-loop and quarter-decay methods will be considered. The former is useful for the majority of loops, and the latter for very slow control loops. Both methods take into account the stability requirements of the loop and provide a final 4:1 subsidence of consecutive controller output response cycles. These methods provide accurate results, because the dynamics of the process and controller are included.

In the closed-loop Ziegler–Nichols method, proportional, reset, and derivative action are first turned off and a strip-chart recorder connected to the controller output. The proportional gain K_C is then increased slowly until the actuator cycles steadily as shown by Figure 8–12. The value of K_C that just produces steady oscillation is called the ultimate gain, K_{CU}. The ultimate period is denoted by P_U. The controller settings

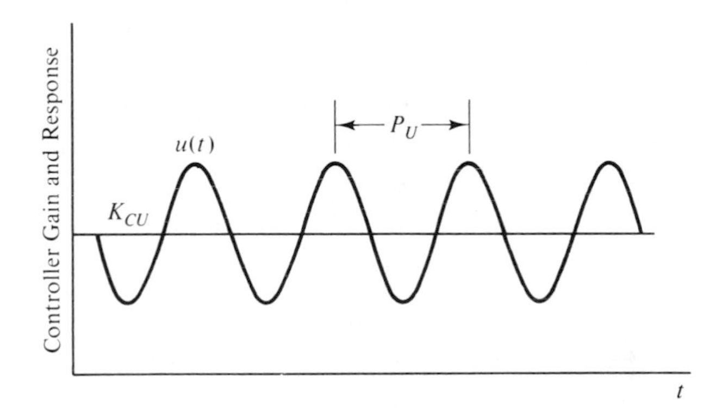

FIGURE 8–12. Ultimate Gain Output Cycling

recommended by Ziegler and Nichols are described by the following equations and require observation of at least four cycles for validity.

$$\text{P:} \quad K_C = 0.5 K_{CU} \tag{8-12}$$

$$\text{PI:} \quad K_C = 0.45 K_{CU} \tag{8-13}$$

$$T_i = \frac{P_U}{1.2} \tag{8-14}$$

$$\text{PID:} \quad K_C = 0.6 K_{CU} \tag{8-15}$$

$$T_i = \frac{P_U}{2} \tag{8-16}$$

$$T_d = \frac{P_U}{8} \tag{8-17}$$

A test of less severity for tuning very slow processes is the quarter-decay method. The preceding Ziegler–Nichols method calls for trial-and-error adjustment to provide a decay ratio of 1. Adjustment for a decay ratio of $\frac{1}{4}$, described by Figure 8–13, requires less time, since only two response cycles must be observed. However, additional measurement and computation is required to extract the decay ratio. An additional advantage of this method is that the controller remains stable because oscilla-

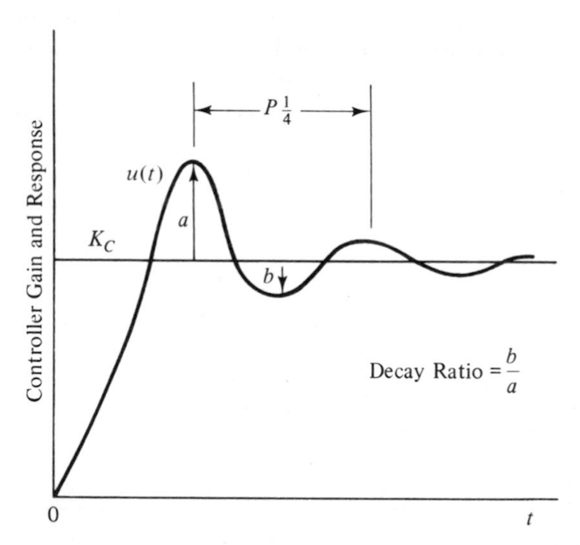

FIGURE 8–13. Controller Response Decay Ratio

tion is not induced. Recommended controller settings are described by the following equations.

$$\text{P:} \quad K_C = K_{C1/4} \tag{8-18}$$

$$\text{PI:} \quad K_C = 0.9K_{C1/4} \tag{8-19}$$

$$T_i = P_{\frac{1}{4}} \quad \text{(and adjust for } \tfrac{1}{4} \text{ decay)} \tag{8-20}$$

$$\text{PID:} \quad K_C = 1.2K_{C1/4} \tag{8-21}$$

$$T_i = P_{\frac{1}{4}} \quad \text{(and adjust for } \tfrac{1}{4} \text{ decay)} \tag{8-20}$$

$$T_d = \frac{T_i}{4} \tag{8-22}$$

The foregoing controller tuning methods involve introducing a disturbance into the system by a step change in the setpoint setting. The controllers are therefore tuned for changes in the setpoint. However, the controller reacts both to setpoint changes and process load changes. Setpoint changes are prevalent in batching processes, and load changes are prevalent in most continuous processes. The setpoint variable is used to introduce the tuning disturbance simply because it is generally more readily available. The principal difference in tuning for load changes is usually a somewhat smaller required integral response. In practice, this can normally be accommodated in the procedures above if the primary function of the controller is to react to load changes.

8-4 APPLICATION CONSIDERATIONS

Analog controllers are available from a number of manufacturers, including Foxboro, Taylor Instrument and Leeds and Northrop. Following selection, they must then be interfaced to process sensors, actuators and the supervisory computer. Controller design generally emphasizes stability and reliability of operation, whether they are pneumatic or electronic devices. The decision of whether to use pneumatic or electronic controllers is an important consideration and frequently is not clear-cut. For explosive or temperature-extreme environments, the pneumatic controller has distinct advantages. For conventional process applications, however, both pneumatic and electronic controllers are surprisingly close in such specifications as accuracy, repeatability, and reliability. Electronic controllers have the edge in computer and electrical sensor interfacing, in resolution, and in speed of response. For the pneumatic controller, delay is on the order of 1 s/400 ft of interconnecting piping, but they have an edge insofar as actuator interfacing, since most actuators are pneumatic devices. Their cost is also about 25% less than comparable electronic controllers. In addition, their speed of response can be improved by placing the controller at the process with remote indication at the control station, but this requires a four-pipe instead of a two-pipe interconnecting arrangement.

Figure 8–14 describes an elemental pneumatic proportional controller, where the setpoint is entered through the dial setting. Many circuit variations exist for electronic controllers, so presentation of a complete schematic would be of minimal utility. A standard electronic controller setpoint interface is either a motor-operated rheostat or digital stepping motor. Alternatively, a D/A converter with a holding register can be interposed between the computer digital output and analog setpoint input. This feature allows the setpoint to be preserved in the event of a computer malfunction. It also provides a continuous signal that can be fed back to the computer for verification of controller setpoint position.

As a result of the continuous operation of most process control systems and the impracticality of constant instrument monitoring by operations personnel, it is normal practice to alarm critical process

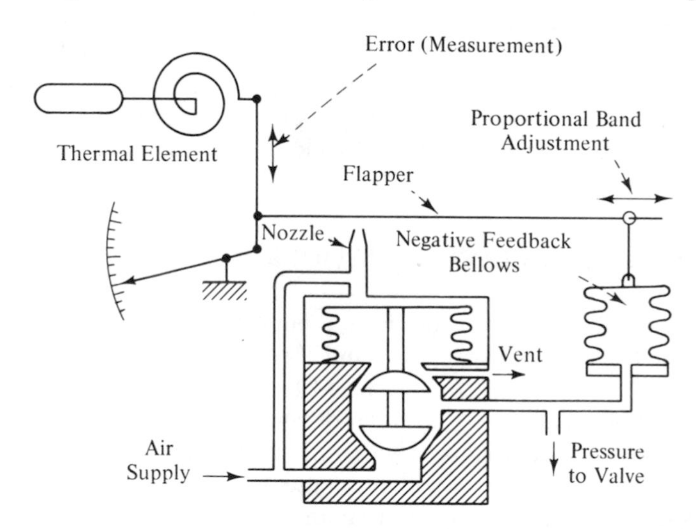

FIGURE 8–14. Pneumatic Proportional Controller (*Courtesy* Chemical Engineering)

variables. For example, most analog controllers include deviation alarms which may be set to trip when the process variable deviates from the setpoint by perhaps ±10%. Dual-limit window comparators, such as the Burr Brown 4115 module, may also be used to monitor process variables. A typical application provides for an alarm to be initiated at the lower of the two limits, and automatic process shutdown at the upper limit. For some slow reaction processes it may be of interest to take the derivative of a process variable in order to enhance the visibility of its rate and direction of change. This can be accomplished either by the process control computer or a simple differentiator. This technique may present difficulty, however, in the presence of process noise.

A useful circuit for computer-supervised analog controllers is a watchdog timer and alarm to signal a computer malfunction to process operations personnel (Figure 8–15). The circuit shown will time out and alarm if not reset by the computer within every 30-s time period. This is usually arranged by a software loop monitoring the computer real-time clock directing an input/output device handler to momentarily ground the watchdog timer reset line. Figure 8–16 shows a typical electronic analog controller with the location of its tuning adjustments, and Figure 8–17 illustrates a complete interface between a supervisory computer and a wind tunnel with four analog controllers. The printed circuit board for the interface of Figure 8–17 is shown in Figure 8–18.

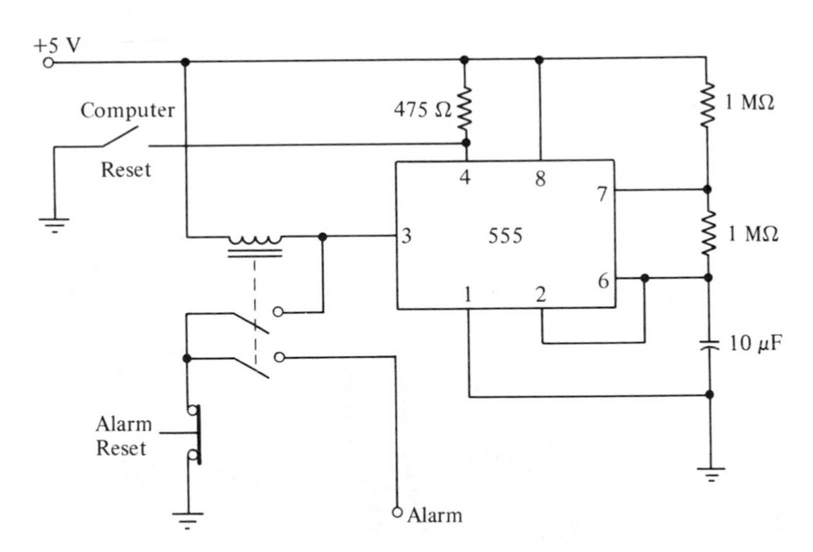

FIGURE 8–15. Computer Watchdog Timer

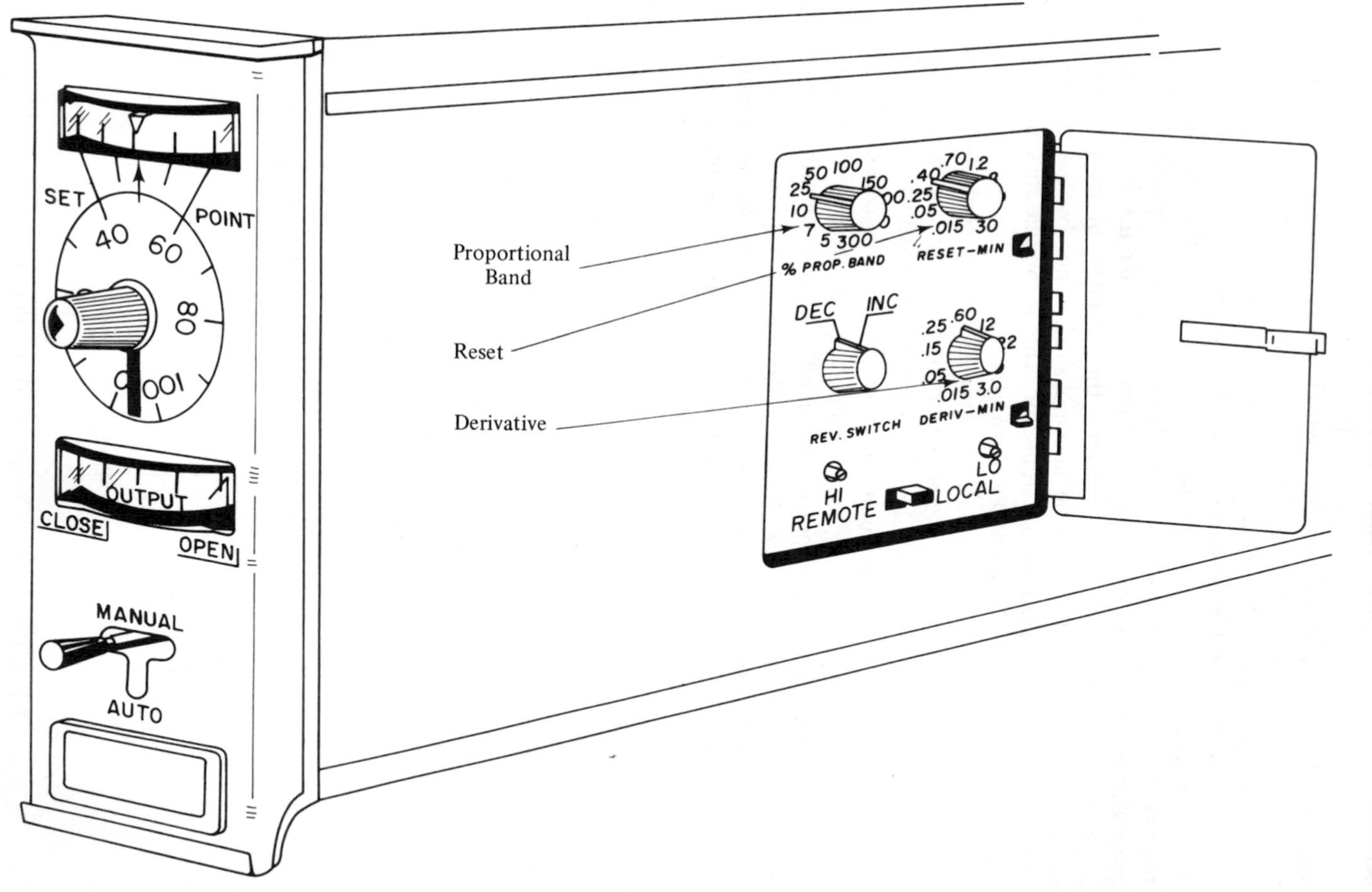

FIGURE 8–16. Electronic Controller Tuning Adjustments (*Courtesy* Foxboro)

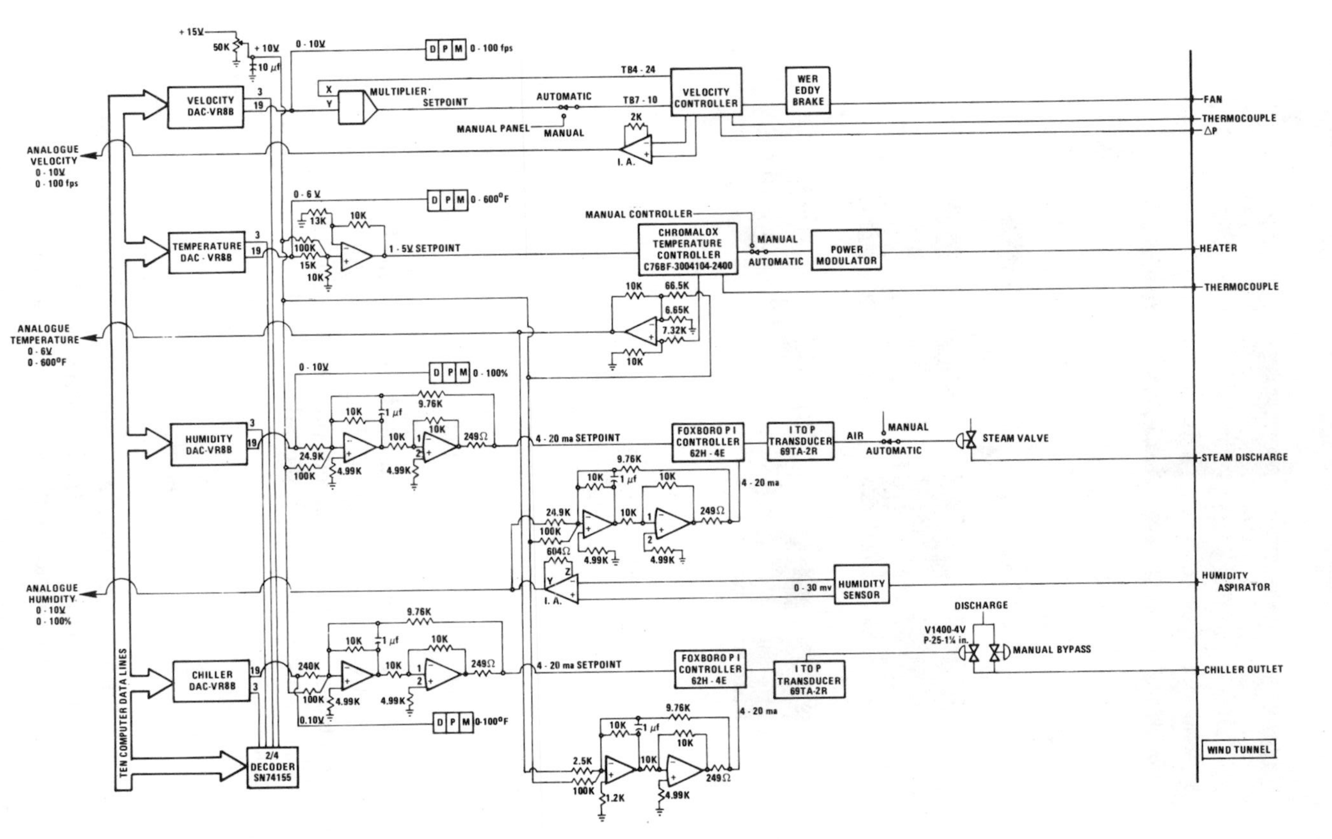

FIGURE 8–17. Example Computer-to-Process Analog Interface

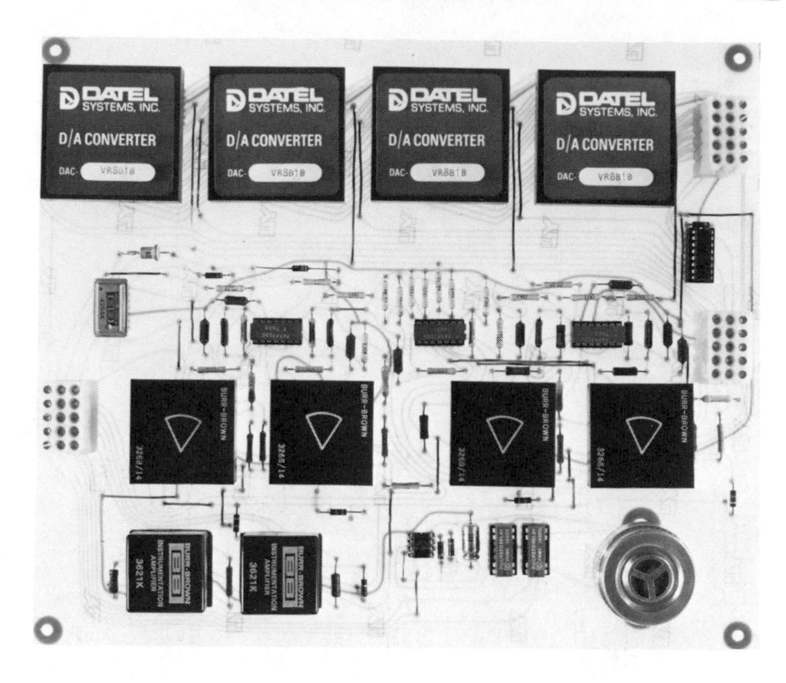

FIGURE 8–18. Analog Interface Circuit Board

PROBLEMS

8-1 Process controllers may be initially tuned from observation of the parameters of Figure 8–3 and application of the equations below. Determine the proportional gain and integral time for a PI controller if a 60% change of full-scale in the actuation signal Δu results in a 30% change in the measured process variable Δx. The process exhibits a dead time of $\frac{1}{2}$ second and a time constant of 1.125 seconds.

$$K_C = \frac{\Delta u}{\Delta x} \cdot \frac{\tau}{L} \qquad T_i = 3.3L$$

8-2 A controller proportional gain setting K_{cu} of 1.2 causes a process to cycle with a frequency of 0.291 cycles per minute. Determine PI controller proportional band and reset rate settings for this process.

8-3 Determine the change in the output manipulated variables Δu for the PI controller of Problem 8–1 for a step change in the error signal of 5%. This occurs following a process load change for a duration of 5 seconds. Utilize the controller adjustments of Problem 8–1 and equation (8–10) in this solution.

8-4 The reactor illustrated in Figure 8–11 has a 12 minute time constant, a 2 minute dead time, a process response to actuator input gain K of unity, and oscillates with a 8 minute period in a closed loop. Since adjustment of the reactor temperature by coolant flow is nonlinear, the use of cascade control overcomes this problem. Determine the tuning adjustments for a PI temperature controller in the outer loop and a P valve controller in the inner loop. The inner loop oscillates with a 30 second period for a proportional band setting of 16%.

8-5 Implement the PID controller of Figure 8–10 using operational amplifier circuitry. Limit the frequency response to 16 Hz, include provision for turning off the integral and derivative terms, provide process deviation and output meters to indicate both ± deviation from the setpoint and percentage of output actuation, and show scale factors and component values.

8-6 Develop circuitry to interface the controller of Figure 8–10 to the output of a thermocouple linearizer providing 1 mV/°C over a 0 to 800°C range for $x(t)$, and an 8-bit DAC of 5 volts full-scale for $m(t)$ representing an input setpoint range of 0 to 500°C. Also convert the actuator signal $u(t)$ to 1–5 volts.

REFERENCES

1. E. C. Barbe, *Linear Control Systems*, International Textbook Company, New York, 1963.
2. P. S. Buckley, *Techniques of Process Control*, John Wiley, New York, 1964.
3. L. A. Drake, "Process Control Design," Short Course Notes, University of Cincinnati, December 1974.
4. M. Hordeski, "When Should You Use Pneumatics, When Electronics," Instruments & Control Systems, November 1976.
5. B. C. Kuo, *Automatic Control Systems*, Prentice-Hall, Englewood Cliffs, N. J., 1967.
6. B. G. Liptak, "How To Set Process Controllers," *Chemical Engineering*, November 23, 1964.
7. A. Lopez, P. Murrill, and C. Smith, "Optimal Tuning of Digital Controllers," *Instruments and Control Systems*, October 1968.
8. P. W. Murrill, *Digital Computer Process Control*, International Textbook Company, New York, 1972.

9. J. R. Ragazzini and G. F. Franklin, *Sampled Data Control Systems*, McGraw-Hill, New York, 1958.

10. E. Savas, *Computer Control of Industrial Processes*, McGraw-Hill, New York, 1965.

11. F. Shinskey, *Process Control Systems*, McGraw-Hill, New York, 1967.

12. C. L. Smith, "Controller Tuning That Works," *Instruments and Control Systems*, November 1976.

13. J. G. Ziegler and W. B. Nichols, "Optimum Settings for Automatic Controllers," *A. S. M. E. Transactions*, November 1942.

9

ELECTRONIC POWER SUPPLIES

9-0 INTRODUCTION

One of the last items to be considered and the first to cause trouble is usually the power supply. Overspecifying power supplies in terms of voltage regulation and output ripple is costly and unnecessary. However, overspecifying the current output capability can provide increased reliability. The decision to build or buy a supply is usually economically in favor of buying in view of the competition and major effort in this area by vendors. Therefore, the purpose of this chapter is to provide insight and design information on present methods and trends in electronic power supplies.

Digital circuits typically require only about 4% line and load regulation, which frequently can be met by a passive ferroresonant-type supply. Linear circuits that operate from symmetrical plus and minus supplies generally possess a power-supply rejection ratio (PSRR) on the order of 60 dB to ripple and voltage variations. Consequently, 1% voltage regulation and ripple levels up to 10 mV rms are usually adequate for all but the most critical applications. With Table 9–1 and later examples it is shown that zener regulation suffices for many applications, and three-terminal regulators are usually more than adequate. Raw supplies, shunt and series regulation, switching regulators, distributed supplies, and thermal design are the principal topics covered.

TABLE 9–1. Power-Supply-Regulator Comparison

Type	Regulation (%)	Ripple Attenuation (dB)
Ferroresonant	2.0	—
Zener	2.0	20
Three terminal	0.1	40
Modular linear	0.01	60
Switching	0.01	60

9-1 RAW POWER SUPPLIES

The fact that the regulator stage will also reduce ripple has resulted in a trend to obtain most of the smoothing in this manner. This is primarily an economics consideration, permitting a smaller and lower-cost raw supply filter. Almost all raw supplies today utilize capacitor input filters, with transformer line isolation and full-wave bridge rectification the norm (Figure 9–1). This relaxes the requirement on transformer and diode ratings in comparison with a center-tapped transformer full-wave design. A delayed-action fuse should be placed on the line side of the raw supply rated about 25% above the supply output volt-ampere rating. Transient protection is important to protect both the rectifier diodes and regulator stage. A varistor such as the General Electric MOV device is useful for clipping line transients. A 0.01-μF 1 kV capacitor across the line also aids in noise reduction.

The voltage, current, and ripple requirements of the load must be described prior to supply design or specification. The raw supply dc output voltage is usually chosen 5–10 V higher than the regulator output voltage, and the raw supply dc output current includes full-load plus

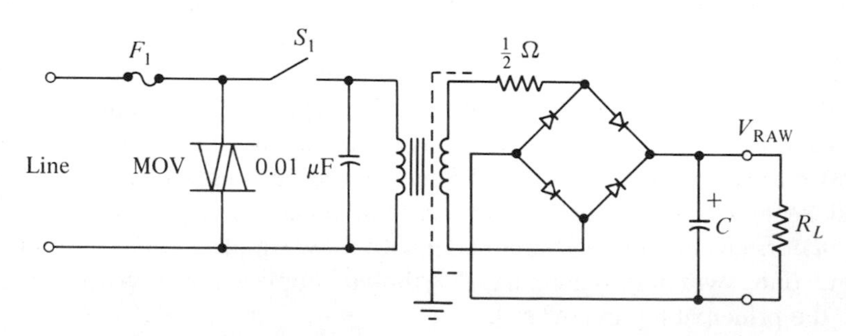

FIGURE 9–1. Raw Power Supply

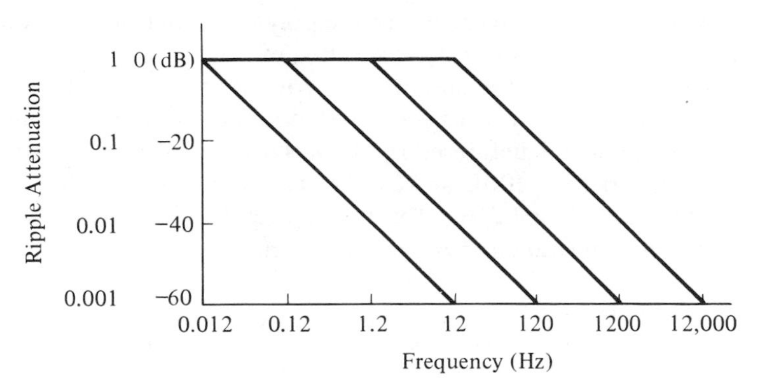

FIGURE 9–2. Ripple Attenuation Versus Filter Cutoff

regulator quiescent current. This dc volt-ampere product is approximately equivalent to the required transformer rms volt-ampere rating for full-wave bridge rectification and a capacitor input filter. A conservative design would specify an additional 20% in the transformer rms volt-ampere rating.

The major design trade-off for raw supply capacitor input filters is achieving good voltage regulation at low ripple and low cost. The capacitor peak voltage rating must be sufficient, and the current inrush allowed for since the uncharged capacitor at turn-on is a short circuit. The diode surge current rating, typically six times the rated value, must also be adequate to handle this inrush. A $\frac{1}{2}$-Ω resistor placed between the rectifiers and transformer secondary is usually adequate for this. The capacitor should then be sized such that excessive ripple current is avoided because electrolytics are lossy in a resistive manner and dissipate real power which can shorten their life due to temperature rise.

An rms ripple of $\frac{1}{2}$% of the dc output voltage is a nominal raw supply design value (Figure 9–2). The minimum output load resistance and filter capacitor $R_L C$ product will provide a −20-dB attenuation per decade to ripple from its cutoff frequency of $1/R_L C$ radians. For full-wave 60-Hz rectification, the most significant ripple is at the 120-Hz second harmonic, and the total rms ripple for a sinusoidal input waveform will be 48% of the dc output voltage (Table 9–2). This is true for both bridge and two-diode center-tapped transformer full-wave rectifier circuits.

TABLE 9–2. Raw Supply Ratings

Parameter	FWB	FWCT	HW
Transformer V-A rating	$V\text{-}A_{sec}$	$V\text{-}A_{sec}/0.7$	$V\text{-}A_{sec}$
Required secondary V_{rms}	$V_{dc}/0.9$	$V_{dc}/0.9$	$V_{dc}/0.45$
Rectifier ripple V_{rms}	0.48 V_{dc}	0.48 V_{dc}	1.21 V_{dc}

By way of example, consider a raw supply dc output of 20 V and 200 mA. This requires an rms transformer rating of 4 V-A, or 5 V-A conservatively. The load resistance and filter capacitor values are determined below to satisfy the $\frac{1}{2}$% raw ripple design criteria. Reduction is obtained by attenuating the 48% unfiltered ripple of 9.6 V to 0.48%, or 96 mV rms, by a filter rolloff to $-40\,\mathrm{dB}$ at 120 Hz. This requires a $1/R_L C$ corner frequency of 7.5 rad, or 1.2 Hz. This method results in a conservative raw supply voltage regulation and ripple reduction.

$$\text{raw supply regulation} = \frac{V_{\text{raw max}} - V_{\text{raw min}}}{V_{\text{raw min}}} \cdot 100\% \tag{9-1}$$

$$R_L = \frac{V_{\text{raw min}}}{I_{L\,\text{max}}} \tag{9-2}$$

$$= \frac{20\text{ V}}{0.2\ A} = 100\ \Omega$$

$$C = \frac{1}{w_C R_L} \tag{9-3}$$

$$= \frac{1}{(7.5\,\text{rad})(100\,\Omega)} = 1232\,\mu\text{F}$$

Occasionally it is of interest to add additional raw supply filtering for further ripple reduction. An *LC*-filter section cascaded with an existing capacitor-input filter will behave as an ac voltage divider to the ripple component (Figure 9–3). And if the inductor dc resistance is small, the

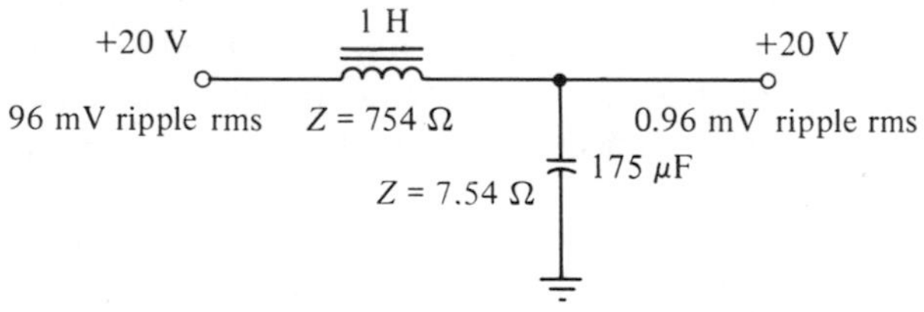

FIGURE 9–3. *LC* Filter Section

effect on the dc output voltage will be negligible. This additional filter section can be designed with the following two equations. First, choose a convenient inductance value equal to or greater than L_c. Then choose the ripple reduction required of the *LC*-filter section and calculate the required capacitor value. For example, to achieve an additional 0.01 ripple attenuation with the previous raw supply, the required L and C

values are obtained as follows.

$$L_c \geqslant \frac{R_L}{1130} \qquad \text{henries} \geqslant \frac{100}{1130} \tag{9-4}$$

$$\geqslant 0.0885\ \text{H} \qquad \text{choose 1 H standard value}$$

$$C = \frac{1}{(\text{attn.})\ \omega^2_{\text{ripple}} L} \qquad \text{farads} \tag{9-5}$$

$$= \frac{1}{(0.01)(2\pi)^2(120\ \text{Hz})^2(1\ \text{H})}$$

$$= \frac{10^{-6}}{0.00569} = 175\ \mu\text{F}$$

The ferroresonant constant-voltage transformer can hold the output voltage to within 1% for a ±15% line voltage variation. The constant-voltage transformer will also provide load regulation to within 2–5% for resistive loads but worsens quickly for reactive power factors. Waveform distortion also increases as the load is lightened. Consequently, these units are operated at half capacity or greater to maintain distortion under 3% or so with the harmonic-neutralized sinusoidal output types.

The constant-voltage transformer consists of four windings: a primary, resonant winding, harmonic compensation winding, and a secondary. A resonant circuit is formed with a capacitor and the resonant winding which acts to absorb changes in the primary voltage in concert with reluctance change in a magnetic shunt path in the core structure. Constant-voltage transformers provide an economically attractive approach that is widely used in raw supplies for digital equipment, since their line and load regulation are frequently adequate without resort to electronic regulation. This approach is generally competitive only at the higher volt-ampere ratings, however.

9-2 SHUNT REGULATORS

It is frequently not appreciated that a shunt zener regulator provides ripple reduction and line and load regulation. Consider the foregoing 200-mA raw supply attached to a 1N3793 15-V $1\frac{1}{2}$-W zener diode which exhibits an impedance of 10Ω at 25 mA zener current (Figure 9–4). Allowing for a nominal ±5% line voltage fluctuation and an output load variation ranging from 70 to 100 mA, ripple reduction and line and load regulation are calculated as shown. The principal drawback of the zener regulator is its efficiency which is typically in the 50% range, as with this example. Nevertheless, it does offer attractive performance, and its mechanization is simple and inexpensive.

where
$$V_{raw} = 20 \pm 1 \text{ V}$$
$$V_{reg} = 15 \text{ V}$$
$$\text{ripple}_{raw} = 96 \text{ mV rms}$$
$$I_{load} = 70\text{–}100 \text{ mA}$$
$$I_Z = 25 \text{ mA}$$
$$Z_Z = 10\ \Omega$$

$$\text{raw supply regulation} = \frac{V_{raw\ max} - V_{raw\ min}}{V_{raw\ min}} \cdot 100\% \tag{9-6}$$

$$= \frac{21\text{ V} - 19\text{ V}}{19\text{ V}} \cdot 100\%$$

$$= 10.5\%$$

$$R_B = \frac{V_{raw\ min} - V_{reg}}{I_{total\ min}} \tag{9-7}$$

$$= \frac{19\text{ V} - 15\text{ V}}{100\text{ mA} + 25\text{ mA}} = 32\ \Omega$$

$$I_{total\ max} = \frac{V_{raw\ max} - V_{reg}}{R_b} \tag{9-8}$$

$$= \frac{21\text{ V} - 15\text{ V}}{32\ \Omega} = 188\text{ mA}$$

$$\text{line regulation} = \frac{(I_{total\ max} - I_{total\ min})(z_z)}{2} \tag{9-9}$$

$$= \frac{(188\text{ mA} - 125\text{ mA})(10\ \Omega)}{2}$$

$$= 340\text{ mV or } 2.3\% \text{ of } V_{reg}$$

$$\text{load regulation} = (I_{load\ max} - I_{load\ min})(z_z) \tag{9-10}$$

$$= (100\text{ mA} - 70\text{ mA})(10\ \Omega)$$

$$= 300\text{ mV, or } 2\% \text{ of } V_{reg}$$

$$\text{output ripple} = \frac{(\text{ripple}_{raw})(z_z)}{R_b + Z_z} \tag{9-11}$$

$$= \frac{96\text{ mV rms}}{4.2}$$

$$= 23\text{ mV rms, or } 0.15\% \text{ of } V_{reg}$$

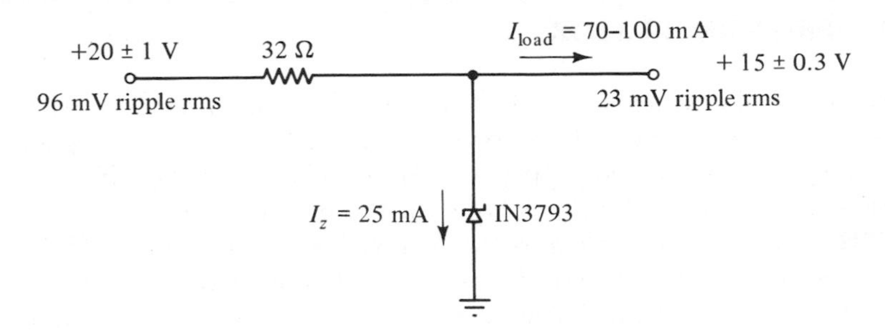

FIGURE 9–4. Zener Regulator Example

A zener-referenced bipolar shunt regulator provides performance on a level with zener regulation, but at a higher power-handling capability and without an expensive power zener (Figure 9–5). Voltage regulation and ripple reduction provided by this circuit are stable and frequently adequate. Efficiency is competitive with the series-type regulator, but its simplicity precludes features typical of the series regulator, such as current limiting and high ripple reduction. The low-power zener should be biased at the zero-temperature coefficient current I_z specified by the manufacturer. Best performance is obtained with a large current gain for the transistor, such as an MJE 1100 device. The following equations specify the circuit components with R_B chosen for adequate power dissipation.

$$I_{total} = I_z + 1.1 I_{load\ max} \tag{9-12}$$

$$R_B = \frac{V_{raw} - V_{reg}}{I_{total}} \tag{9-13}$$

$$R_1 = \frac{0.6\ \text{V}}{I_z - \dfrac{0.1 I_{load\ max}}{h_{FE}}} \tag{9-14}$$

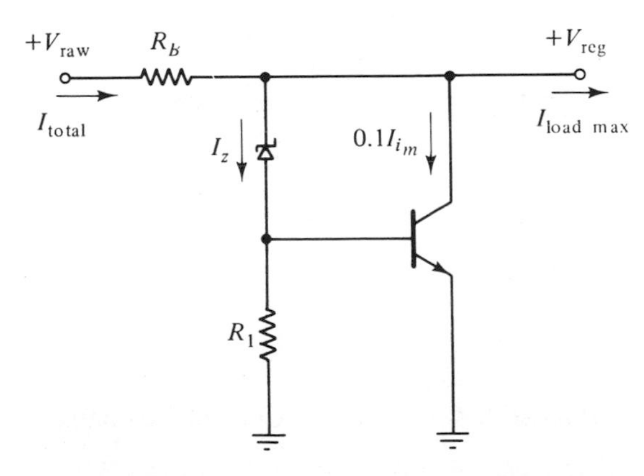

FIGURE 9–5. Bipolar Shunt Regulator

9-3 SERIES REGULATORS

A recent trend in voltage regulation is to distribute the filtered raw supply voltage to user circuits with an on-board linear three-terminal regulator providing final regulation, ripple reduction, and decoupling. The newest designs emphasize low-current types in the 100-mA range in low-cost TO-92 plastic packages such as the National Semiconductor LM78LXX series devices. Most of these devices are self-contained ICs with short-circuit protection, thermal shutdown, and are available as dual-tracking plus and minus regulators. Modular linear supplies with remote-sense lines terminated at the circuit board provide the same result. With this approach it is good practice to connect 100-Ω resistors between the output and sense terminals at the supply to preclude overvoltage in the event that either sense line is broken. In general, the use of modular regulated supplies is more expensive than the distributed raw supply and on-board regulator approach. These self-contained modular supplies typically use a 723-type IC regulator and are convenient for powering small systems, however.

Three-terminal regulators are available with output voltages from 5 to 40 V and currents from 100 mA to 3 A. Line and load regulation are typically 0.1% to 1% with about 40 dB of ripple rejection. The primary utility of these devices is their ability to provide economical local on-board regulation with decoupling, output protection, and circuit simplicity. And several regulators may be operated from a single raw supply, all supplying different regulated voltages as required. A tantalum input capacitor is normally required which will be specified by the manufacturer to ensure unconditionally stable operation. An additional feature is their flexibility for configuration as a constant-current source (Figure 9–6). Output voltage adjustment is possible by elevating the ground reference terminal above 0 V. Remote switching is also feasible and is described by Figure 9–7.

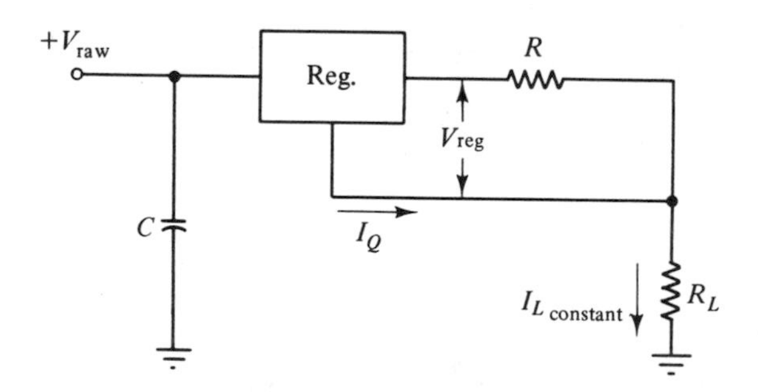

FIGURE 9–6. Constant-Current Regulator

$$I_{L\ \text{constant}} = \frac{V_{reg}}{R} + I_Q \tag{9-15}$$

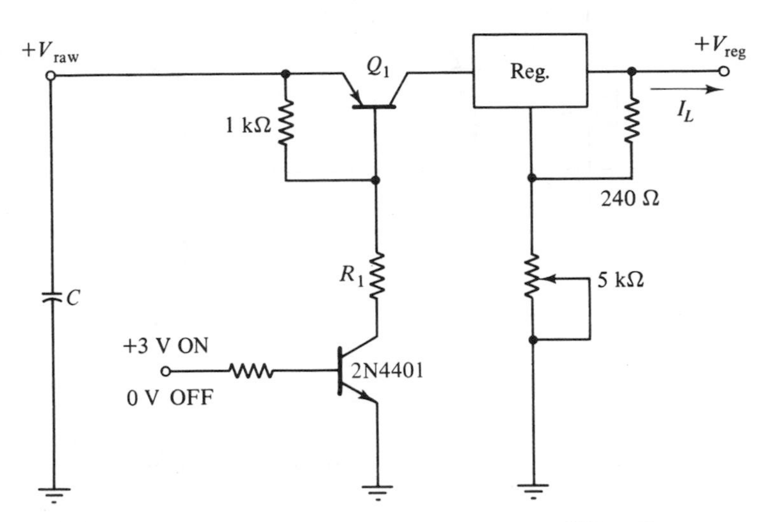

FIGURE 9–7. Adjustable Remote Turnoff Regulator

$$R_1 = \frac{V_{raw}}{I_L} \cdot h_{FE_{Q1}} \tag{9-16}$$

The basic linear series regulator shown by Figure 9–8 forms the heart of both the three-terminal and modular devices. The typical circuit includes a constant-current source Q_1 that provides line regulation by maintaining I constant with a varying V_{raw}. Error amplifier Q_5 shunts current away from the Darlington output pass stage with an increase in output voltage, thereby increasing the drop across the series pass transistor Q_3. Zener diode D_1 provides the error amplifier reference voltage, and Q_4 provides output current limiting by conducting when forward-biased by excessive current through R_s which cuts off Q_2 and Q_3. Capacitor C_2 limits the error amplifier bandwidth to ensure stability and prevent the regulator from becoming a power oscillator. The principal limitation of the linear series regulator is the power dissipation in the pass stage Q_3, which must maintain operation in the active region of its transfer characteristic. Efficiency is typically in the 40–60% range. Overvoltage devices are also available which conduct and bypass the regulator to ground in the event of an overvoltage condition. These optional components, placed at the regulator output, are good insurance against catastrophic circuit damage from a shorted pass transistor which would connect the raw supply voltage to the load.

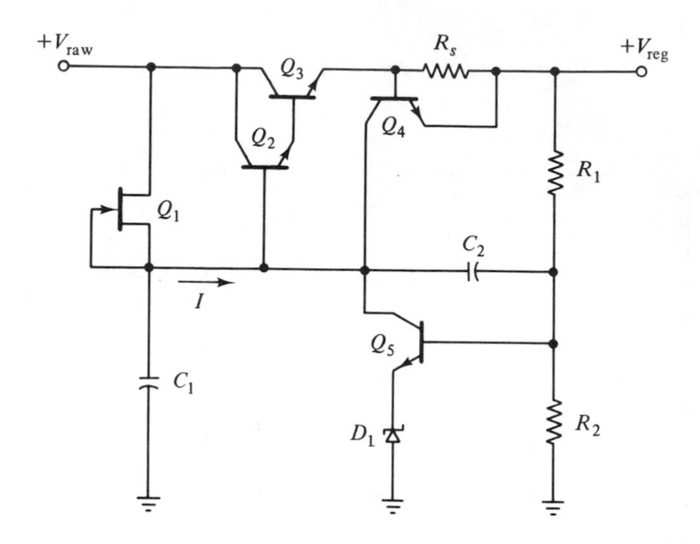

FIGURE 9–8. Basic Linear Series Regulator

Crowbar overvoltage protection is generally implemented by means of an SCR device (Figure 9–9). The purpose of the crowbar is to protect the load from damage if the power-supply-regulator pass stage shorts and applies the full raw supply across the load. The SCR anode is connected to the raw supply to prevent destroying the pass stage in the event of a false crowbar firing. The zener is selected to equal the maximum supply output voltage permitted. A capacitor protects against rate effect and false SCR firings. A fuse is always included in this circuit to provide assured clearing of the overvoltage condition. The SCR ensures blowing of the fuse.

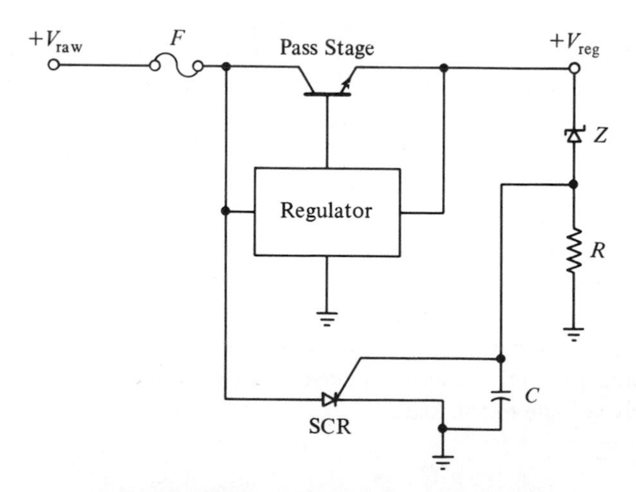

FIGURE 9–9. Overvoltage Crowbar

9-4 SWITCHING REGULATORS

Switching supplies are two to three times more efficient and complex than linear supplies with a typical efficiency around 80%. With the advent of reliable switching transistors and improved output filtering, low-output noise versions appeared with regulation to 0.01% and total noise and ripple of 1 mV rms (Figure 9–10). The incoming line is rectified if it is ac, and the dc then chopped at a 25kHz to 50 kHz rate by bipolar switching transistors. This square-wave voltage is then stepped up or down as required, usually by a toroidal transformer, and then rectified to provide the output voltage of interest. Efficiency is high because the cutoff-to-saturation transitions of the transistors result in negligible dissipation, toroidal transformer efficiency is high, and no large output filter components are required because of the high ripple frequency. Regulation is achieved by means of a feedback trigger circuit which controls the duty cycle of the switching transistors to maintain the load voltage at the rated value. Some high-power switching regulators omit the line transformer for even greater efficiency. The output filter is an important section of the switching supply and is usually an *LC* type for high power efficiency.

Similar to the application of on-board three-terminal regulators, the dc-to-dc convertor is a switching supply that can also be used on each circuit board in a system all fed from a common supply. This becomes economically attractive when two or more regulated voltages are required by one board and additional voltages by other boards in a system. An example of such an application is a sensor-based microprocessor system requiring different voltages for the processor, data conversion, and perhaps auxiliary logic circuits. This method of power distribution is described by Figure 9–11.

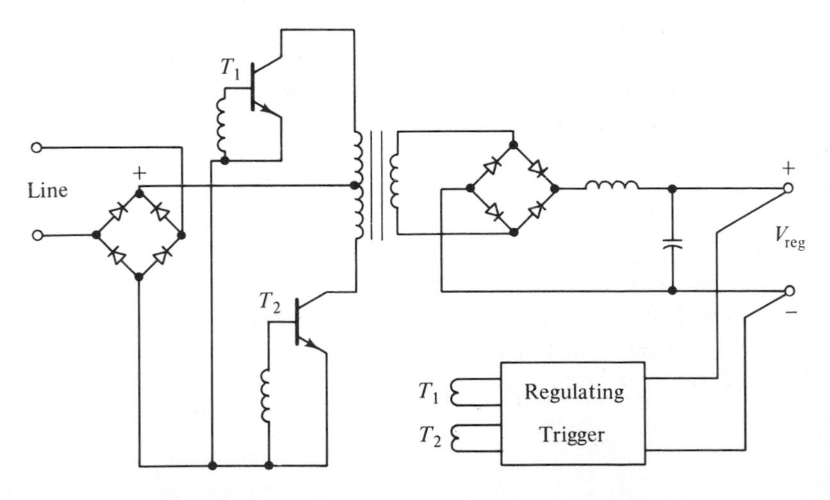

FIGURE 9–10. Basic Switching Supply

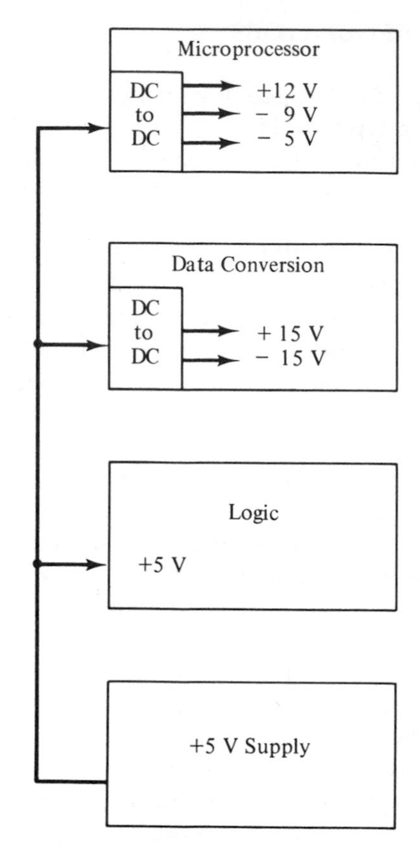

FIGURE 9–11. DC-to-DC Convertor Power Distribution

The greatest frequency of series regulator failures is attributable to overdissipation in the pass transistor and its driver. In high-current supplies using the standard 2N3055 pass transistor, substitution of a 2N3772 provides better performance, owing to its higher gain. With switching regulators sputtering of the output filter capacitors due to heating caused by ripple across the capacitor's effective series resistance (ESR) can result in destruction of the switching control circuitry. This phenomenon is prevalent with tantalum capacitors in high-frequency switchers, because the maximum permissible ripple for these capacitors decreases with frequency. Even well-designed supplies generate heat that must be removed to avoid heat prostration of the supply. This is the subject of the following section.

9-5 THERMAL DESIGN

All electronic equipment needs cooling to maintain the temperature of each component below its safe operating value. Heat always flows from hotter components to cooler ones, and the temperature of each component will rise until it is hot enough to transfer its heat. This section provides information to aid in the thermal design and heat transfer for electronic equipment. In all cases the cooling of such equipment consists of the conduction of heat from components to the cooling medium and the transfer of this heat to the ambient environment. This problem is summarized in equation (9-17).

$$T\,(\text{component}) = \Delta T\,(\text{conduction}) + \Delta T\,(\text{transfer}) + T\,(\text{ambient}) \qquad (9\text{-}17)$$

Because most electronic components operate over a range of power-dissipation values, the concept of thermal resistance Θ is very useful. Thermal resistance permits component temperature to be determined at any arbitrary power dissipation and is normally specified by the manufacturer for semiconductor devices. This parameter is expressed by equation (9-18) aided by Table 9–3.

TABLE 9–3. Thermal Conductivity

Material	K (W/in.°C)
Aluminum	5.5
Copper	10.0
Steel	1.7
Still air	0.0007
Thermal compound	0.01
Glass	0.02
Mica	0.018
Teflon	0.005

$$\Theta = \frac{\Delta T}{Q} = \frac{\lambda}{K\alpha} \qquad \text{°C/watt} \qquad (9\text{-}18)$$

where Q = conducted heat, watts
λ = heat conduction length, inches
K = thermal conductivity, watts/inch °C
α = cross-sectional area, square inches

The mounting of electronic components on a heat sink can present heat-transfer problems if the surfaces only touch at their high points.

Either soldering or the use of thermal heat sink compound plus mechanical compression between the component and heat sink are essential. In the case of cooling fins, heat conduction through the fins is not constant but decreases along the fin from base to tip. The temperature difference required to transfer the heat to the ambient depends upon the number and geometry of the fins and the heat-transfer method, such as radiation and natural convection or forced air.

Consider the following heat-transfer example for a 2N3055 series regulator pass transistor. This device is rated by its manufacturer to dissipate 100 W at a maximum junction temperature of 50°C. With a TO-3 case, the Θ_{JC} is 1.5°C/W and Θ_{CS} is 0.35°C/W for a mica washer and thermal grease. For 48 W maximum device dissipation, determine the required heat-sink thermal resistance. Linearly derating to 50 W dissipation with the aid of Figure 9–12 allows a 125°C junction temperature.

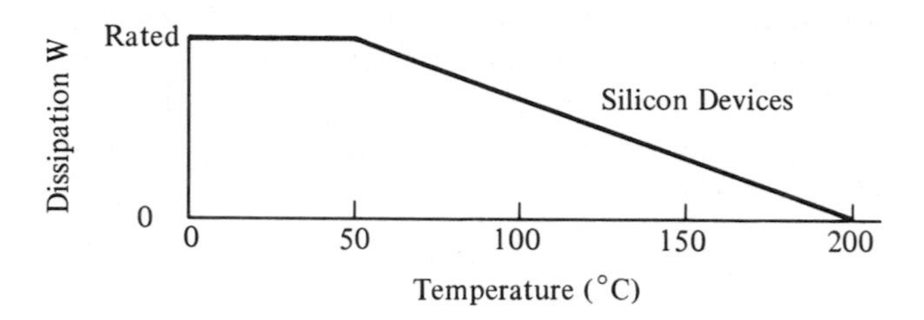

FIGURE 9–12. Junction Temperature Versus Dissipation Derating

Assume that the ambient temperature is at 25°C and select a convection heat sink having an Θ_{SA} equal to or less than the calculated value. The thermal resistance diagram for this example is described in Figure 9–13.

$$T(\text{component}) = \Delta T(\text{conduction}) + \Delta T(\text{transfer}) + T(\text{ambient}) \qquad (9\text{-}17)$$

$$T_{J_{max}} = P_{\text{dissipation}}(\Theta_{JC} + \Theta_{CS} + \Theta_{SA}) + T(\text{ambient}) \qquad (9\text{-}19)$$

$$125°\text{C} = 48\text{ W}(1.5°\text{C/W} + 0.35°\text{C/W} + \Theta_{SA}) + 25°\text{C}$$

$$\Theta_{SA} = \frac{12°\text{C}}{48\text{ W}}$$

$$= 0.25°\text{C/W}$$

Approximately an order-of-magnitude increase in heat transfer can be achieved with the use of forced air rather than relying on radiation and natural convection. When the heat to be transferred is above about 50 W, forced air cooling may provide a better system design because of the

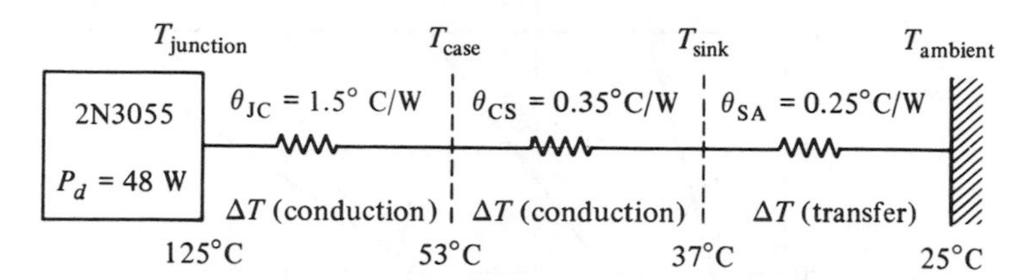

FIGURE 9–13. Thermal Resistance Diagram

excessive size of convection heat sinks. Air always should be blown into an enclosure through a filter rather than exhausted, to avoid dust entrainment. Because of the complicated nature of air flow, a simple formula is not available for calculating the air pressure required to flush a given amount of air through an enclosure. Further, the temperature of the air rises as it absorbs heat, and component temperatures accordingly rise to be hotter than the surrounding air in order to continue to transfer heat. However, increasing the air flow has limitations because of the buildup of back pressure.

Nevertheless, an approximate design guide is available with reference to Figure 9–14, which relates airflow to thermal resistance. From the preceding transistor cooling example, the heat sink could be reduced in size to a Θ_{SA} of 1°C/W if 40 ft^3/min of air is directed over it. But note

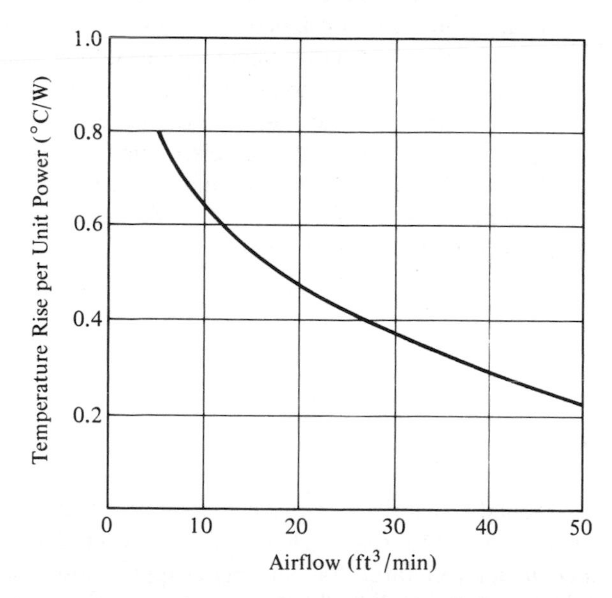

FIGURE 9–14. Forced-Air-Cooled Heatsink (*Courtesy* Wiley-Interscience)

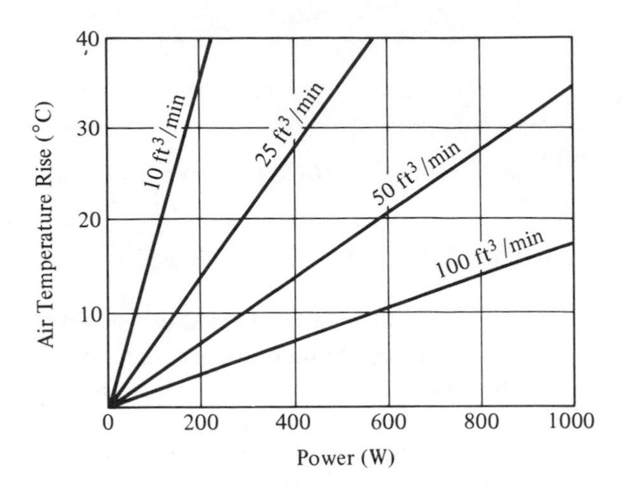

FIGURE 9–15. Enclosure Air Temperature Rise (*Courtesy* Wiley-Interscience)

that the curve has a knee around 18 ft^3/min, which is attributable to the previously mentioned back pressure. Therefore, a Θ_{SA} of 0.5°C/W and 18 ft^3/min would result in the same cooling, with greater economy in the size of the fan. For an enclosure containing several circuit boards or subsystems, each unit should be designed to operate satisfactorily on the bench with only conduction and natural convection cooling. A cooling fan is then specified to ensure that enough air flow is provided to limit enclosure temperature rise to the desired value. For example, with reference to Figure 9–15, a total internal dissipation of 200 W and an 18-ft^3/min air flow will limit the enclosure internal air temperature rise to 20°C above the ambient. A satisfactory cooling design and fan selection can be developed with the aid of this figure.

PROBLEMS

9-1 A center-tapped full-wave rectifier is to supply 1 A at 100 V with no more than 1 V RMS ripple. For a 2 Henry choke of 10Ω DC resistance in an LC filter for this raw supply, determine: (a) the required capacitance value, (b) the transformer V-A rating, and (c) the voltage regulation from no load to full load. Ignore rectifier voltage drop and label the completed circuit.

9-2 Design a zener regulated microprocessor power supply to provide +12 V and −9 V at 100 mA each. For an output ripple of 10 mV RMS, determine: (a) R_b, (b) the raw supply filter capacitors, and (c) the dual-secondary transformer total volt-ampere rating. Allow 10 mA in each zener, assume a 60 Hz line frequency, each secondary $V_{rms}=20$ V, $Z_z=10\Omega$, and show the completed circuit.

9-3 Show how the output voltage of a three-terminal regulator circuit can be raised above its rated value by the addition of two resistors. Derive an equation expressing the output voltage for such a circuit arrangement.

9-4 A potential problem exists with the basic regulator circuit of Figure 9–7 at low output currents. When the collector-to-base leakage current of Q_3 is adequate to supply its base current at low regulator output currents, the regulator may fail due to the loss of control by Q_2. Provide a solution for this problem.

9-5 The Class A germanium audio output stage of a well-known automobile radio manufacturer has a $\Theta_{JC}=0.9°\text{C/watt}$ mounted on a heat sink of $\Theta_{SA}=2°\text{C/watt}$. For a maximum junction temperature of 70°C, an ambient temperature of 50°C and a $\Theta_{CS}=0.6°$ C watt, determine: (a) the allowable device power dissipation, and (b) the transistor case temperature at this dissipation.

9-6 A microcomputer enclosure designed for convection cooling contains a CPU which dissipates 7.2 W to which is added an analog I/0 board dissipating 3.1 W. An auxiliary hardware multiply/divide board is then added which dissipates 4.4 W. Finally, a megabyte of semiconductor memory is included on 16 boards each dissipating 6.6 W. Determine the forced air flow necessary over these circuit boards to limit their temperature rise to 10 degrees above the ambient air temperature.

REFERENCES

1. L. Accardi, "Super Stable Reference Voltage Source," *Electronic Design News*, May 15, 1972.

2. *DC Power Supply Handbook*, Hewlett-Packard, 100 Locust Avenue, Berkeley Heights, N.J. 07922, 1970.

3. E. Dilatush, "Power Supplies Special Report," *Electronic Design News*, April 5, 1976.

4. E. R. Hnatek, "Use Integrated Circuits in Transformerless DC-to-DC Converters," *Electronic Design News*, February 5, 1973.

5. A. Kusko et al., "Designing Reliability into Power Circuits," *Electronics*, March 8, 1976.

6. L. Mattera, "Powering Up with Linear IC's," *Electronics*, February 3, 1977.

7. R. S. Olla, "Switching Regulators: The Efficient Way to Power," *Electronics*, August 16, 1973.

8. *Power Supply Handbook*, Kepco Incorporated, Flushing, N.Y. 11352, 1965.

9. A. W. Scott, *Cooling Of Electronic Equipment*, Wiley–Interscience, New York, 1974.

10. *Voltage Regulator Handbook*, National Semiconductor, 2900 Semiconductor Drive, Santa Clara, Calif. 95051, May 1975.

11. R. L. Young, *Linear and Digital Electronic Devices, Circuit, Filter, and Subsystem Design*, Short Course Notes, University of Cincinnati, March 1974.

10

RELIABILITY OF ELECTRONIC SYSTEMS

10-0 INTRODUCTION

The need for higher levels of reliability in electronic equipment increases year by year for various reasons, including the demand for increased performance and the economic consequences of downtime resulting from equipment failure. The reliability of hardware systems is concerned with the prediction of equipment performance over a specified interval, including the reserve strength against stress. Accordingly, methods are available for calculating the average time between failures for component parts and systems and the probability of completing system operation over a given time period.

One purpose of this chapter is to present the basic relationships that define the reliability behavior of components and systems. Then the development of design considerations is pursued through which reliability can be improved, such as from an informed choice of components and derating for stress reduction. Finally, reliability enhancement methods are evaluated, including preventative maintenance, redundant paths, and standby systems. The application of these principles will enable the designer to estimate the reliability of specific systems, identify and improve critical areas, and determine the best allocation of resources for maximizing system availability within given cost constraints.

10-1 THEORETICAL BASIS OF RELIABILITY

As a qualitative description, reliability can be defined as the probability of a system performing its intended mission satisfactorily when it is required to. Experience has shown that it is more productive to design reliability into equipment than to determine it by testing. Consequently, functional relationships have been developed for valid mathematical prediction of reliability behavior. Three clearly definable periods form the composite life cycle of components and their extension into systems: the early failure period, the useful life period, and the wearout period. These three intervals generate the bathtub reliability curve of Figure 10–1, wh

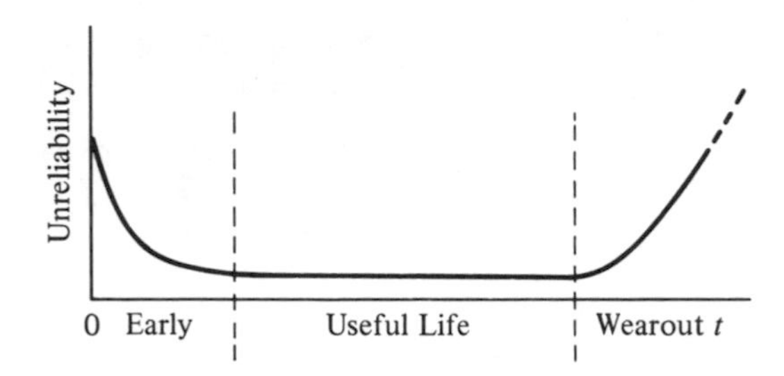

FIGURE 10–1. Bathtub Reliability Curve

each segment is defined by a probability density function unique to the behavior during that interval. Early and useful life reliabilities are characterized by exponential functions and progressive wearout by the normal probability density function.

$$\text{unreliability} = 1 - \text{reliability} \tag{10-1}$$

$$\text{early reliability} = \exp\left(-\frac{n_e t}{m_e}\right) \tag{10-2}$$

$$\text{useful life reliability} = \exp\left(-\frac{t}{m}\right) \tag{10-3}$$

$$\text{wearout reliability} = 1 - \int_0^T \frac{\exp\left[-(T-m)^2/2\sigma^2\right]}{(2\pi\sigma^2)^{1/2}} \tag{10-4}$$

where n_e = number of substandard components
m_e = substandard mean time between failures
m = good component mean time between failures
σ = wearout standard deviation
M = wearout mean life
T = total elapsed operating time

The mean time between failures (MTBF), m, is usually available from the manufacturer and is a necessary parameter required before reliability evaluation can be attempted. However, if a quoted MTBF is not supported by actual tests of a statistically valid number of components, it can be wrong by orders of magnitude when based only on intelligent guesswork. Also, testing a couple of units until they evidence trouble is equally meaningless for acquiring a valid MTBF. If an experimental MTBF is to be made, the nonreplacement method is generally preferred for its efficiency. This method is defined by equations (10-5) and (10-6) and provides results possessing a 90% confidence.

$$m = \sum_{i=1}^{r} \frac{t_i + (n-r)t_r}{r} \tag{10-5}$$

$$n = \frac{30}{1 - \exp(-t_r/m_s)} \tag{10-6}$$

where m = MTBF
n = sample size
t_i = elapsed time to individual failures
t_r = total test time much less than mean life M
M = estimated or specified mean life M
m_s = estimated or supplied MTBF
r = sum of failed units to time t_r

Early failures are normally eliminated within the first 20–200 h by burn-in or debugging procedures. When completed, reliability is not further affected by this cause. Debugging time can be expressed in terms of the harmonic progression of equation (10-7). For 10 substandard components and an early failure MTBF m_e of 10 h, this formula predicts the average time required to clear 63% of early failures. And since this behavior follows an exponential decay relationship, $5E$ provides for a 99% debugged system.

$$E = m_e\left(1 + \frac{1}{2} + \frac{1}{3} + \cdots + \frac{1}{n_e}\right) \tag{10-7}$$

$$= 30 \text{ h} \quad \text{for 63\% debugging}$$

$$5E = 150 \text{ h} \quad \text{for 99\% debugging}$$

For components and systems in general, reliability usually implies the operating time span between the debugging of early failures and before wearout effects become appreciable. During this useful-life period failures occur at random and cannot be further reduced by component replacement. Although these chance failures are not predictable, their frequency of occurrence is constant and defined by the inverse of MTBF, $1/m$. Consequently, during the useful-life period reliability will be the same for equal operating periods, regardless of the starting point. This is described by the exponential probability distribution of equation (10-3). It can easily be shown, therefore, that useful life failures will remain below 10% if the operating time t is held to one tenth of m. However, if components are not replaced until $t=m$, only a 37% survival chance exists (Figure 10-2a). Extending this to a more complex example, consider the reliability calculation of equation (10-3) for an electronic circuit where the operating time to maintain not less than 99% reliability is of interest (Table 10–1). The interpretation of this result is that 99 out of every 100 operating periods of 110 h will be completed without chance failure. However, the circuit can fail in any one of the 100 periods. Note that the expected hourly failure rate for this circuit is determined from the sum of the contributions of each component.

TABLE 10–1. Electronic Circuit Hourly Failure Rate

Components	MTBF	Failure Rate
10 diodes	$\div m$ of 5×10^5 h	$=2\times10^{-5}$/h
4 transistors	$\div m$ of 10^5 h	$=4\times10^{-5}$/h
20 resistors	$\div m$ of 10^6 h	$=2\times10^{-5}$/h
10 capacitors	$\div m$ of 10^6 h	$=1\times10^{-5}$/h
Expected hourly failure rate Σ^1/m		$=9\times10^{-5}$/h

$$\text{useful life reliability} = \exp(-9\times10^{-5}t) \qquad (10\text{-}3)$$

$$=0.99 \quad \text{for 110 operating hours}$$

Wearout is usually of more consequence than either early or chance failures. As component strength deterioration sets in wearout failures rise above the chance failure level, thereby defining the useful life–wearout boundary. From Figure 10–2 it is apparent that an exponentially behaving population of components suffers its greatest losses in the period before m. The normally behaving population, in comparison, suffers its greatest losses around the mean life, M. And in almost all instances $M<m$. Therefore, the end of the useful life period can nominally be defined to occur at the time $M-3\sigma$, which also corresponds to $\frac{1}{2}$% of the area under the normal probability distribution curve described by equation (10-4).

Considering the previous electronic circuit example with an expected hourly failure rate of 9×10^{-5} per hour, it is of interest to determine the combined reliability due to chance and wearout failure contributions. The total age T is taken to be 800 h of operation, the mean life M is 1000 h, and the standard deviation σ is 100 h. Combined reliability is equal to the

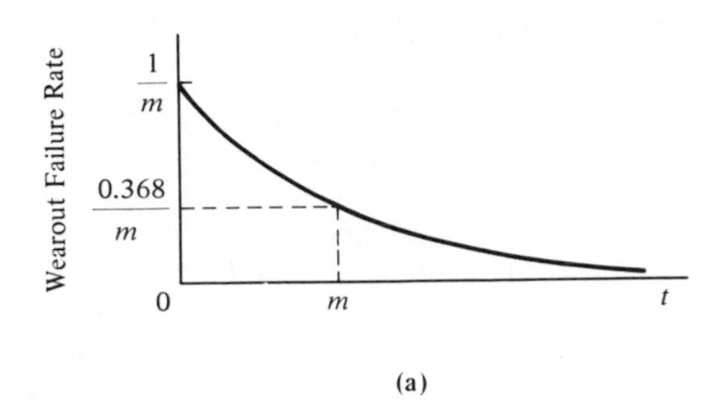

(a)

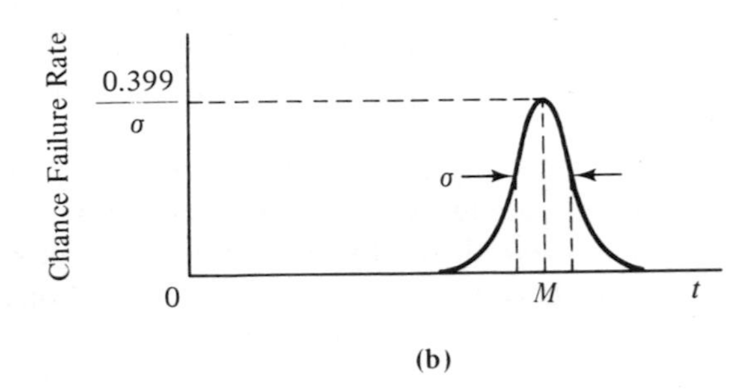

(b)

FIGURE 10–2. Chance and Wearout Failure Behavior

product of the individual reliabilities, and integration of the normal distribution requires resort to tabulations of the error function available in most mathematical handbooks.

$$\text{combined reliability} = \text{useful life} \cdot \text{wearout} \tag{10-8}$$

$$= \exp\left(\frac{-t}{m}\right) \cdot \left[1 - \int_0^T \frac{\exp\left[-(T-M)^2/2\sigma^2\right]}{(2\pi\sigma^2)^{1/2}}\right]$$

$$= \exp(-9 \times 10^{-5} \cdot 800)$$

$$\cdot \left[1 - \int_0^{800} \frac{\exp\left[-(800-1000)^2/2 \cdot (100)^2\right]}{\left[2\pi(100)^2\right]^{1/2}}\right]$$

$$= (0.93) \cdot (1 - 0.023)$$

$$= 0.91$$

10-2 COMPONENT-PART BEHAVIOR

The designer has two useful tools at his disposal in designing for reliability —reliability calculations employing component failure rates, and the derating of components for stress reduction. The reliability of electronic systems is mostly series-type reliability, with little redundancy involved. Consequently, component derating is essential for the achievement of high reliabilities. And because the reliability of a series system is determined by the sum of the component failure rates, design simplification is important. There is a distinct difference between design for high reliability and fail-safe design. A single-engine aircraft is an example of the former, and the Lunar Excursion Module is an example of the latter, which included considerable complexity in the form of redundant paths and functional overlap.

To carry out the reliability calculations, a design is partitioned into its equivalent series and parallel paths and the calculations performed on these paths in accordance with the following rules. The product law for series-connected elements is defined by equation (10-9). Equation (10-10) defines the relationship for parallel-connected elements for the case of two paths. Whether the calculations include only the useful life reliability of equation (10-2) or the combined useful life and wearout relationship of equation (10-8) is determined by the component useful life–wearout boundaries for each path.

$$R_s = R_1 \cdot R_2 \cdots R_n \qquad (10\text{-}9)$$

$$R_p = R_1 + R_2 - R_1 \cdot R_2 \qquad (10\text{-}10)$$

The purpose of preventative maintenance is to develop a program designed to eliminate wearout through component replacement and overhaul. Preventative replacement is essential for reliable operation of long-life systems. For example, the scheduled periodic overhaul of aircraft with replacement of fatigued components ensures their continued integrity and high reliability during operation. Therefore, only the useful life reliability is involved and is typically 0.99999 for each hour of flight. In contrast, if components are replaced only as they fail, then a system of many components will exhibit an elevated and constant failure rate. An aging automobile is an example of equipment that is usually serviced only when required and eventually stabilizes at a high and continuous component failure rate.

Since it is normally of interest to maximize both the reliabilty and cost effectiveness of a system, the choice of replacement or overhaul time is an important consideration. Accepted practice to avoid wearout contributions to system reliability is to replace components at $M-3\sigma$, when both mean life and standard deviation are known. Unfortunately, these data usually are not available. With this lack, but the probable availability of MTBF, a user is confronted with the situation of trying to deduce some relationship between M and m. Such intelligent guesswork has no basis in fact and is impeachable for a number of reasons including the possibility of varying stress levels over component lifetime. However, observation suggests that a range of wearout times may be postulated for solid-state

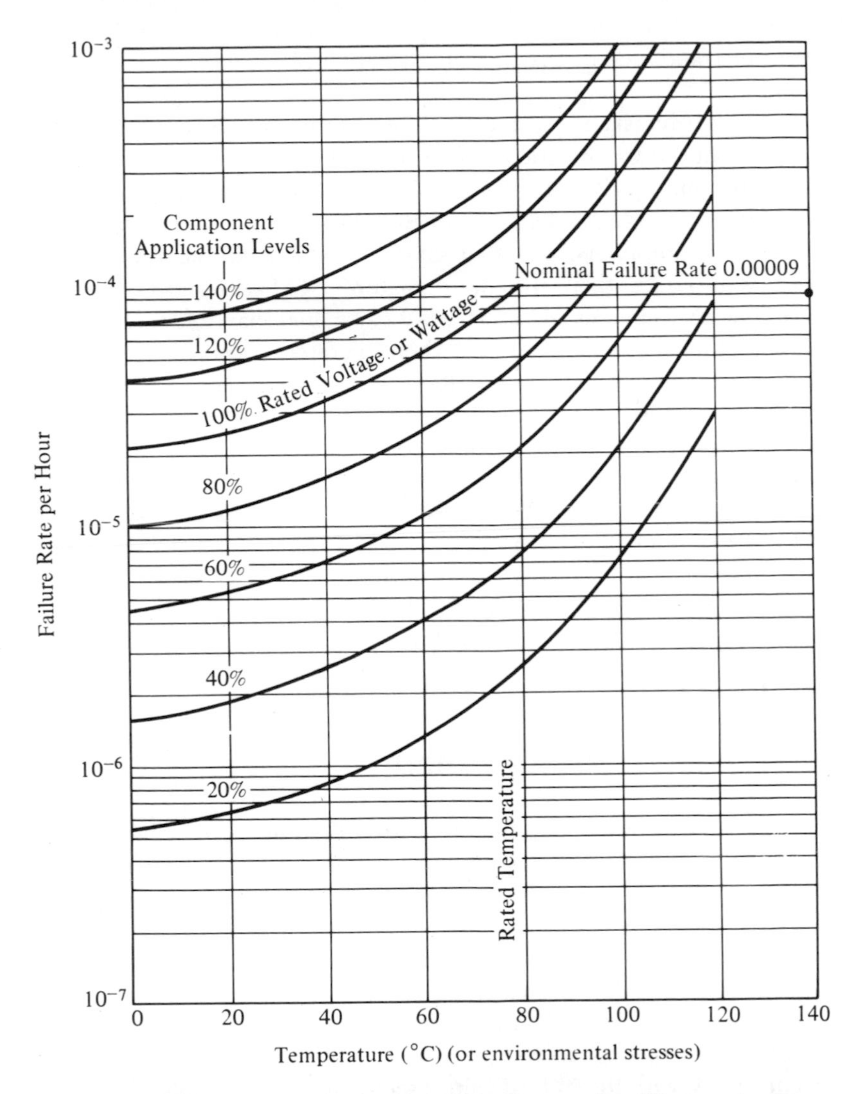

FIGURE 10–3. Failure-Rate Derating Curves for Electronic Components (*Courtesy* Prentice-Hall)

systems, extending from about 5000 to 50,000 h. The higher value would apply to conservatively designed and operated circuits such as digital computers, and the lower value to cost-competitive circuits such as television receivers.

The dependence of component failure rates on temperature and dielectric stresses approximately follows the Arrhenius law, which states that the rate of chemical reactions doubles with each 10°C rise. Figure 10–3 shows failure-rate derating curves for electronic components, from which it is evident that derating components by about one third in both temperature and voltage results in an order-of-magnitude failure-rate reduction.

A frequently asked question is: What performance improvement is available from the specification of high-reliability components beyond the derating technique? Recent studies[5,6] indicate that discrete transistors have about a 25% greater failure rate than linear integrated circuits such as operational amplifiers, and that CMOS digital logic has up to a 4:1 greater failure rate than the more mature 5400 series TTL devices. Passive devices such as resistors and capacitors have failure rates a fraction of those of active devices when operated within their specified ratings, although capacitors do fail at nearly three times the rate of resistors because of the greater variety of materials and number of assembly steps used in their manufacture.

Both linear and digital active devices are available in commerical and military reliability grades. There are additional categories within the military grade, depending upon the extensiveness of the tests performed, such as precap visual, X-ray, and burn-in tests. However, the most expensive devices do not always provide the highest reliability, owing to their reduced production runs. The lowest military category, unscreened mil temp, is a good value and has an excellent history of low failure rates.

10-3 RELIABILITY ENHANCEMENT

Reliability and modular design are two different approaches to the reduction of maintenance costs. Reliable design reduces the frequency of repair, while modular construction reduces the service cost per failure and increases maintenance effectiveness. These two concepts may also be combined for additional benefit, as shown in the following development. A modularly designed color television receiver has its largest voltage and temperature stresses associated with the horizontal sweep subsystem. This is essentially a series connected arrangement of three modules, described by Figure 10–4, with the MTBF values shown for each module.

The expected hourly failure rate sum for this subsystem is $1/m = 1.4 \times 10^{-5}$ per hour. Assuming that the set is operated a nominal 1000 hours per year, then from previous developments wearout will not contribute to the failure rate until about 5000 h, which is equivalent to 5 years of operation. Consequently, the warranty period may safely extend to 1 year with freedom from wearout contributions to the failure rate. This leaves the chance failure or useful life reliability which is calculated for a 1000-hour operating period.

$$R_s = \exp(-2\times10^{-6}\cdot10^3)\cdot\exp(-10^{-5}\cdot10^3)\cdot\exp(-2\times10^{-6}\cdot10^3) \quad (10\text{-}9)$$

$$= (0.998)(0.99)(0.998)$$

$$= 0.986 \quad \text{per 1000 operating hours}$$

Synch → Horizontal Oscillator $m = 5\times10^5$ h → Horizontal Output $m = 10^5$ h → High Voltage and Regulator $m = 5\times10^5$ h → CRT

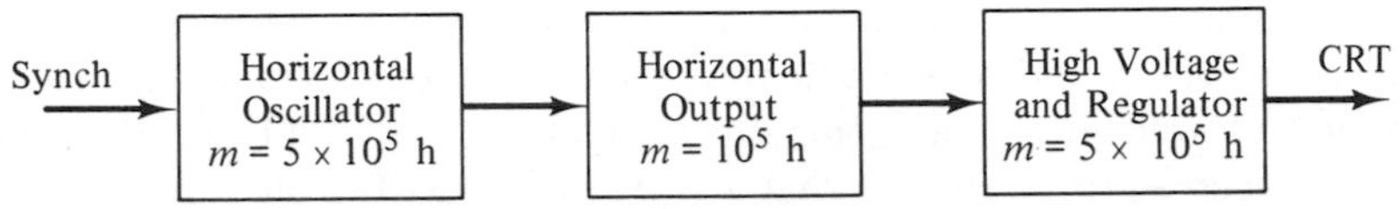

FIGURE 10–4. Horizontal Sweep Subsystem

Ideally, at the end of 5000 h of operation preventative replacement should be exercised. Within this operating period, however, the chance failure reliability can be enhanced by operating two horizontal output modules in parallel (Figure 10-5), each sharing the stresses and where the overall subsystem reliability is now described by equation (10-10) embedded in equation (10-9). Reliability is seen to be increased due to the redundant configuration of the horizontal output stage. The MTBF for equal output modules operated in parallel is defined by equation (10-11).

$$R_s = R_{osc}\cdot R_p\cdot R_{HV} \quad (10\text{-}9)$$

$$= \exp(-2\times10^{-6}\cdot10^3)\cdot\big[\exp(-10^{-5}\cdot10^3)$$

$$+\exp(-10^{-5}\cdot10^3) - \exp(-10^{-5}\cdot10^3)$$

$$\times\exp(-10^{-5}\cdot10^3)\big]\cdot\exp(-2\times10^{-5}\cdot10^3)$$

$$= (0.998)\cdot[0.99+0.99-(0.99)(0.99)]\cdot(0.998)$$

$$= 0.996 \quad \text{per 1000 operating hours}$$

$$m_p = m + \frac{m}{2} + \cdots + \frac{m}{n} \quad (10\text{-}11)$$

$$= 10^5 + \frac{10^5}{2} = 1.5\times10^5\,\text{h}$$

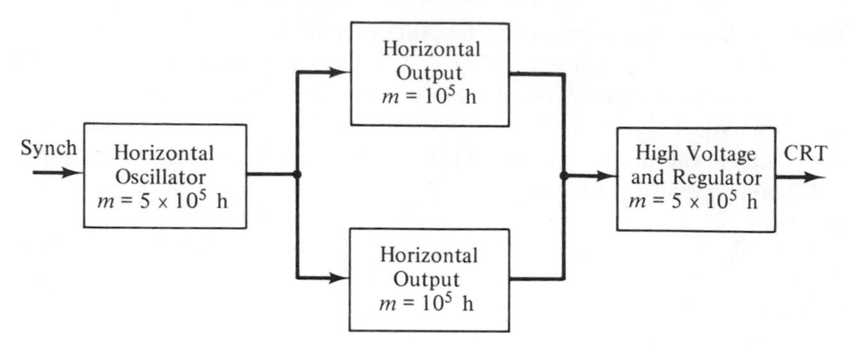

FIGURE 10–5. Redundant Module Operation

Redundant operation of systems usually is not economically justifiable, however. Standby reliability offers reliability enhancement similar to redundant reliability and generally at a lower cost, and an additional benefit accrues from the fact that a replacement part in standby does not accumulate wearout. But an acceptable transfer or replacement method must be worked out within the limits of permissible system outage or downtime following a failure. For example, an acceptable downtime for a television receiver may be a day. However, for a standby power system, allowable outage time may be less than 1 s, necessitating a more complicated transfer scheme.

For identical modules or components, one operating and the remaining standing by, their combined reliability is defined by the Poisson distribution of equation (10-12). For a single standby unit, which is more often the situation, standby reliability is described by equation (10-13). Considering the horizontal sweep subsystem now with a single standby horizontal output module and a 1000-h operating period, the chance failure reliability is determined to be 0.996, which is identical to the previous redundant configuration. Of course, this assumes a correct failure diagnosis and efficient changeover method.

$$\exp(-X)\cdot\left(1+X+\frac{X^2}{2!}+\frac{X^3}{3!}+\cdots\right)=1 \qquad (10\text{-}12)$$

$$R_{SBY}=\exp\left(\frac{-t}{m}\right)\cdot\left(1+\frac{t}{m}\right) \qquad (10\text{-}13)$$

$$=\exp(-10^{-5}.10^3)(1+10^{-5}.10^3)$$

$$=(0.99)(1.01)$$

$$=0.9999 \quad \text{per 1000 operating hours}$$

$$R_s=R_{osc}\cdot R_{SBY}\cdot R_{HV} \qquad (10\text{-}9)$$

$$=(0.998)(0.9999)(0.998)$$

$$=0.996 \quad \text{per 1000 operating hours}$$

10-4 SYSTEM RELIABILITY AND AVAILABILITY

Reliability has been examined both at the component and subsystem levels. The concepts presented are now extended to the system level, where it is of interest to determine the expected reliability for specific operating intervals. A process control system having a computer that supervises four similar controller channels over a dedicated line and multiplexed interface provides a useful example. It is of interest to determine the reliability of this system, shown by Figure 10–6, per monthly 720-h operating periods. It is assumed that there are no wearout contributions to the failure rate. Representative reliability data are presented in Table 10–2 and a total series connected system is also assumed, where a failure in any controller channel is considered a system failure. The allocation of resources to improve the system reliability determined by equation (10-3), where the MTBF for this series connected system is obtained from equation (10-14), could include a redundant computer and/or interface. However, the cost effectiveness of this action would likely be marginal.

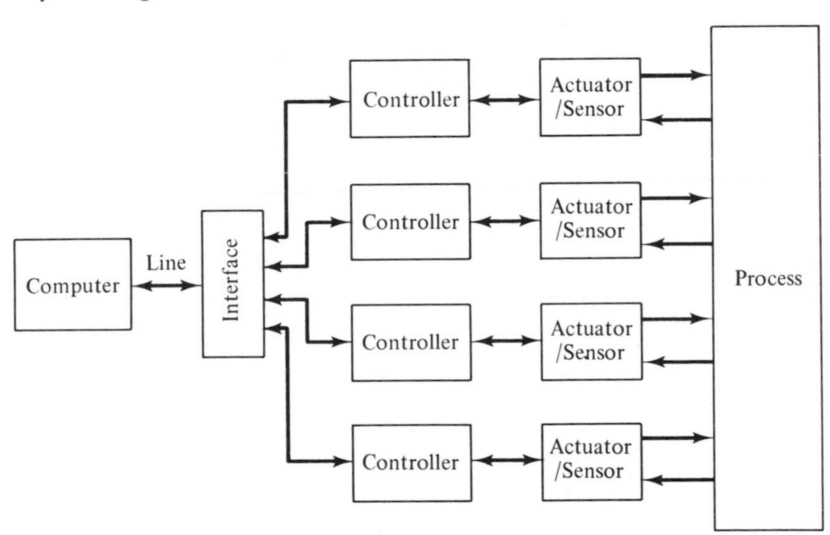

FIGURE 10–6. Process Control System Diagram

TABLE 10–2. Reliability Data

Device	MTBF (h)	Failures per Month(720 h/month)
Computer	10^4	0.0720
Line	10^6	0.0007
Interface	10^4	0.0720
Controller	10^5	0.0072
Actuator/sensor	10^5	0.0072

For industrial applications a conservative system design, component specification, and operating philosophy is usually linked with a well-conceived maintenance program to accommodate in-service system failures. Accordingly, a system availability function A can be defined which links MTBF with the mean time to repair (MTTR) for components. Availability defines the percentage of average time a system is available for service. For example, if the foregoing process control system requires an average of 8 h of maintenance per failure, determined from service records, then its availability will be 99.7%, from equation (10-15).

$$M_s = \frac{1}{\dfrac{1}{m_1} + \dfrac{1}{m_2} + \cdots + \dfrac{1}{m_n}} \text{ h} \qquad (10\text{-}14)$$

$$= \frac{1}{\dfrac{1}{10^4} + \dfrac{1}{10^6} + \dfrac{1}{10^4} + \dfrac{4}{10^5} + \dfrac{4}{10^5}}$$

$$= \frac{1}{10^{-4} + 10^{-6} + 10^{-4} + 4 \times 10^{-5} + 4 \times 10^{-5}}$$

$$= 3560 \text{ h}$$

$$R = \exp\left(-\frac{t}{m_s}\right) \qquad (10\text{-}3)$$

$$= \exp\left(-\frac{720}{3560}\right)$$

$$= 0.816$$

$$A = \frac{\text{MTBF}}{\text{MTBF} + \text{MTTR}} \qquad (10\text{-}15)$$

$$= \frac{3560 \text{ h}}{3560 \text{ h} + 8 \text{ h}}$$

$$= 0.997$$

In summary, the single most effective contribution to the design of reliable electronic systems is derating of the component parts. System operation at stress levels below component ratings provides substantial reliability improvement. Second, an understanding of the behavior of physical systems throughout their life cycle is useful, and the preventative replacement or overhaul of components before they enter wearout is essential. This action maintains system reliability at the useful life, or chance failure, value where it is constant for equal operating periods. Finally, simple design is crucial to reliable systems. And when system reliability must be further improved or critical areas exist in a system, redundant paths or standby units provide worthwhile reliability enhancement with advantage generally in favor of the standby approach.

REFERENCES

1. I. Bazovsky, *Reliability Theory and Practice*, Prentice-Hall, Englewood Cliffs, N. J., 1965.
2. E. Deyer and C. Jobe, "For the Real Cost in Design, Factor in Reliability," *Electronics*, August 30, 1973.
3. D. R. Doll, "How To Calculate Network Reliability," *Data Communications*, January/February 1975.
4. D. R. Doll, "Where To Spend Money To Improve System Availablilty," *Data Communications*, Nov/Dec 1974.
5. E. R. Hnatek, "High Reliability Semiconductors," *Electronics*, February 3, 1977.
6. L. Mattera, "Reliability Revisited: Failure Rate Comparisons," *Electronics*, December 25, 1975.
7. *RADC Reliability Notebook*, Publication RADC-TR-65-330, Rome Air Development Center, New York. 1965.

APPENDIX A

GAIN, BANDWIDTH, AND DISTORTION MEASUREMENTS

The gain of an amplifier should never be obtained from the direct application of an input signal. If the amplifier gain is high, the required input signal to maintain output linearity may be too small for accurate measurement. Also, the gain–bandwidth characteristic of the voltmeter may vary on different ranges. The use of an input attenuator solves these problems and transfers the measurement accuracy to the precision of the attenuator used. Usually, amplifier input impedance will be much higher than the typical 50-Ω attenuator termination impedance. Consequently, 50 Ω connected in shunt with the amplifier input will provide the correct termination, but introduces an additional 6-dB loss. The attenuator is adjusted to obtain equal readings in switch positions 1 and 2. Voltage gain is then equal to the attenuator setting plus 6 dB. Alternatively, an amplifier operating characteristic may be plotted between the amplifier noise level and overload points.

Square-wave rise-time measurements may be obtained on the device under test to ascertain its bandwidth and frequency-domain performance characteristics. A wideband oscilloscope is necessary for adequate resolution and time-base calibration. The input attenuator prevents input overloading, and the initial measurement t_{ro} provides for system calibration. This method is valid for devices that contain no inductors.

Harmonic and intermodulation distortion characterize the effects of nonlinearities and curvature associated with the transfer characteristics of active devices. Intermodulation distortion consists of sum and difference products of the input signal frequencies. Harmonic distortion consists of a sum of frequencies harmonically related and increasing upward from each input frequency. Consequently, intermodulation distortion will typically be on the order of twice the harmonic distortion. The signal generators used for distortion measurements must be capable of providing low-distortion sinusoidal signals (Figure A-3). Two generators are required for intermodulation measurements with their outputs summed.

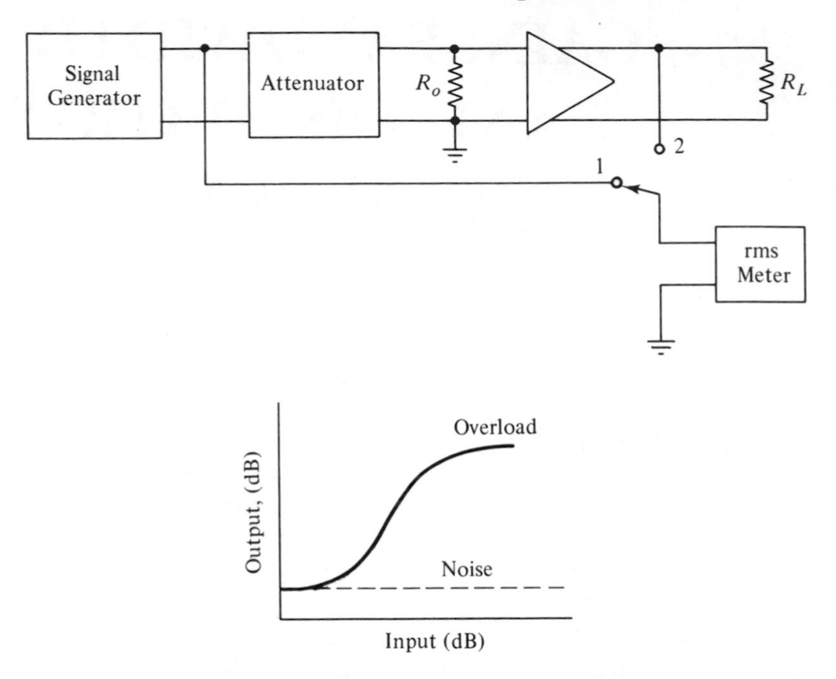

FIGURE A–1. Gain Measurement

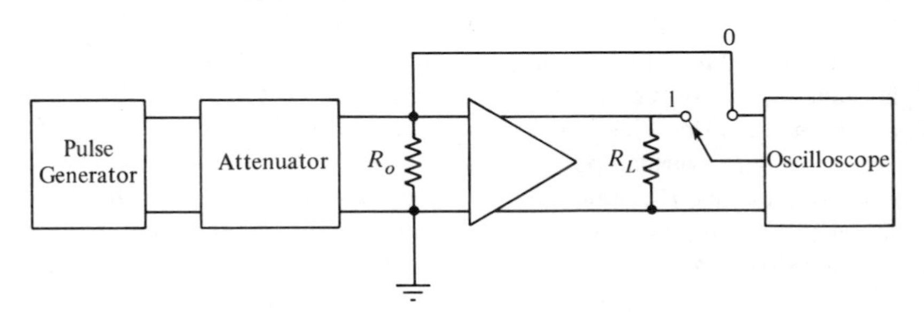

$$\text{Bandwidth} = \frac{0.35}{\sqrt{t_{r1}^2 - t_{r0}^2}} \text{ Hz}$$

FIGURE A–2. Bandwidth Measurement

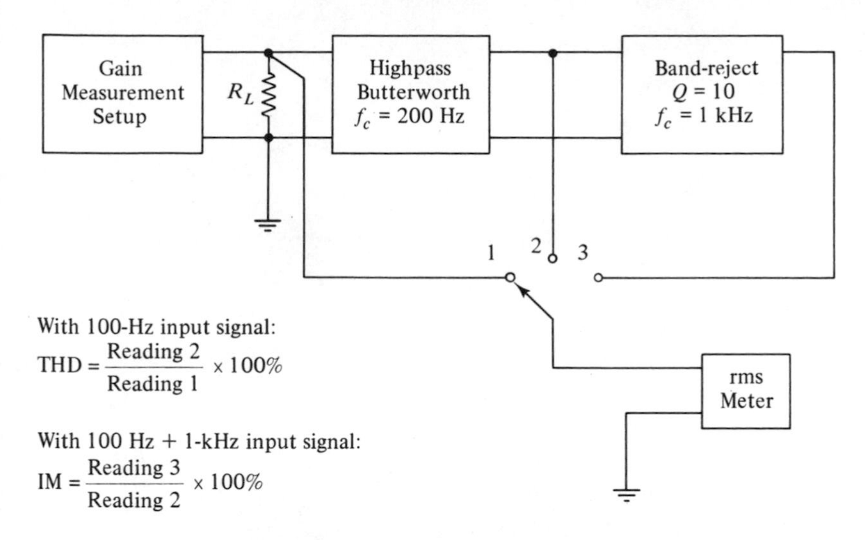

With 100-Hz input signal:

$$\text{THD} = \frac{\text{Reading 2}}{\text{Reading 1}} \times 100\%$$

With 100 Hz + 1-kHz input signal:

$$\text{IM} = \frac{\text{Reading 3}}{\text{Reading 2}} \times 100\%$$

FIGURE A–3. Distortion Measurement

APPENDIX B

REVIEW OF DECIBELS

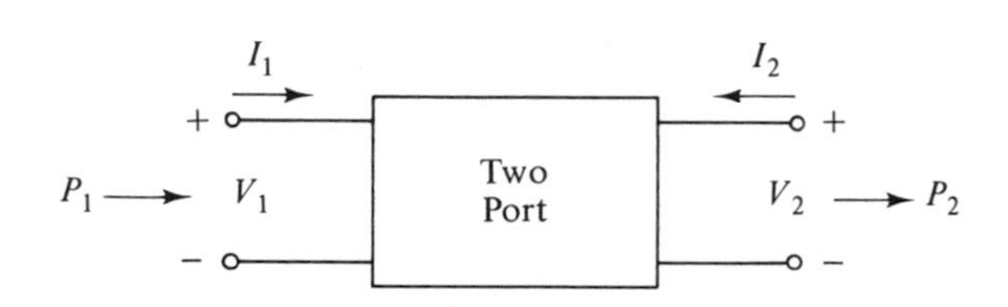

$$A_{dB} = 10\log_{10}\frac{P_2}{P_1} \qquad \textit{power gain}$$

$$= 10\log_{10}\frac{V_2^2/R_2}{V_1^2/R_1}$$

$$= 10\log_{10}\left(\frac{V_2}{V_1}\right)^2 \cdot \frac{R_1}{R_2}$$

$$= \underbrace{20\log_{10}\frac{V_2}{V_1}}_{\text{voltage gain}} + \underbrace{10\log_{10}\frac{R_1}{R_2}}_{\text{impedance gain (zero for } R_1 = R_2)}$$

$$A_{dB} = 10\log_{10}\frac{I_2^2R_2}{I_1^2R_1} \qquad \textit{power gain}$$

$$= \underbrace{20\log_{10}\frac{I_2}{I_1}}_{\text{current gain}} + \underbrace{\log_{10}\frac{R_2}{R_1}}_{\text{impedance gain (zero for } R_1 = R_2)}$$

APPENDIX C

SIGNAL PLUS NOISE CONVERSION

In the experimental evaluation of signal to noise ratios, the situation usually exists whereby only a signal-plus-noise to noise measurement can be made. This occurs because the noise cannot be removed when making a signal measurement as the signal can when measuring the noise level. However, the following mathematical manipulation converts signal-plus-noise/noise measurements $(S+N/N)$ into signal/noise ratios (S/N). Consider a 5dB $S+N/N$ measurement and equate to the following expression:

$$(S+N/N)|\mathrm{dB}=10\ \log\left(\frac{S+N}{1}\right)$$

$$5\,\mathrm{dB}=10\log\left(\frac{S+N}{1}\right)$$

$$3.16=S+N$$

Evaluating;

$$(S/N)\,\mathrm{dB}=10\log[(S+N)-1]$$

$$=10\log[3.16\text{–}1]$$

$$=3.34\,\mathrm{dB}$$

INDEX